LLEWELLYN'S

2011

Magical Almanac

Featuring

Elizabeth Barrette, Deborah Blake, Calantirniel,
Dallas Jennifer Cobb, Ellen Dugan, Denise Dumars,
Emyme, Sybil Fogg, Abel R. Gomez,
Marcus F. Griffin, Magenta Griffith, Elizabeth Hazel,
James Kambos, Deborah Lipp, Lupa, Melanie Marquis,
Graham Miller, Mickie Mueller, Paniteowl,
Susan "Moonwriter" Pesznecker, Kelly Proudfoot,
Diana Rajchel, Raven Digitalis, Janina Renée,
Suzanne Ress, Michelle Skye, Harmony Usher, Katherine
Weber-Turcotte, Tess Whitehurst, and Gail Wood

Llewellyn's 2011 Magical Almanac

ISBN 978-0-7387-1132-4. Copyright © 2010 by Llewellyn. All rights reserved. Printed in the United States. Llewellyn is a registered trademark of Llewellyn Worldwide, Ltd.

Editor/Designer: Nicole Edman

Cover Illustration: © Tammy Shane/Langley Creative

Calendar Pages Design: Andrea Neff and Michael Fallon

Calendar Pages Illustrations: © Fiona King

Interior Illustrations © Carol Coogan: pages 13, 20, 22, 24, 62, 77, 135, 137, 215, 265, 269, 279, 305, 330; © Chris Down: pages 27, 31, 94, 234, 237, 293, 296, 299, 335, 337, 339; © Kathleen Edwards: pages 51, 53, 99, 102, 131, 216, 219, 272, 277, 317; © Paul Hoffman: pages 68, 106, 258, 261, 321, 325, 326; © Wen Hsu: pages 17, 71, 74, 122, 127, 249, 254, 286, 290, 342, 348; © Mickie Mueller: pages 42, 47, 79, 82, 241, 246, 313; © Sabrina the Ink Witch: pages 37, 57, 87, 90, 111, 117, 225, 281, 282.

Illustration pages 143–146 by Llewellyn Art Department.

Clip Art Illustrations: Dover Publications

Special thanks to Amber Wolfe for the use of daily color and incense correspondences. For more detailed information, please see *Personal Alchemy* by Amber Wolfe.

You can order Llewellyn annuals and books from *New Worlds*, Llewellyn's catalog. To request a free copy of the catalog, call toll-free 1-877-NEW-WRLD or visit our website: www.llewellyn.com

Astrological data compiled and programmed by Rique Pottenger. Based on the earlier work of Neil F. Michelsen.

Llewellyn Worldwide Ltd.
2143 Wooddale Drive
Woodbury, MN 55125

About the Authors

ELIZABETH BARRETTE has been involved with the Pagan community for more than twenty years. She served as managing editor of *PanGaia* and Dean of Studies at the Grey School of Wizardry. Her *Composing Magic* explains how to write spells, rituals, and other Pagan material. She lives in central Illinois and enjoys magical crafts and gardening for wildlife. She has done much networking with Pagans in her area, including coffeehouse meetings and open sabbats. Other writing fields include speculative fiction and gender studies. http://ysabetwordsmith.livejournal.com/ http://gaiatribe.geekuniversalis.com http://reviewarchive.iblog.my

DEBORAH BLAKE is a Wiccan High Priestess who has been leading Blue Moon Circle for many years. She is the author of *Circle, Coven and Grove, Everyday Witch A to Z, The Goddess is in the Details*, and *The Everyday Witch A to Z Spellbook*, all from Llewellyn. Deborah was a finalist in the Pagan Fiction Award Contest and her short story, "Dead and (Mostly) Gone," is included in *The Pagan Anthology of Short Fiction*. She is also working on a number of novels, most of them featuring a Witch, of course. When not writing, Deborah runs The Artisans' Guild and works as a jewelry maker, a tarot reader, an ordained minister, and an Intuitive Energy Healer. She lives in a hundred-year-old farmhouse in rural upstate New York with five cats who supervise all her activities, both magickal and mundane.

LISA ALLEN/CALANTIRNIEL has been published in many Llewellyn annuals and has practiced many forms of natural spirituality since the early 1990s. She currently lives in western Montana with her husband, teenage daughter, and three young cats, while her older son is in college. She is a professional astrologer, tarot card reader, dowser, flower essence creator and practitioner, a ULC Reverend, Usui Reiki II, and a certified Master Herbalist. She has

an organic garden, crochets professionally, and is co-creating Tië eldaliéva, "the Elven Path," a spiritual practice based on J. R. R. Tolkien's Middle-Earth stories. www.myspace.com/aartiana

RAVEN DIGITALIS (Montana) is the author of *Planetary Spells & Rituals*, *Shadow Magick Compendium*, and *Goth Craft*, all from Llewellyn. He is a Neopagan Priest and cofounder of the "disciplined eclectic" tradition and training coven Opus Aima Obscuræ, and is a DJ. Also trained in Georgian Witchcraft and Buddhist philosophy, Raven is a Witch, Priest, and Empath. He holds a degree in anthropology and is also an animal rights activist, photographic artist, Tarot reader, and the co-owner of Twigs & Brews Herbs. www.ravendigitalis.com www.myspace.com/oakraven

ELLEN DUGAN, the "Garden Witch," is an award-winning author and psychic-clairvoyant. A practicing Witch for more than twenty-seven years, she is the author of many Llewellyn books; her newest are *A Garden Witch's Herbal* and *Book of Witchery*. Ellen encourages folks to personalize their spellcraft, to go outside and get their hands dirty, so they can discover the wonder and magick of the natural world. Ellen and her family live in Missouri. www.ellendugan.com

REV. DENISE "DION-ISIS" DUMARS, M.A. serves Thoth as a writer, a professor of writing, and a writer's representative. She is a founder of the Iseum of Isis Paedusis, which was chartered by the Fellowship of Isis in 2001. She and the other Iseum Adepti hold seasonal rituals at Pacific Unitarian Church in beautiful Rancho Palos Verdes, California. She hopes to visit Egypt some day, but in the meantime she volunteers for the American Cinematheque at Grauman's Egyptian Theatre on Hollywood Boulevard.

EMYME is a solitary practitioner who resides in a multigenerational, multicat household in southern New Jersey. Hobbies that renew her are: gardening, sewing and crafts, and home care and repair. Emyme has self-published a children's book about mending fami-

lies after divorce and remarriage. She is an avid diarist; dabbles in poetry; creates her own blessings, incantations, and spells; and is currently writing a series of fantasy fiction stories set in the twenty-fifth century. Her personal mantra is summed up in four words: Curiosity, Objectivity, Quality, Integrity. catsmeow24@verizon.net

Sybil Fogg, also known as Sybil Wilen, has been a practicing Witch for more than twenty years. She chose to use her mother's maiden name in Pagan circles to honor her grandparents. She's also a wife, mother, writer, teacher, and belly dancer. She lives in Portland, Maine, with her husband and their plethora of children. www.sybilwilen.com

Abel R. Gomez is a student, writer, performer, and ritualist ecstatically devoted to Maa Kali. His practice is rooted in a deep reverence for the intricacies of Nature, a constant reminder of the mystery and wonder of humanity and the world. Abel is passionate about musical theatre, permaculture, animal rights, and social justice. He studies Shakta Tantra with SHARANYA, a local Devi Mandir (Goddess temple), and is a member of the San Francisco Reclaiming community of Witches.

Marcus F. Griffin is a prolific author and has penned critically acclaimed works in a wide variety of genres. He is author of *Advancing the Witches' Craft, WISP-Paranormal, Spooky Streets and Haunted Highways,* and the novel *Slaughter.* Marcus is an active member of the Horror Writers Association. He is also a regular contributor to *Circle Magazine* and the UK's *Paranormal Magazine,* and writes monthly feature columns for Ghostvillage.com. Marcus lives with his wife in northern Indiana in a haunted home located on their sanctuary, Nevermore Gardens. www.marcusfgriffin.com

Magenta Griffith has been a Witch more than thirty years and a High Priestess for more than twenty. She is a founding member of the coven Prodea, which has been celebrating rituals since 1980,

as well as being a member of various Pagan organizations such as Covenant of the Goddess. She presents classes and workshops at a variety of events around the Midwest. She shares her home with a small black cat and a large collection of books.

ELIZABETH HAZEL is an astrologer, tarotist, artist, and mystic scholar. She is the author of *Tarot Decoded* and *The Whispering Tarot*, and writes horoscopes, feature columns, and articles. Liz is the editor of the *ATA Quarterly Journal* and has lectured in the United States and Britain. She officiates open community sabbats in the Toledo area in partnership with the Unitarian Church. www.kozmic-kitchen.com

JAMES KAMBOS is a regular contributor to Llewellyn's annuals. Born and raised in Appalachia, his magical traditions have been influenced by the folk magic ways of Appalachia and by his Greek heritage. When not writing, he enjoys painting and cooking. He currently lives in the beautiful hill country of southeastern Ohio.

DEBORAH LIPP has been Wiccan since 1981 and is a priestess, teacher, and author. She writes about Wicca and the occult, as well as entertainment. She is the author of *The Elements of Ritual, The Way of Four, The Way of Four Spellbook,* and *The Study of Witch-craft.* Deborah is a blogger and Tarot reader, and a passionate movie buff. She lives in suburban New York.

LUPA is a Pagan and (neo)shaman living in Oregon with her husband, their two kitties, and lots of books and art supplies. When not working on her master's in counseling psychology, Lupa enjoys gardening, hiking, environmental activism, reading, artwork, and video games. She's written several books. www.thegreenwolf.com http://therioshamanism.com http://paganbookreviews.com

MELANIE MARQUIS is a full-time Witch and writer. She's the founder of United Witches global coven, and she also organizes a Pagan group in Denver. She's written for many New Age and

Pagan publications. A nondenominational Witch, she specializes in practical spellwork, tarot, and spirit communication, teaching a personalized approach to the magickal arts. injoyart@yahoo.com

GRAHAM MILLER is a practicing solo eclectic Pagan. He is the author of *The Busy Pagan* and two novels, *The Loch* and *The Madman's Guide to Britain*. He is also a professional tarot and Rune reader. In his spare time, Graham gardens, makes jewelry, carves stone, and casts statues from melted aluminium cans. He has a fascination for stone circles and prehistory. Graham lives in a small village in rural Kent in the southeast of the United Kingdom with his wife and three children.

MICKIE MUELLER is an award-winning and critically acclaimed Pagan spiritual artist. She is Co-High Priestess of Coven of the Greenwood, an ordained Pagan Minister. She is also a Reiki healing master/teacher in the Usui Shiki Royoho tradition. Mickie is the illustrator of *The Well Worn Path* and *The Hidden Path* and the illustrator/writer of *The Voice of the Trees: A Celtic Ogham Oracle.* She is a regular article contributor to Llewellyn's periodicals, and her art is published internationally. www.mickiemuellerart.com

Jacci Sutton, simply known as Owl or **PANITEOWL** in the Pagan community, lives in the foothills of the Appalachians. She and her husband have acres of natural woodland and are developing a private retreat for spiritual awareness and host two annual events on Owl Mountain. She is founder and Elder High Priestess of the Mystic Wicca Tradition. Jacci has given workshops at Pagan events on the East Coast and in Canada. Her articles and poetry have been published in various Pagan periodicals and websites, as well as in Llewellyn's annual publications. Look for her on Facebook!

SUSAN "MOONWRITER" PESZNECKER has practiced Earth-based spirituality for three decades; she currently teaches Nature Studies and Herbology in the online Grey School of Wizardry. She

is a registered nurse, holds a master's degree in nonfiction writing, and teaches college composition, creative writing, and English. Sue has published several nonfiction essays and the books *Crafting Magick with Pen and Ink* and *Gargoyles*; her work has also appeared in the Llewellyn annuals and calendars. She lives in beautiful northwest Oregon, a perfect temperate setting for her works with herbal and natural magicks.

Originally from Australia, **KELLY PROUDFOOT** now lives in Nashville, TN, and is working on a self-help book about LifeMapping and two novels. She's been a practicing Numerologist and Tarot reader for twenty years, a solitary eclectic Wiccan, and is interested in magickal herbalism, Norse mythology, dream therapy, and quantum mechanics. She hopes to soon start her own herbal farm.

DIANA RAJCHEL lives in Minneapolis, where she engages with the city spirit daily. A full-time writer, artist, and priestess, she enjoys the world around her and connects to the spiritual through her creative efforts. http://dianarajchel.com

JANINA RENÉE is a scholar of folklore, psychology, medical anthropology, the material culture of magic, ritual studies, history, and literature. She has written *Tarot Spells, Playful Magic, Tarot: Your Everyday Guide, Tarot for a New Generation,* and *By Candlelight.* Janina continues to work on multiple books, including ongoing research projects into the ways folk magic and medicinal techniques relate to medical hypnosis, as well as the modulation of Asperger syndrome and other sensory processing problems. http://TarotMagicAdventures.blogspot.com.

SUZANNE RESS has been writing nonfiction and fiction for more than twenty-five years. She is an accomplished self-taught gardener, beekeeper, silversmith, and mosaicist. She lives in the woods at the foot of the Alps in northern Italy with her husband, daughter, two dogs, three horses, and an elusive red stag.

MICHELLE SKYE is a Pagan Priestess. She teaches classes, leads workshops, and founded both Massachusetts Pagan Teens and Sisterhood of the Crescent Moon. Skye is the author of three books by Llewellyn, *Goddess Alive!*, *Goddess Afoot!*, and *Goddess Aloud!* Her articles have appeared in *Circle Magazine*, *SageWoman*, *Llewellyn's Herbal Almanac*, and *Llewellyn's Magical Almanac*. Skye lives in Massachusetts.

HARMONY USHER is a freelance writer, researcher, and social worker in small-town Ontario. She shares her world with two creative, dynamic teenagers and is blessed to celebrate life, love, and the phases of the Moon with a fantastic circle of like-spirited women.

KATHERINE WEBER-TURCOTTE is a freelance writer and regular contributor to *Herb Quarterly* magazine. Her passions include herbal medicine, gardening, and animals. She is a student of Clayton College of Natural Health. Katherine writes from her Enchanted Wood surrounded by a bevy of Cocker Spaniels. www.enchantedwoodmusings.blogspot.com or Kathy@enchantedwoodherbs.com

TESS WHITEHURST is an advocate of self-love, self-expression, and personal freedom. She's a Llewellyn author, columnist for *NewWitch* magazine, intuitive counselor, and feng shui practitioner. Her Web site and e-newsletter *Good Energy* include simple rituals, meditations, and musings for everyday magical living. Tess lives in Venice Beach, CA, with two magical cats, one musical boyfriend, and a constant stream of visiting hummingbirds. www.tesswhitehurst.com

GAIL WOOD has been a Witch, Priestess, and Tarot Reader for nearly thirty years. She is a High Priestess and Elder in the RavenMyst Circle, a tradition of American Wicca. She is the author of four books and numerous articles on Pagan and Wiccan themes. www.rowdygoddess.com or darkmoonwitch@earthlink.net

Table of Contents

Earth Magic

City Kids and Mother Earth

by James Kambos

In this era of text messaging and e-mailing, many children have lost touch with Mother Earth. Unlike many adults who have been raised in small towns, or who had relatives in rural areas, many kids today are being raised in urban environments. As a result, they have lost connection with the natural world. Since we're quickly becoming further removed from our agrarian roots, we adults have a responsibility to show our children how we are all connected to Mother Earth and how fun a little earthy "magic" can be. Here are some Earth-oriented activities to share with your child.

The Gift of Food

Getting children involved in food preparation is a good way to introduce them to the blessings of Mother Earth. When children help in the kitchen, they not only enjoy participating but they're also more likely to eat food that's good for them.

Including kids in the kitchen can be done in several ways. Have young ones help prepare a salad. Let them tear clean lettuce leaves into a bowl. Have some presliced or shredded salad ingredients on hand—tomatoes, cucumbers, carrots, radishes, and so forth. Let them toss the ingredients so they can see the textures and colors. Next, have a few fragrant herbs chopped so they can sprinkle them over the salad as a garnish—chives, dill, and mint are good choices. Encourage your kids to smell the herbs as they work with them.

Older children can help by measuring ingredients or slicing fruits and vegetables. Cooking simple foods, such as pasta, is another chore you could delegate to an older child.

Allow your children to set the table. Tell them the table is like an altar; setting the table is a way to show respect for Mother Earth and for the gift of food.

Before long, your children will come to view mealtime as a pleasant family ritual and a time to give thanks for the Earth's bounty.

Let's Get Dirty

Teaching your children how to plant flowers, herbs, or vegetables can be an excellent way to show a child how Mother Earth provides beauty and food. You don't need to cultivate an entire garden to do this; a small plot or a pot will do fine. Not long ago at a garden center, I met a man who wanted to purchase one tomato plant for his son, just to teach him where food comes from. Good idea!

To get started, take your kids to a garden shop and let them pick out one or two plants or seed packets. Don't forget any supplies you may need: soil, pots, watering cans, etc.

Decide whether to buy established plants or seeds—seeds will take more time but may offer more lessons about the miraculous job Mother Nature does. Here are some tips:

• For flowering plants, I suggest marigolds, begonias, petunias, and zinnias. They're tough and bloom over a long season.

• If you want to try seeds, California poppies, cosmos, and zinnias are good choices for a children's garden. They germinate quickly, so kids can see results in a short time.

• Basil and dill are good choices for some easy-to-grow herbs.

• And for vegetables, like the gentleman I mentioned earlier, one tomato plant is an ideal choice. Tomatoes take up little space and some varieties can even be grown in a container.

Whatever plants you choose, watching something they've planted grow gives children a sense of accomplishment and connection to Mother Earth.

Visit a Fair

As summer fades into autumn, county and state fairs begin to celebrate the harvest season with rides, food, exhibits, and produce displays. Behind the carnival atmosphere, though, fairs actually began in ancient times as serious Pagan celebrations to thank the Earth for her bounty. Pagan deities such as Feronia, Mercury, and Diana were honored at some of these fairs.

Children love to go to fairs, so attending a fair as a family can become a fun way to educate your children about our dependence on the Earth for our survival.

As you stroll through the exhibition hall, children will see award-winning foods and produce. They'll quickly learn that our food doesn't originate on a supermarket shelf, but from hard work and nature. And while you're there, make sure they see the farm animals. Seeing a cow or a lamb up close for the first time is a memorable experience for any child. Children especially love the baby animals of any species.

Down on the Farm

Most areas have pick-your-own farms open to the public, offering a wide variety of fresh fruits and vegetables in season. In most North American regions, the picking season begins with strawberries in June. As the growing season progresses, you'll be able to find berries of all types, then peaches, apples, and pumpkins. Search the Internet and sites like pickyourown.org to find farms near you.

Picking your own produce is a fun, economical way to let your kids experience the bounty of nature. Harvesting your own food in this manner benefits a child in more than one way. Not only will they receive hands-on

experience collecting their own food, but they'll experience the beauty of nature in other ways. Perhaps they'll see wildflowers and butterflies. They'll also gain a sense of what earlier generations had to do to survive off the land, before supermarkets and fast food joints.

And, as an added bonus, you shouldn't have any trouble recruiting your kids to help you make a delectable cobbler or pie from the fruit they've picked!

Decorate with Nature

Kids love to decorate, especially with natural materials they've collected themselves. Rocks, leaves, pine cones, and seashells are just a few popular items that are easy to find. Kids can make almost anything into art, so let them be creative.

When your children bring home some of these natural treasures, it's the perfect time to point out the magical powers the various items are believed to possess. You can also help them display their earthy items—an empty canning jar could hold interesting rocks or seashells, or an old bowl on the kitchen table could showcase leaves and pine cones. Turning their finds into "art" will inspire kids to look at the natural gifts of our planet with a new appreciation.

Thanking Mother Earth

After a child begins to see how we're connected to the Earth and that the Earth provides so much for us, show your children appropriate ways to thank Mother Earth for her generosity. Before digging or cultivating, for example, silently ask the Earth permission to turn the soil. And after planting or harvesting, instruct your children to leave an offering as a symbol of thanks. This could be as simple as sprinkling the area with water or leaving a bit of bird seed on the ground.

~

For most of us, living directly from the land is a thing of the past. That is why it's so important for adults to teach children who've only known urban environments how dependent we are upon Mother Earth for our survival. Eventually, even city kids will begin to understand our connection to Mother Earth and the magic of her seasons.

Pagan Permaculture

by Abel R. Gomez

Many people were drawn to the Pagan and occult paths for their emphasis on connection with nature, a sense of beauty and wonder in the world, and a deep reverence for the interconnectedness of the universe. As Witches, we can engage in these mysteries through magic, intentionally shifting consciousness and opening to the extraordinary. We can also engage in these mysteries in everyday life through our actions—the choices we make and the way we treat one another and Mother Earth, herself. One of the richest models of such a lifestyle is permaculture.

Permaculture is a philosophy of ecological design and a set of Earth-based principles that allow us to live in greater harmony with the natural world. Coined by naturalist Bill Molison and his student David Holmgren in the 1970s, *permaculture* refers to the concepts and methods that allow us to design and create sustainable human communities. These communities draw upon the best of indigenous wisdom and modern science to create worlds of true abundance and beauty. Since its inception, permaculture has become an international grassroots movement, fostering a sense of community and connection to the sacred cycles of life. Observation of the natural world is of utmost importance in permaculture. In fact, it is what sets permaculture apart from other ecological philosophies and design sciences. Permaculturists observe the Sun cycles, the flows of wind and rain, and the habits of native plant and animal species to understand the greater ecosystem as a whole. By observing first, we are able to more fully understand how the natural systems work in a particular ecosystem before setting out to partner with those systems. We must first observe the flow of energy before attempting to direct it toward a particular end, a principle demonstrated in group ritual or energetic healing.

Because permaculture is rooted in observation, it seeks to create systems that are mutually beneficial to the entire ecosystem. Everything is connected in permaculture. The entire world is a vast web of interdependence. In these systems, every element has a specific function, contributing valuable resources and actually

19

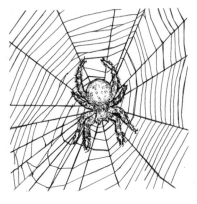

improving the flora and fauna of the ecosystem while accomplishing human goals. Designers strategically include elements that build topsoil, encourage native plants to thrive, and catch and store energy for the greatest abundance.

In this way, permaculture creates systems the same way nature creates systems—through relationship. Patrick Whitefield, a noted permaculture teacher and designer, calls permaculture "the art of creating beneficial relationships," observing the patterns of the natural world and mimicking them in smaller, controlled ecosystems. All things in nature function through relationship to everything else. Magic itself works through relationships, allowing us to tap into powers greater than ourselves, transforming our will into reality. The same is true in permaculture. Permaculture designers observe the patterns of nature and integrate them into designs to create self-sufficient systems that have the strength and resiliency of the natural world.

The most fundamental relationship in permaculture, however, is the one between humankind and the natural world. Permaculture teaches us that we are intimately connected to the rhythms of nature. Indigenous people have lived in harmony with the natural world for eons, cultivating the land through agriculture, controlled fires, and other means. It is only recently that humanity has created imbalance in nature. We must remember that we have co-evolved with nature and that what we do to her, we do to ourselves. We are a part of nature, born of the Earth, and the decisions we make and actions we take ripple out into all of our relations. Ecosystems never work as isolated objects but as part of an interdependent dance. Humans are a part of this dance as well.

Our connection to nature is at the heart of Earth-based spirituality. Through ritual and magic, we create containers to experience the Great Mystery at the core of our being. Permaculture allows us to take these mystical experiences out into the world using systems that honor the things we hold sacred.

Finding a Sit Spot

Though permaculture can be used as a model for sustainability, a guide for understanding the patterns of nature and human life, and a philosophical approach to experiencing the world, it is most often used as a design science to create edible landscapes. It is through our food that we experience the deepest connection with the natural world. No matter how seemingly divorced society becomes from Mother Nature, we depend on the cycles and forces of the natural world for sustenance. With this in mind, permaculture designers create systems that work with nature to provide us with the greatest abundance while taking into account effects on the entire system. These designs are based upon three simple principles called the permaculture ethics: care of Earth, care of people, and share of the surplus.

The first step in any permaculture design project is creating a "sit spot" where you can observe the flows and patterns of a particular space before beginning to work its natural systems. An outdoor ritual space near the area you plan to work with can be particularly powerful as a sit spot. If you don't have a ready-made sit spot, create one. Find an area close to the place you wish to work and ritually establish it as your observation area. Cast a circle and erect a ritual space, calling upon the gods and the spirits of the land for guidance and blessing. You may wish to create an altar or shrine to the land spirits to show your willingness to partner with them. More than simply a place to plan out a garden, your sit spot will become the center from which you understand the deeper patterns and mysteries of Nature.

Renowned author and priestess Starhawk once referred to permaculture as the way in which we become indigenous to a place. We become more attuned to the land, to the cycles of life, and to the way things work through our observation of the natural world, especially when the observation becomes an ongoing pursuit. Make your sit spot a part of your daily spiritual practice, if possible. Visit your area in silence and listen to the sounds of the intricate network around you. Notice the animals and plants that live there, the patterns of sunlight and shadow, and the way the wind moves through the space. Give offerings to the spirits of the land and allow them to whisper their wisdom to you as you build a deeper relationship with the land.

Because permaculture is rooted in observation, the work we do in our sit spot is of utmost importance. It is typical to spend up to a year studying the patterns of a particular ecosystem before implementing change. Though this may seem like a long time, it is truly an invitation to build relationship and understand the way nature works. Take notes on the microclimates and how seasonal shifts affect the growth of plant life. Pay attention to the areas that get the most and least amounts of sunlight and the way water flows in the given area. The more we know, the easier it will be to create a system that works with natural patterns and grants us the highest yield.

Creating an Herb Spiral

One of the easiest permaculture projects to create is an herb spiral. Drawing upon several permaculture principles, creating an herb spiral maximizes one's planting space, creates useful edges, and is aesthetically pleasing. An herb spiral also allows for several microclimates (based on the herbs' placement in relation to sunlight and soil moisture) in which the herbs on top have full drainage and the ones below hold more water. Nature is our model in permaculture. In this case, we will be using the ancient spiral pattern, symbolic of both growth and renewal, as our inspiration for our herb garden. It is also an opportunity to grow your own magical herbs, especially if you have limited space.

The first step, after you decide on a space and record your observations, is to lay down a circular piece of cardboard about six feet in diameter. The cardboard will help promote good soil, defend against weeds, and provide a guide for building your spiral. Begin by drawing a spiral on the cardboard, beginning in the center and spiraling clockwise to the edge. There should be about eight inches between the spiral loops. (The exact proportions will depend on how large you intend your spiral to be. More detailed information can be found in the recommended reading at the end of the article.)

Next, stack short bricks (full-size bricks may be hard to use in small circles) or medium stones along the line of your spiral, starting at the outside end of the spiral and building your line of stones higher as you move toward the center. Picture a rough cone shape and you'll get an idea of what you are aiming for. After you add soil, you'll have a continuously sloping bed in which to plant your herbs.

The next step involves layering and watering. Within the spaces of the bricks or stones in the spiral, create layers of bark mulch, straw, and soil, respectively. The layers will be thin on the outside loops, while the inside loops will need thicker layers to build up to the proper height. These layers will build soil while also creating drainage. Be sure to water each layer thoroughly before adding the next.

You can now begin to plant your herbs. Because this is permaculture, make sure that the herbs on the lowest levels enjoy muddy soil and the herbs above prefer to be mostly dry, since any water will naturally flow downward. A simple search online will provide you with a good list of appropriate herbs. Once all of the herbs are planted, you may wish to say a little prayer to welcome the spirits of the plants into your garden. This is especially important if you plan to use the herbs in any sort of magical work. As

we know, the natural world and the magical world are based on relationship, so the stronger your relationship with the herbs, the more powerful the magic will be.

Delving Deeper

The herb spiral is merely a small piece of the vast world of permaculture. As we continue to listen to the natural world, we can gain deeper understanding and reverence for the great intricacies of nature. If permaculture calls to you, you may wish to take a permaculture design course. Typically these courses are two-week intensives, but other models also exist. At the end of the course, participants are awarded a permaculture design certificate. Pagans and magic workers may be especially drawn to Earth Activist Training, a permaculture design course taught by Starhawk, grounded in Earth-based spirituality, activism, and magic.

At its core, permaculture is a celebration of deep interdependence with all life. It is about finding the sacred in the rhythms of the natural world and partnering with them to create true beauty and abundance. As Witches, we can utilize permaculture as a practice and a way of life that can further our relationship to the natural world and inspire us to live in the fullness of our humanity. Permaculture allows us to manifest a world of justice and reverence for all life, a world that can nourish us and the future generations to come.

For Further Study

Flores, Heather Coburn. *Food Not Lawns: How to Turn Your Yard into a Garden and Your Neighborhood into a Community.* White River Junction, VT: Chelsea Green, 2006.

Hemenway, Toby. *Gaia's Garden: A Guide to Home-Scale Permaculture.* White River Junction, VT: Chelsea Green, 2009.

Holmgren, David. *Permaculture: Principles and Pathways Beyond Sustainability.* White River Junction, VT: Chelsea Green, 2003.

Starhawk. *The Earth Path: Grounding Your Spirit in the Rhythms of Nature.* New York: HarperCollins, 2004.

Recommended Web sites:

Earth Activist Training: Planting the Seeds of Change. www.earthactivisttraining.org (accessed September 21, 2009).

The Permaculture Activist. www.permacultureactivist.net (accessed September 21, 2009).

Connecting to the Land: Modern Paganism, Bioregionalism, and the Genius Loci

by Lupa

When you think of where Neopagans get their inspiration, what locations come to mind? Ireland? Egypt? Malta? India? Some other faraway, exotic locales? If you're like a lot of Pagans, you find the prospect of places like these—whether their past or their present existences—to be exciting and spiritually inspiring. Why else are there guided tours around Stonehenge, the Egyptian pyramids, and the Maltese ruins? Sure, a lot of the people visiting are just tourists, but there's a growing trend toward catering to those with a more spiritual focus to their travels, whether they are would-be shamans seeking remote Amazonian villages or Goddess worshippers looking for evidence of the Great Mother in the world of the ancients.

Even those of us without huge travel budgets sometimes get wrapped up in the "over there" aspects of Paganism. Look at the huge boom in popularity of Celtic this and that in the 1990s. And many Pagans take their inspiration from ancestors and others long-gone, in far-off places. Often, the search for connection to places and cultures that are temporally and geographically removed causes a serious disconnect with one's own time and place, to the point that you have people who are all too seriously convinced they were born in the wrong century on the wrong continent!

This is just one facet of a greater trend in Western cultures, which have the greatest cultural influence on modern Neopaganism. The trend is that of taking one's own home territory for granted, and the result is that we don't care nearly enough for what we have while we're distracted by what we feel we lack. This isn't just evidenced by people who wish to be in another place and another time; it's also manifested by those who pretend to be removed from nature while seeking ever-greater technological distractions, who stubbornly remain ignorant of the reality

26

of our limited natural resources while pretending that someone else will fix every problem. And by people who are so intent on looking out for Number One that it never occurs to them that they can never entirely detach themselves from an intricate web of interdependence they are a part of simply by being alive.

There have been a number of attempts to help Pagans appreciate their immediate environs more. Notable examples are the various books on urban Paganism, such as *City Magick* by Christopher Penczak and *Urban Primitive* by Raven Kaldera and Tannin Schwartzstein. These books are influential in helping Pagans appreciate not just the open spaces—the woods and fields—but also the wilderness and nature found within the city and the urban environment.

This appreciation can be taken further, though. Ultimately, it doesn't matter whether you're a rural or urban Pagan; what's important is the appreciation of the place you're in right now. Too many Pagans overlook the magic right under their noses while daydreaming about places they may never see in person. One of the most important ways to reframe where you live and what's important about it is the bioregion.

What is Bioregionalism?

Bioregionalism is the defining of a community—not limited to humans—based on the features of the biological landscape they inhabit. Cities, for all the changes they may cause on a given bioregion, are still a part of that bioregion. Take, for example, the Cascadia bioregion, which includes my city: Portland, Oregon. Cascadia is largely composed of temperate rainforests and mountain ranges, though it gently segues through land converted to farming and out to the coast. (Being often rocky and chilly, it's not quite a "beach" as many think of beaches.) Washington, Oregon, and British Columbia are generally considered to be within Cascadia, though sometimes northern California, at least part of Idaho, and even the southernmost portion of Alaska are included.

More specifically, I live in the Columbia River estuary, the land that feeds water into that particular major river. And even more locally, I'm in the Johnson Creek watershed. This doesn't even take into account other natural phenomena, such as the area's geology. However, waterways make convenient and noticeable boundaries for bioregions, and ecosystems are often centered around water sources.

A bioregion is not merely a geographic and ecological delineation, however. It also carries significant implications for how we approach culture, politics, economics, and other areas of our lives. Bioregionalism strongly favors local economies; sustainable relationships with the natural environment as well as human communities; valuing not only the human residents of the bioregion, but the nonhuman ones as well; and an opposition to artificial boundaries created with "power" or control in mind, rather than the best interests of the inhabitants.

While Cascadia is the best-known bioregion (largely due to the fact that so many of us here are avid environmentalists who love this sort of thing), everyone lives in a bioregion. I won't spend this essay explaining how to define your bioregion in detail. However, good starting points for research are discovering your watershed, geology, climate, and weather patterns.

Keep in mind that cities are a part of their given bioregions. The Willamette River, for example, still runs through Portland

and still has an effect on us, and our electricity is supplied by hydroelectric dams on the Columbia. In addition, many of the weeds that grow in the open lots and nooks and crannies in the city are also native, as are many of the smaller animals found within city limits. We have changed the landscape, but we haven't—and can never—entirely divorced ourselves from our bioregion.

The Genius Loci

Bioregions do have a personality. Some of their character comes from the people who live in them, but this is not the sum total of what's important. As mentioned before, bioregionalism takes into account every aspect of the region, not just the human population. All this together comprises the spirit of the place—otherwise known as the *genius locus* (or *genius loci*, plural).

In my experience, there is never just one single genius locus of a place. Instead, they overlap and enclose each other like Russian nesting dolls. For example, there is the genius locus of the wetlands near my home. Then there is the genius locus of the Johnson Creek watershed, of which the wetlands are a part. Both are enveloped by the genius locus of the Columbia River estuary, and finally, all are enclosed by the Cascadia bioregion. Each genius has its own personalities, and yet they flow into each other as well. Even the smallest genius locus I mentioned, the wetlands, is made of the presence of numerous other spirits—the plants, the animals, the waters, both incarnate and discarnate. (It's helpful to allow for permeable, mutable boundaries when dealing with land spirits.)

Thinking of the land in terms of bioregions instead of only human-made boundaries (though these also have their importance) can be a great help when working with genius loci. The land is not only defined by humans, and while cities may have a more human feel than more rural areas, they are hardly the only important places to connect with. Within cities, though, there are parks and other "natural" areas[1] that, while they may

---

1. I hesitate to delineate between "natural" and "unnatural" because I see it as a false dichotomy that encourages humans to think of ourselves as divorced from nature, when we clearly are anything but.

be hemmed in by human structures, possess qualities that are not human at all. And, as mentioned, the rivers and the climate and the basic geology of a place are only dependent on humans to a certain degree, so even thinking of cities as "human" isn't quite accurate. Anyone who has spent time in rural areas knows that the fields and woods are not solely defined by the fences humans build; neither are cities.

So when we work with land spirits, it's important to keep in mind everything that genius loci are composed of, not only the most apparent parts. A good example would be when you move to a new place and want to get to know it better. Many people, when they move to a new location, spend a lot of time driving from one place to the next, then parking and walking around for a limited amount of time before getting back into the car. This is often only to get to know the human parts of a place, such as stores, restaurant, and entertainment venues.

Those of us who are avid hikers and walkers know that you miss a lot when you only drive, and some details are only evident when you take the time to get to know a place at a slower pace. You get to see things you wouldn't even notice when driving by at thirty, forty, fifty miles per hour. When you're exploring a place on foot, you have the time to pay more attention, and you aren't distracted by the road.

Walking also exposes you more to the genius loci in your area, providing a fuller and more varied experience than just getting to know those areas mostly attuned to human activities. If you set out to explore a place with all of its parts and layers in mind—as a bioregion instead of just a human habitation—you're going to get a much more complete picture of who's there and what they're about. You'll also gain a better appreciation for the diversity and resources a place offers, which can be incredibly helpful, especially if you aren't exactly thrilled about the place you've just moved to. You may find yourself surprised by what you didn't know was there! Try drawing a map of your own bioregion to get a better understanding of the natural boundaries and smaller regions within it.

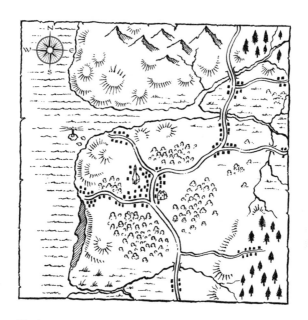

Ethical and Ecological Implications

I started this essay by speaking of the fundamental disconnect that many humans, particularly in postindustrial cultures, have from their environment and some of how that can manifest in Neopaganism. By becoming more aware of our bioregion and the genius loci within it, we are not only gaining more knowledge, we are also taking on more responsibility.

Responsibility is not a bad thing. Yes, it does ask more of us, but we all benefit in the end. The majority of ecological problems we face—"we" meaning not only humans but Beston's "other nations"[2]—are due to the human tendency to ignore the implications and effects of our actions on ourselves and everything else.

Too often, Pagans have the tendency to take and take from the spirits and other beings who help us; too often, we forget to make offerings. Or if we do make offerings, they're rote and prescribed and present little practical aid to the spirits. While

---

2. ". . . the animal shall not be measured by the man . . . They are other nations . . . fellow prisoners of the splendor and travail of the earth." –Henry Beston, *The Outermost House.*

there's nothing inherently wrong, for example, with leaving a place for the genius loci at the table at a feast to celebrate the harvest, this does nothing to benefit the actual soil that grew the food at that feast. We offer the spirits the "spiritual essence" of what we have benefited from, but we do nothing physical to help the physical phenomena that these spirits are attached to. In that, these sorts of offerings are somewhat of an empty gesture if we take both spiritually and physically, but only give back spiritually.[3]

If we're going to really connect to the land, we need to know what the land needs from us, not just what we need from it. This means being more aware of some unpleasant realities, including the fact that our very presence on that land is harmful to it. Even if you don't have a car, live in a tiny apartment, and eat organic food, you're still using resources from the land, resources that are most likely already either heavily drawn on and/or damaged by the land (and, potentially, land elsewhere). This doesn't mean you should move, but it does mean that this awareness should be part of what guides your growing relationship with the place.

How this guides your actions depends on who you are and on your circumstances. In Portland, activism is incredibly common; there are multiple nonprofit organizations dedicated to various watersheds in the area, all of whom are looking for volunteers (and often donations as well). Your area may not be quite as obviously active, but check around for opportunities. Even picking up garbage on your own, with no official recognition from the human community, can be rewarding when working with the genius loci.

Make yourself as aware as possible of the local environmental issues. Some areas' newspapers are really good about reporting on such things; others wouldn't run a story on the environment even if there was nothing else to print. All but the smallest communities tend to have at least some sort of environmental

---

3. Some folks like to leave out food from the feast for wild animals as an offering, but encouraging wild animals to do something mutually dangerous like associate humans with food isn't perhaps the best offering, especially when it was the soil and not the animals that made the crops grow.

network. You may have to look hard for like-minded people, but they're almost always there.

You can also tailor your everyday choices to reducing your tread upon the ground. Look into ways you can reduce your demand on the local natural resources, ways that are compatible with your income, health, and schedule. You may not be able to add a gray water system to your home's plumbing, but anyone can take a plastic bottle filled with water and stick it in the toilet tank to reduce the amount of water used with each flush.

And you don't need to stop with the ecological level of the bioregion, either. Issues of social justice and civil rights are equally integral, for example. Whatever you can do to make the place you live a better place to be counts for a lot with the genius loci of your home. The important thing is to ask the genius loci what they and their land need the most, both through communicating with them, and through observing the daily occurrences in your area.

For Further Study

Cascadian Bioregion, http://cascadia-bioregion.tripod.com/ (accessed September 21, 2009).

McGinnis, Michael Vincent, ed. *Bioregionalism.* New York: Routledge, 1999.

Nature Journaling

by Susan "Moonwriter" Pesznecker

If you're a worker of magick, you've probably kept one or more journals as part of your magickal life—a book of spells, a dream journal, or even a tarot log. One of the most satisfying types of journaling is a nature journal. Combining writing, images, objective recording, and even scrapbooking, the nature journal has something for everyone and is an incredibly satisfying way to enrich one's magickal workings. It's a cornerstone of practice for those of us who work with "green," nature-based magicks, but it's also a rich adjunct for everyone else. Nature, after all, is the wellspring from which all magickal energy emerges. Experiences and observations may be etched into our memories, but while memory is a lovely personal carry-along, it's also imperfect. That's where journaling comes in: to help us keep track of the details.

Your nature journal can take whatever size or shape works for you and can capture anything from the complete subjectivity of describing a bird song to the absolute objectivity of a carefully sketched map. Your nature journal is personal and there's no right or wrong method of recording your experiences. Some people keep a single journal that combines both rough and polished notes; others use one journal for initial notes and sketches, then transfer their creations to a "final," more formal notebook. Still others work electronically, creating a paperless record. Whatever the format, each journal becomes a work in progress and a working record of a unique magickal journey.

And let's note the commonality of the words *journal* and *journey*, which share Latin and Old French roots, roughly translating into "a day's travel" or "a day's portion." Nature journaling comes with a rich, important history via the explorers and adventurers who carried journals and logs to record the details of their trips. Consider that in recording your own "green" magickal path, you're creating a durable record of your own journey.

Making Written Entries

First and foremost, nature journals begin with written notes about one's observations and experiences. Why should you use journaling as a way to document adventures in nature? Journaling is a wonderful way to increase your powers of observation, to learn more about the world around you, and to extend your own magickal reach. Earth has many lessons to teach, and nature journaling provides a superb way to listen, apply, and learn those lessons.

Learning to Observe

Speaking of listening . . . most of us humans aren't very good observers. Our lives are packed and busy and we're often engaged with moving from one place or activity to another as quickly as we can—so quickly that we often fail to simply look around. But good powers of observation are an important part of good journaling, and fortunately, observation is a skill that improves with intention and practice.

When you observe, focus on being as quiet and still as possible. This is especially important in the natural setting, as your ability to be silent—in terms of sound and movement—makes it more likely that you'll see and hear the trees, plants, animals, and energies around you without disturbing them. Good observation slows down time. Be present in the moment; pull in your energy and imagine yourself melting into your surroundings until you're almost invisible. Now open your senses: feel the sights, smells, sounds, textures, and even tastes around you. Open your magickal sixth sense to the powers close by and welcome them in. (Obi-Wan was right: the Force is all around us.)

Finding a Day Sign Exercise

Each day, preferably early in the day, go outside. Open your powers of observation and look for something that speaks to you. It might be a brightly colored bird, a broken branch, a stone in your path—anything. This is your "day sign." Once you find it, consider what it means. Is it telling you something you need to know? Does it suggest an allegory or story? A portent? Spend five to ten minutes recording your discoveries.

Freewriting

Freewriting is another important writer's tool. When you freewrite, you simply take up paper and pencil (or keyboard and screen) and begin to write. You can write about a specific idea—a prompt—or just start writing. Write continuously, without stopping. Don't correct spelling or punctuation, and don't even worry about writing in whole sentences; just let your mind dump ideas onto the paper. Write for five or ten minutes, then stop and look at what you've written. Your words might find their way into a journal entry or might provide the beginnings of a reflection.

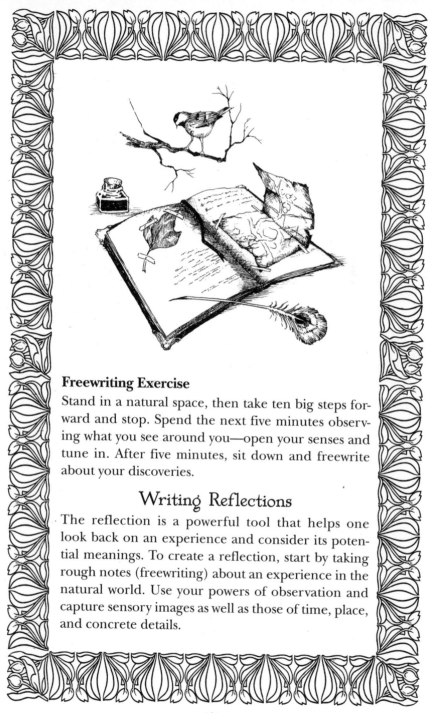

Freewriting Exercise

Stand in a natural space, then take ten big steps forward and stop. Spend the next five minutes observing what you see around you—open your senses and tune in. After five minutes, sit down and freewrite about your discoveries.

Writing Reflections

The reflection is a powerful tool that helps one look back on an experience and consider its potential meanings. To create a reflection, start by taking rough notes (freewriting) about an experience in the natural world. Use your powers of observation and capture sensory images as well as those of time, place, and concrete details.

Then, put the notes away to "steep" for at least a few days—the longer, the better. Once some time has passed, pick up the writing, reread it, and refine the work, expanding the ideas and considering their larger meanings. Your reflection can take any form, from a structured piece of writing to a field book entry or even a piece of poetry. Consider the ways in which nature speaks to you through your notes. By allowing time to pass between the initial note taking and the later writing, you'll gain "reflective distance," allowing you to objectively review the experience and better understand the possible meanings within.

Reflection Exercise

Go outside on a clear night after dark and spend twenty to thirty minutes looking at the night sky. Take notes as you watch—you might also sketch what you see overhead. After the time passes, go inside and make additional notes to fully capture the experience. Put the writing away for several days, then go back and create a reflection. What messages and inspirations did you find in the night sky?

Working with Images

One of the most fun parts of nature journaling is the artistic aspect. Even those of us who aren't artists can enjoy adding images and color to our nature journal. A good sketch, map, or diagram or a special font can explain or expand a written entry immensely. Even a simple border adds interest and beauty to your pages.

<u>Sketches and diagrams</u>: Use pencil or ink to create simple artwork. Add figure legends or use arrows and "bubbles" for explanation. Not the artistic type? Turn to a drawing book for instruction (see For

Further Study). I like to keep a folder of simple images and practice copying them; I'm not very good at creating my own drawings, but I do pretty well at copying simple sketches.

Maps: A good map can come in very handy in a nature journal. You might map the location of a magickal glade, capture the layout of a campsite, or detail a specific map showing your favorite spot for wildcrafting (making crafts from found natural objects). Use a magnetic compass to note direction and a 100-foot cord, knotted at 10-foot intervals, to estimate distance. Graph paper works well for mapping. Cut out the finished map and glue into your nature journal.

Graphs and tables: In some cases, a graph, chart, or table will be a handy addition to your nature journal, particularly if you include Earth-based study and sciences in your green workings. You might choose to track weather conditions, note the time and place of moonrise/moonset over a period of time, or record the details of crystal testing. Use a ruler to create these additions, and finish with a title and legend.

Papers and Tools

It's fun to experience with papers, inks, and other materials. Try different colors of ink and variously textured papers for both writing and drawing. Use a glue stick to attach photographs or other materials to your journal pages. Stickers, rubber stamps, adhesive letters, and other scrapbooking paraphernalia make decorative additions for your journal. You might even try making your own paper or ink. Make a simple ink by using a candle to blacken the under-

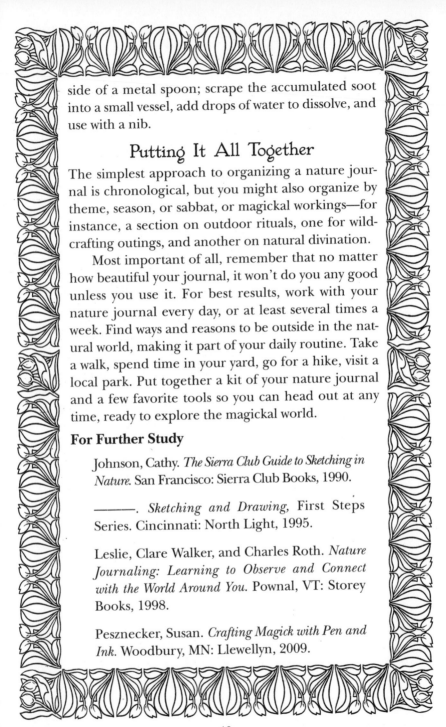

side of a metal spoon; scrape the accumulated soot into a small vessel, add drops of water to dissolve, and use with a nib.

Putting It All Together

The simplest approach to organizing a nature journal is chronological, but you might also organize by theme, season, or sabbat, or magickal workings—for instance, a section on outdoor rituals, one for wildcrafting outings, and another on natural divination.

Most important of all, remember that no matter how beautiful your journal, it won't do you any good unless you use it. For best results, work with your nature journal every day, or at least several times a week. Find ways and reasons to be outside in the natural world, making it part of your daily routine. Take a walk, spend time in your yard, go for a hike, visit a local park. Put together a kit of your nature journal and a few favorite tools so you can head out at any time, ready to explore the magickal world.

For Further Study

Johnson, Cathy. *The Sierra Club Guide to Sketching in Nature*. San Francisco: Sierra Club Books, 1990.

———. *Sketching and Drawing*, First Steps Series. Cincinnati: North Light, 1995.

Leslie, Clare Walker, and Charles Roth. *Nature Journaling: Learning to Observe and Connect with the World Around You*. Pownal, VT: Storey Books, 1998.

Pesznecker, Susan. *Crafting Magick with Pen and Ink*. Woodbury, MN: Llewellyn, 2009.

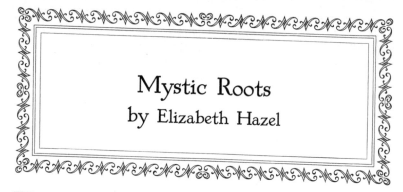

Mystic Roots
by Elizabeth Hazel

Earth magic is familiarly associated with prosperity, abundance, stability, patience, and endurance. The mysticism and magic of the Deep Earth—the realm of invisible underground roots and chthonic underworld gods—is less familiar. Roots are used as a metaphor for invisible, pre-existing human structures. People have family roots, spiritual roots, and karmic roots. The calm silence of the Deep Earth is a gentle and supportive source of aid and renewal, as well as an invaluable part of a magical palette.

The esoteric and mythological concepts surrounding death, the underworld, and the afterlife are also amazingly consistent in diverse pantheons across the globe. Gods or goddesses traveling to the underworld are a metaphor for the seasons and an explanation for winter's fallow period. These tales were generated as lifestyles centered on farming and domesticated livestock replaced migratory hunting and gathering. The gods and stories from this transition are thought to be between five and ten thousand years old.

Myths are poetic and dramatic narratives that often animate common sense and survival skills. On the surface, underworld stories seem to involve grieving and a keen sense of loss. Yet good farmers know that the soil must rest between growing seasons. Winter rain and snow soften the soil for spring planting. Ancient farming peoples needed gods who were willing to offer their bodies to revitalize the invisible roots of plants that fed humans and animals during the growing season.

Journeys to the underworld represent a process of restoration. The body of the submerged god or goddess is a battery that recharges the soil and roots. Various underworlds are depicted as vast, invisible complexes intertwined with life on Earth. Plant

roots are anchors, nutrition-gathering and -storage systems, and the underworld provided much the same function for human life in a metaphysical context. For instance, in Blavatsky's Theosophical system, the Akashic Records form a karmic root system that connects past, present, and future and acts as a storehouse of rewards, debts, and soul patterns.

Underworld Gods

The extremely ancient god Osiris actually pre-dates Egyptian civilization, and his name means "the hidden one." This god was once a great king who taught his people how to sow seeds and harvest the riches of the soil. After his earthly life, Osiris became an earth god associated with corn, trees, and fertile soil. In later centuries, he transmogrified into the ruler of the Egyptian underworld, Duat. Then as now, the Moon was considered quite magical, and Osiris' legend includes his body being torn into pieces and made whole again. As plant growth often coincides with lunar cycles, Osiris was affiliated with the Moon in his earliest role.

The history of the Greek god Cronus (the Roman god Saturn) contains many similar elements. Cronus is a very, very old god, and the earliest statues of him date to 7000 BCE. He was once a living king who taught agricultural techniques. Like Osiris, Cronus became an earth god associated with the harvest and then relocated (willingly or forcibly, depending on the source) to the edge of Tartarus, the Greek underworld. Cronus' son Pluto (a.k.a. Hades) is the lord of the underworld, but his first identity was Ploutos (Roman Plutus), the son of Demeter and her demigod consort, Iasion. Ploutos is the god at the roots of the Earth and he is associated with wealth.

The most familiar myth of underworld journeying is that of Demeter and Persephone. After her daughter was abducted by Hades, Demeter blanketed the world with cold and refused to allow anything to grow until her daughter's return. Winter is Demeter's revenge. Persephone is an embodiment of feminine life-giving energies. While her presence is needed above the Earth during the growing months, her visit to the underworld in the winter is purposeful. To early peoples, spring "rose" from the Earth, so she needed to be beneath it to make her big entrance on the Earth's stage at the Spring Equinox.

Persephone's tale echoes that of Inanna, the Sumerian goddess who endures a similar journey to the underworld. She offered her consort to the underworld demons and he remained as their king. In later Orphic revisions, this god (called Zagreus, Sabazios, or Dionysus) returns to life in the spring.

Yule lore features underworld journeys by the Sun or the Holly King. In Nordic lore, this journey is made by the gentle Sun god Balder. These figures travel to the dark realm so that the life-giving energy of the Sun can be reborn. As may be expected with the more explosive drama associated with male deities, fierce battles ensue to ensure their return. Male deities enact the return of the Sun, while female deities enact the renewal of Earth's fertility. Both roles are important since the fight for life occurs both on the Earth and in the sky.

The Fates

The Fates are consistently associated with the life-and-death axis, which is sometimes called the World Pillar, the World Tree, or the Spindle of Necessity. In Nordic myth, the Norns are stationed at the roots of the World Tree, Yggdrasil. It is their job to water Yggdrasil to keep it healthy and growing, since an evil dragon is constantly chewing at its roots. The Norns were said to weave webs of life from east to west, and sometimes appeared as swans or mermaids to give mortals advice or to foretell the future. The Norns' weaving was done blindly according to Ørlög, the external laws of the universe that determined turns of fate (much like kismet, karma, or fate). Ørlög was an older power than the Norns and was applied to group destiny as much as personal fate. The well-being of the group was essential to survival, and a person who carried bad fate could spoil the group's luck.

The Greeks had a similar notion: The Fates, or Moirae, were placed atop the Spindle of Necessity to spin, weave, and cut the threads of life. Necessity, personified as the goddess Ananké, joined with Kronos (Time) to give birth to Aether, Chaos, Erebos (Darkness), and Heimarmene (Fate or Destiny). Fate is created through Necessity and Time. Yet like the Norns, Necessity and Time were older and more powerful forces that dictated the spinning of the threads of life.

The Fates are entwined with birth and death, so they are generally placed near the entrance or exit of souls in cosmological architectures. In the late classical period, Prothyraia was the goddess of the doorway, the portal between life and death. Orphic rituals use this name as a designation for either Artemis or Hecate. Selket and Amentet are portal guardians in Egyptian lore.

Location, Location, Location

Osiris was provided with a ladder, the Djed, to climb into the underworld, and this ladder goes up, not down. Occult and esoteric lore places the underworld in the vast darkness of the night sky. As the outermost visible planet, Saturn mediates the portal between life and death. In Platonic and Hermetic thought, human souls are created in the cosmos and made of the same stuff as the stars. When a soul is incarnated, it becomes entwined with *Anima Mundi*, the World Soul. After death, illuminated souls return to the cosmos. Developing souls return to new bodies for further learning and improvement.

In Hermetic thought, the cosmos was regarded as a massive recycling system. Souls originate from the maker of the cosmos, the "origin and root of all." Immortal souls are placed in mortal bodies, giving mankind a dual nature. The Great Creator exists in eternity and created the cosmos, which functions with strict order and creates Time. Time is change, and is the source of generation, the cycles of life and death on Earth. The Earth gives birth to changing forms, which are dissolved and renewed. In the *Corpus Hermeticum*, Trismegistus writes ". . . for life is not birth, but perception; death is not change, but forgetting." This means that knowledge of the soul cannot be taught, but can be remembered.

The path of the dead and the underworld are associated with specific locations in the sky. At Midsummer and Yule, the Earth and Sun are aligned with the "root" of the galaxy, the Galactic Center, an invisible star nursery. The solstices are soul portals. The solstices link the ends of the Milky Way along the path of the dead. The two cosmic bears, Ursa Major and Ursa Minor, circle with the North Star, Polaris, around the top of the World Axis, while the ship *Argo*'s rudder, the star Canopus, marks the bottom of the axis. While the soul portals are north and south, death is sometimes associated with the Sun setting in the west.

Other sabbats are associated with death and the underworld, particularly Samhain. The Fates may be evoked at Imbolc for divination. Memorials to the dead are offered at Lammas. Deep Earth and root-working magic can be included in any of these sabbats.

Deep Earth Rituals

Ancient Earth-renewing rituals often took place in caves or underground sanctuaries and featured symbolic enactments of seeding, growth, death, and rebirth, as well as blood mysteries. The entrance of an underground sanctuary symbolized the shift from light into darkness and required consent from the guardian of the portal. Although a child exiting the womb goes from dark into light, the soul entering the body goes from light into darkness, losing its fiery etheric form as it is cloaked within the body.

Underworld deities and the Fates have great symbolic consistency. Goddesses of fate are invariably depicted with needles, spindles, mirrors, rudders, globes, or wheels. Goddesses who journey to the underworld have pomegranates and are associated with frogs, snakes, and lizards. Underworld gods are associated with trees: pine trees, sycamores, tamarisks, cypresses, and willows. The pine cone is a common tribute. Ladders or stairways serve to connect the Earth with the underworld. Libations to underworld gods are poured with the left hand. Oaths are witnessed by underworld gods when the oath-taker stomps on the ground three times with the left foot.

Magical rituals that involve Deep Earth and/or the underworld can focus on several areas: to get to the root of old problems, to heal difficult karma from past lives, to petition for aid or strength from dead relatives or ancestors, or to gain justice in disputed wills and estates.

The underworld is invisible, dark, and mysterious, so silence and darkness are critical components necessary for performing Deep Earth magic. Prepare a votive candle in a glass holder and submerge it in soil placed in a larger glass jar. This symbolizes taking a light into this dark realm.

Rituals should begin with evoking a gatekeeper deity before directly contacting the underworld. Set the stage by moving from light into darkness; extinguish all light except the candle submerged in soil. Once the connection has been made, ask for the needed aid, or express desires for healing, cleansing, justice, rejuvenating, or karmic remediation. In ancient Greek thought, the dead needed food to reawaken. Dig a hole in the ground and offer milk, honey, wine, bread, or blood. If the ritual includes a petition, place it in the soil after the offerings have been made. Complete the process by pushing the soil back into the hole. The final step is to acknowledge the gatekeeper when returning to the light.

Gemstones and semiprecious stones are found in the earth, and can be worn or carried as protective amulets. Bury the amulet in a jar or bowl filled with soil. Sprinkle the surface of the soil with appropriate root powders or herbs and charge it beneath the Moon or night sky. Magical roots, which are generally used in powdered form, include mandrake, lotus, goldenseal, comfrey,

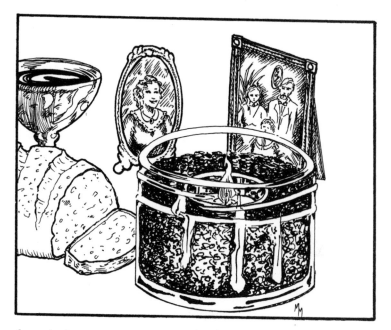

galangal, ginger, and ginseng roots. An underworld-charged amulet serves as a reminder of the presence of deceased relatives or mentors as a source of aid and protection, and offers a tool for invoking these connections when needed.

Place a crystal at the roots of an herb, flower, or tree when it is planted. When these herbs are harvested, they can be used in rituals. Make a tea of these herbs or burn it as incense to enhance the connection to the underworld realm.

Create an underworld "telephone" connection to get advice from a deceased loved one or mentor. Tie crystals to both ends of a string. Bury one crystal, and leave the other above the ground. Concentrate on a photograph or mental image of this person before sleeping, and request aid or advice through the medium of dreams. Remove the crystals from the soil when the answer has been received.

Since the underworld is associated with darkness, perform underworld rituals during the fourth-quarter Moon phase (waning Moon). Hecate is associated with earth, sea, and sky, but she also has significant lunar and underworld powers. Her chthonic, nocturnal, ghostly aspect is Antaia ("she who encounters you");

as goddess of crossroads, she is called Enodia or Trioditis (having three heads or bodies). Hecate and Artemis are both associated with black dogs. Bury dog hair with a crystal, petition, or food offerings, or fashion a small dog of clay to include with buried offerings.

Underworld Cuisine

Root vegetables are welcome additions to winter sabbats. These organic sources of energy-sustaining carbohydrates help the body ward off cold. Create your own version of Persephone Potatoes, Yama Yams, Tellus Turnips, or Belili Beets as a way of honoring the underworld gods and acknowledging the wealth found in their realm.

Ginseng and ginger are both useful, health-sustaining roots. Ginseng roots mimic the shape of a human, and the Chinese believe this root contains the powers of the Great Spirit. Ginseng is credited with sustaining good health and longevity. Ginger can be used as both a flavoring and as a tea. Keep ginger tea around in case anyone gets a stomach ache, as ginger settles the belly (especially those troubled from overindulging in feasts!). Ginger tea is also a gentle remedy for babies with colic. Use lotus or arrowroot in place of corn starch as a thickening agent.

~

As the health of the roots determines a plant's ability to flourish and flower, the health of one's personal roots is the key to sustaining a productive life that is well-grounded in the past and present, and prepared for the future. The nurturing and feeding of one's spiritual roots ensures that these invisible sources of life are revitalized and eager for fruition and fertility. Consider doing a root-healing ceremony during a personal fallow period to ensure that vibrant growth will follow.

Ancient Egyptian Earth Deities

by Denise Dumars

The earth deities of ancient Egypt are the deities of life and death. The cruel heat and dryness of the desert contrasted with the fertile soil of the inundation of the Nile River make this dichotomy abundantly clear.

Probably the most important Egyptian earth deity is Geb (sometimes spelled Seb), consort of the sky goddess Nut (see "Ancient Egyptian Air Deities" in this volume) and personification of the Earth itself. Not only were five new gods born of Geb's union with the sky goddess, but his body is seen as the life-giving force of all animals on Earth, who are said to "rest on Geb's back," and he nurtured and protected animals. One story finds Geb mourning dead animals until Nut explained to him the cycle of death and rebirth. After that, he understood that to die meant to "go into the body of Geb." Pharoahs ruled from "the throne of Geb," and Geb himself was the Great Pharoah, the father of Osiris, from whom Osiris took wisdom and by whom he was counseled. The sexual aspect of Geb is evident—as is true of many other "earthy" gods of Egypt—as he is usually depicted as a man in a sexually aroused state, gazing at his mate, Nut, who is above him in the sky.

In Geb's death aspect, he was seen as being responsible for the existence of poisonous snakes and earthquakes. Some sorcerers of Egypt believed that they could control poisonous snakes by petitioning Geb for protection, but a contrasting myth states that Ra, the creator deity, made snakes poisonous when Geb once got too big for his britches and tried to take over the throne of Ra. Ra sent a fiery serpent to bite him and drive him away, and poor old Geb has been herding snakes ever since!

Second only to the god Thoth in intellect among the Egyptian gods is Ptah, the god of architecture, building, engineering, craftsmanship, and inventor of tools of all kinds. Ptah is often shown wearing a skullcap and sometimes bound in mummy wraps, like Osiris. His name means "force captured in form," which is a good way of explaining how a house—or a pyramid—comes into being. When a sculptor in ancient Egypt made a statue of a deity out of clay, he would ask Ptah to breathe some life into it. Thoth's word was the intellectual idea of an object; Ptah's word was literally the object itself. It could be said that Thoth is the divine blueprint maker, and Ptah constructs the building outlined by the blueprint.

No wonder Ptah was so important to the Egyptians, as they created some of the most important and enduring feats of engineering and building in the ancient world. Those who work in architecture, construction, engineering, and as craftspersons today can consider Ptah as a patron, as was done in ancient times.

I once misread an e-mail from a friend in New York City. I had asked him how he got to work, and I thought he wrote that he "took the Ptah train." He said he had meant the "Path" train, but when he looked at the e-mail again, he found that he had indeed typed "Ptah." I told him it might well be a sign from Ptah to thank him for helping engineers create an efficient way of getting to work in overcrowded New York.

Imhotep was an architect, a builder, and something of a philosopher who lived during the twenty-seventh century BCE, and he is one of very few mortals who was deified in ancient Egypt. He was viewed as something of a demigod or a helper of Ptah who seemed to embody Ptah's traits in the form of a mortal man. One story calls him a son of Ptah conceived upon a mortal woman, a beautiful singer named Kherduankh. Imhotep was a popular deity during

the Roman period, a time when he was believed to have invented architecture and the plans for the pyramids. He was also considered a philosopher and a healer, and it was believed that he had a dialogue with Thoth in which he learned some of the secrets of Thoth's magic and medicine. The Greeks identified Imhotep with Asclepius, the god of medicine.

Imhotep sometimes appeared to people in their dreams as a shining scarab, and the scarab beetle god, Khepera, is another deity identified with the element of earth. The common dung beetle, a type of scarab, was observed in Egypt to roll balls of dung and to "give birth" to new scarabs as if spontaneously from the dung. Of course, the beetle merely lays its eggs in the dung, and they emerge when hatched. Egyptians, however, saw this process as symbolic of the Earth creating life, but also of the Sun as it "rolls" from the east to the west each day across the sky. Khepera is drawn as a scarab beetle or as a man with a scarab for a face, and sometimes Ra himself is portrayed with the face of a scarab, as god of all creation.

While the humble dung beetle and the June bug (another type of scarab) may appear drab, there are many types of scarabs that are beautiful metallic or iridescent colors. It is this latter type of scarab that is found in the designs of Egyptian jewelry. Scarabs are found all over the world. Large scarabs with iridescent green wings are common where I live in southern California, where they graze on native fruit and are colloquially known as "fig eaters." If you have seen an episode of the original *Twilight Zone* TV series called "Queen of the Nile," then you have seen one of these native Californian scarabs—the title character retained her youth and immortality by using scarabs to drain the life force of others! The mysteries of ancient Egypt endlessly inspire creativity.

Another god known for his "earthiness" is Min. He is portrayed as a standing figure with a large, erect penis! Min was originally a protector of fields and a god of animal husbandry and agriculture, but one legend states that he was promoted to being the "god of sex" when he allegedly made love to all of the women of Egypt while the men were away at war. In the Coffin Texts, he helped men to achieve sexual prowess and helped women to conceive when they ate lettuce, his sacred plant, as the juice of some varieties resembles semen. It is no surprise that the bull is one of Min's most sacred animals.

When the Greek cosmogony became predominant in Egypt, Min of course came to be identified with Osiris, the god who magically impregnates Isis after death. The Greeks saw Min as a version of Pan, an extremely randy deity.

The best-known Egyptian earth god is of course Osiris. As both god of the fertile soil of the Nile inundation and

god of the underworld, Osiris takes his role as both life-giving god and god of the dead without irony. "Eat of my flesh" was an early pronouncement of Osiris' and it referred to "The Black Land," Al-Khem, as Egypt was known. Without the rich black silt that was deposited by the Nile's flood, there would be no agriculture and hence no civilization in Egypt. And since Osiris is killed very early on in the myth of the origins of the gods of Heliopolis, a great amount of the mythology about him deals with his resurrection and his kingdom in the afterlife. The best-known surviving texts of Egypt are the texts of Osiris, variously called The Book of the Dead, the Opening of the Mouth, or The Book of Coming Forth By Day. All who died in Egypt would expect to be brought before the throne of Osiris, and, once judged worthy, would be invited to live with him eternally in the afterlife, where the dead would reawaken and live forever.

Osiris is usually depicted as a mummified man wearing the crown of a king and carrying the crook and flail of the pharoah. As a symbol of death and resurrection, his worship became central to the religion of the Egyptians after the Fourth Dynasty, and their religion then revolved around the myth of Osiris' birth, death, and resurrection, and the avenging of his death by his son, Horus. An elaborate ceremonial culture of death, including mummification and all the accoutrements with which the dead were buried and the elevation of a whole set of funerary gods then came to the fore, and this is the aspect of ancient Egyptian religion that we are most familiar with today.

Nephthys, an earth goddess in that she is associated with the funerary god Anubis, her son, is the dark twin of Isis (sister-wife of Osiris). They are identical, but where Isis wears a headdress that resembles a throne, Nephthys wears a headdress that resembles a small house, or possibly a tomb. Nephthys is the long-suffering consort of Set, and mother of Anubis by either Set or Osiris, with whom she is in love. She is a chief mourner for Osiris along with Isis, and the two of them are often shown together, either mourning Osiris or guarding the current pharaoh.

The son of Nephthys, Anubis, is portrayed as a black jackal or as a man with the head of a jackal. Anubis' priests wore jackal masks, as did embalmers, since Anubis was thought to protect the spirit of a dead person as the body was prepared for mummification and delivered safely to Osiris. Anubis and his shadowy counterpart, Wepwawet, the wolflike god of Lycopolis (unusual in that there are no native wolves in Egypt) are the guard dogs of the afterlife.

It is ironic that modern people know the Egyptian gods of death better than the gods of life, yet they are often two sides of the same coin. Egyptian funerary designs have been popular motifs in British and American cemeteries since the Victorian era. Isis, Osiris, Horus, and Anubis seem as popular with Egyptian culture aficionados as they were in 2300 BCE.

In Hollywood, California, two larger-than-life statues of Anubis guide moviegoers into the darkened auditorium of Grauman's Egyptian Theatre. The living willingly enter to view those who have been made immortal not by embalming, but by the magic of embedding moving images onto film.

For Further Study

Clark, R. T. Rundle. *Myth and Symbol in Ancient Egypt.* New York: Thames and Hudson, 1995.

Clark, Rosemary. *The Sacred Magic of Ancient Egypt,* St. Paul, MN: Llewellyn Publications, 2003.

Harris, Eleanor L. *Ancient Egyptian Divination and Magic.* Boston, MA: Weiser Books, 1998.

Regula, deTraci, *The Mysteries of Isis.* St. Paul, MN: Llewellyn Publications, 1999.

Broom Magic and Folklore

by James Kambos

Brooms have been associated with folk magic and witchcraft since ancient times. Among the earliest known magical rites involving brooms were fertility rituals that people performed to encourage abundant crops. And since broomsticks are phallic symbols, it's easy to understand why they were used in fertility magic. During these rituals, farmers would mount brooms and sometimes pitchforks, then ride them like hobbyhorses through the fields. As they rode their brooms, they would dance and leap, believing that this would make their crops grow tall. This magical rite of jumping high into the air while riding a broom probably became the basis for the belief that Witches could fly on their broomsticks. Female Witches and the occasional male sorcerer were depicted riding brooms, but men were more likely shown riding pitchforks.

We may never know for sure how the belief came about that Witches could fly on brooms. Some theories suggest it may be related to astral projection. But the image of a Witch and a black cat riding a broom, silhouetted against a Full Moon, remains a classic symbol of the Craft and magic.

The magical qualities that brooms are believed to possess have continued to capture our imaginations well into modern times. Even major films have paid tribute to the magical qualities of brooms. The Walt Disney film *Fantasia* (1940) entertains us to this day with a sorcerer's magic broomstick. And of course Harry Potter has brought the enchanted flying broom into the twenty-first century.

Brooms and Household Magic

Eventually brooms were used for more than just fertility magic. In time, both Witches and non-Witches found many magical uses for the broom in and around the home.

One reason brooms became popular as magical tools in the home is because they could be disguised as an ordinary household item. For example, brooms were used as wands to direct magical energy or to cast a magical circle. During the Burning

56

Times, anyone could be persecuted, even executed, for possessing a magical tool, yet the broom could be left out in the open. Its magical use would never be suspected.

Brooms were also used to protect the home in several ways. Placing a broom across the threshold to repel negative magic is a very old custom. And sprinkling salt near the broom was believed to add even greater protection.

When misfortune was thought to have entered a home, one old German custom was to sweep the home, thus sweeping away any negativity. Each family member would grab a broom and begin sweeping. Starting at the center of the home, they'd sweep outward toward all exterior doors. As they swept, they'd open their front and back doors and sweep out the negativity.

To get rid of an unwanted guest, try this old folk magic charm: Place your broom so that the handle is leaning toward your guest and visualize them leaving. It's believed the person will soon feel uncomfortable and move on their way.

Since broomsticks are symbols of fertility and domesticity, they're used to bring good luck to the home. To bless a new home or the home of a newly married couple, try this bit of broom magic: Crush a few almonds and blend them with a drop or two of honey to make a paste. Next, dab a bit of this mixture on the bristles of a new broom as you think happy, peaceful thoughts. Sweep the front threshold of the home to seal in positive vibrations. Your new broom can now be used for daily or magical use, as you see fit.

To smudge a space or purify your home, remove three bristles from

your broom and light them like a candle. Carry them in a clockwise direction around your home (or only one room) to clear away any negativity.

Even though brooms are thought to bring good fortune, many people still consider it unlucky to sweep after sunset. It's believed that during the fourteenth century, Witches in the British Isles would choose that time of day to perform magic with their brooms by "sweeping" a magic spell toward someone or toward another home. Since it was a serious crime during that era to perform magic of any type, many people refused to sweep outside after sunset in order to avoid being suspected of witchcraft. This eventually led to the belief that sweeping after twilight would lead to misfortune. To this day, my mother and grandmother will never let me use a broom or shake out a rug after dark!

Another interesting folk belief is that you should never sweep around the feet of a single person. It was believed that they'd never marry.

Brooms and Marriage Rituals

As I've said earlier, brooms are good luck and fertility symbols, so it's easy to understand their role in marriage and handfasting ceremonies.

"To marry over the broomstick" is an old term meaning that a couple was joined in a common-law union by jumping over a broomstick together.

Jumping forward and backward over a broomstick is a custom at many Gypsy (Roma) weddings. Another age-old wedding custom is having the newlyweds enter their home by stepping over a broomstick.

Materials For Brooms

The earliest brooms were known as *besoms* and were made by simply tying the broom plant around a stick.

Ash was later used for the handle, birch twigs for the brush (also called a spray), and willow for the binding. Sometimes hazel was used for the handle, oak twigs for the spray, and birch for the binding.

It's interesting to note that the materials used to make early brooms have magical significance. Ash is known for strength and as a symbol of the World Tree, birch is sacred to the Goddess, and willow is associated with Moon magic and Hecate, goddess of magic. Hazel signifies wisdom and is used for wands, while oak symbolizes strength, fertility, and the God aspect.

Collecting Brooms

Brooms are fun to collect, whether you want to use them for magic or for their decorative charm. There are many styles to choose from. The cottage broom is the standard household broom. Whisk brooms are the smallest type of broom. Cindersweeps are also small, but the bristles are bound at an angle, which makes them handy to use if you want to clean around a hearth or wood-stove. One of my favorites is called a cobweb sweep. It's narrow with flexible bristles that are up to two feet long. Due to its size and long bristles, it's good to use for cleaning corners or beneath furniture. And if you're so inclined, it's easy to use for casting a magic circle.

If you're crafty, you can make your own broom, but if you want a broom made in the traditional manner, you can still find trained broom makers. You can sometimes find them at farmers' markets or at agricultural heritage shows. A good online source is www.bereacollegecrafts.com.

~

Brooms are among the oldest of all household items. Their over-all appearance has remained almost unchanged for centuries. It's one of the traditional tools of both the Witch and the home-maker. No matter if you wish to use your broom for the magical or the mundane, remember: the more you use your trusty broom, the more it will be imbued with your personal power.

Using Your Home as a Magical Tool

by Diana Rajchel

Have you considered the way your home affects you on a magical level? Is each space adapted to your needs, both mundane and metaphysical? If you have your home set up for ease of use, are you making the most of that comfort to assist your magical goals? You can organize your space to invite magic, even without your constant physical presence.

The Chinese are well-known for the art of feng shui. It's a living and décor style that taps into some wonderful principles of energy management, but it doesn't always fit with the motif of the ever-colorful Pagan. However, it is possible to combine feng shui–style decluttering with Western energy management. You just need to clean up, clear out, and understand these basic principles: energy needs to flow freely and energy needs a way to build up before you release it for a specific purpose.

Gauge how "full" your home feels. If your house feels bursting, it needs an energy release. If you come home to a cluttered house, you wind up going out into the world and on into a cluttered life—as within, so without. Organization at home echoes in the outside world: you are less forgetful and things run just a bit more smoothly in your daily life.

Before you begin rooting out your excess, create a plan for your space. Start with your daily needs and finish with your long-term desires. Sometimes the magical purpose is the same as the practical; for instance, better sleep is a popular goal. Along with the health benefits, it ties neatly into magical development: you have a better chance of dream recall and lucid dreams, and once good sleep is established you can try dream incubation to plant symbols and intents in your subconscious. If you only have one magical goal, put your effort into that.

Once you have your plan, begin evacuation. Abandon all excuses for hanging on to items you haven't touched in over a year. Items easily disposed of include stockpiled candles and stones, outdated electronic equipment, and old magazines and books. Sell, donate, or recycle as much of your excess as possible.

Decluttering will cause an energetic upheaval. You'll find objects that trigger memories—some good, some bad—that will leave a residue. Since you want to create a fresh new reality, you'll need to sweep that residue out. A house cleansing should refresh your space after your junk detox. Banish the old energy with a symbolic sweeping of the broom in each room, and light a smudge stick to invite the type of energy you want to fill your space.

Once you've cleansed, it's time to fill in empty spaces with the energy you desire. If you have a goal that affects your entire space, try doing something small in each room to prepare for that new reality. For instance, if you'd like a new love or a new friend, create a space that allows for two or more people. You don't need to buy a larger bed if you can't afford one, but you can do small things like adding another pillow or a second throw to your couch. You can include a few more glasses and plates in your kitchen cupboard, the better to serve guests the traditionally proffered drink. You can place images around your home showing people engaged in the activities that you want happening in your space. If you can buy artwork for your walls, that's fantastic, and I encourage you to invest in some lovely pieces from local artists. If you are not so endowed at this time, a simple work-around is to print images you find online that speak to you, or cut pictures from magazines. They don't need to be in full color; you can make a magical project out of coloring in the images yourself, assigning colors that further empower the images with your purpose.

Whether you use a single room or your entire home to build energy, take charge of that space. Evaluate everything from your furniture to your coat hangers; if any item in your home doesn't serve its purpose perfectly, find something that fills your need exactly. Hunt online, in thrift stores, and in dollar stores. Expect a delay of gratification. You may have to take makeshift mea-

sures for the meantime while you save for what you need or work around the requirements of a lease.

Whole-house magic requires an up-front investment of time and money, which will pay off in every minute you don't have to spend looking for something you misplaced, and in the feeling you get when you come home from work and can simply do what you looked forward to doing all day. Patience is a big part of the initial price of your efforts.

Ultimately, what you do is to empower your space with your intent is up to you. The following suggestions are simply guidelines based on common Western magical correspondences. There is no absolute formula, but touching on alignments that other people have invested the energy of their belief into will mean less work for you in the long run. If you're unable to paint a room or obtain a specific piece of furniture, innovate! You can always hang fabrics or tapestries, take images from magazines and make collages on poster board, or even display your own art projects that express your desires and put forth your intention. You can buy or make floor pillows to enhance seating. If you hate a certain color, don't use it; if you have profound positive psychological associations with a color, apply it!

Prosperity: Fill your home with greens, golds, oranges, and pinks. Living plants that are well cared for encourage abundance, as do fish. Good pet choices include goldfish, which are associated with wealth, and guppies because of their well-known fertility and abundance. Add rich fabrics and/or rich textures in the form of pillows, throws, and wall art, and make the space as comfortable and cushy as you can, especially any workspace you spend time in. The keyword behind prosperity is *comfort*: people want riches so that they can live with greater ease.

Love (Romantic): Make space for two or more people in your home. Hang images on your wall of happy couples (somewhat difficult to find in modern art, but surprisingly available in tarot decks and in online images.) Try to choose couples that have characteristics you would like in a lover and in a relationship. For instance, if you would like a relationship based on consideration and respect, an image of a knight and his lady would bring in that type of energy. Be sure your bed is ready to receive an additional person: add a second pillow, and perhaps buy the highest thread-count sheets you can afford. Put items around your home that reflect sensual pleasure and companionship, such as a book you enjoy reading out loud, soft fuzzy things to touch, or items for self-pleasure. Use pinks and roses, reds, and oranges. When choosing pictures of famous lovers and the passion you want, make sure you know the full history of the art's subject—very few women would truly want a lover who emulates the relationship habits of Zeus, Don Juan, Casanova, or Donald Trump. Also, keep in mind that the affair between Romeo and Juliet ended quite badly.

Sleeping/Dreaming: Make sure the spaces you sleep in have excess light blocked out. Populate the room with soothing colors, such as lavenders, blues, greens, and pastel shades. Images of people sleeping or the Greek god Morpheus are also helpful. If you are not prone to allergies, gentle herbal smells (like a sachet of mugwort, rosemary, and peppermint) can also enhance your dreams. Also add a few psychological sleep aids—a dream journal and a before-bed journal can empty the mind when it's difficult to sleep, and a picture book, such as an illustrated copy of *Children's*

Garden of Verse by Robert Louis Stevenson can help imprint a sense of safety and happiness that can ease the mind into sleep.

~

The above are suggestions, rather than formulas. Shape your space to suit you and your purposes. You'll find that all areas of life flow more easily after you've put your home in order and worked out the best way to keep it in order. You'll sleep better—no need to stay up hunting for that misplaced item or all the items you need for the next day! You'll be more likely to have your bills paid on time, to make all your appointments, and to accomplish one or two of those extra little things that you put off. These conveniences alone are simply the magic of cleaning and staying organized. When you do perform rituals, the energy will flow quite easily through your space to your intended goal, all thanks to the magic of organized living. Your organized home becomes a powerful magical tool. Even when you're out working and living your life, your home will be generating energy for you that you can come home to, tap into, and enjoy.

Spiritual Housecleaning: Integrating the Magickal and the Mundane

by Deborah Blake

If you have ever read any of my books, you will already know that I talk a lot about the importance of integrating your spiritual beliefs as a Witch with your mundane, day-to-day life. For one thing, I am a strong advocate of "walking your talk"—that is to say, acting on your values instead of just talking about them. But beyond the credibility issue, there are many benefits to adding magick to the mundane on a regular basis.

One of the best examples of this is what I like to call "spiritual housecleaning." I realize that most of us don't think of doing the chores around the house as an uplifting experience. Personally, I'd rather read a book than mop the floor any day of the week. On the other hand, since I *have* to clean the house, I try to take advantage of some witchy tools to make the job more enjoyable and more effective.

Why Do It?

Turning regular housecleaning into spiritual housecleaning takes a little extra thought and effort—so why should we bother?

There are two obvious benefits. The first is practical: you can clean and protect your house on a magickal level at the same time you are doing a necessary chore. Spiritual housecleaning goes beyond the dirt and clutter to address the underlying negative energy and psychic disorder that can create unseen problems in your home. Additionally, you can add in protection work to keep yourself, your loved ones, and your belongings safe.

The second benefit is less noticeable, but equally valuable. The more we practice our craft, the better at it we get, and the more in tune we are with our own spiritual paths. So if you can combine a few of your witchy practices with your sweeping, mopping, and dusting, you will not only end up with a cleaner house, but as a stronger Witch as well.

Starting with the Basics

As with most magickal work, spiritual housecleaning can be as simple or as complicated as you want to make it. You can create an entire ritual, wear special garb, and cast a formal circle before ever picking up a dust rag. Or you can start with a few basic techniques and add in more complex workings on special occasions when they are needed.

The simplest element to add to your everyday cleaning approach is the one at the core of all magickal practice: intent. All it takes to change mundane cleaning into magickal cleaning on a fundamental level is the intent to do so. Take a few minutes before starting your cleaning chores and do some visualization work.

Light a candle or some incense if it helps you to concentrate and close your eyes. See yourself sweeping or mopping or whatever form of physical cleaning you will be doing. Then visualize yourself washing away all negative energy that might linger from old arguments, fears and worries, or unpleasant guests. Once this image is set in your mind, go about your chores, remembering periodically to focus on ridding yourself of any lingering negativity.

If you want to toss another witchy tool into the mix, try using herbs and plants. Many of the herbs that are used magickally for clearing and cleansing also have practical cleaning properties. The citrus plants (lemon, orange, grapefruit, and the like) are all magickal energy cleansers and boosters, and they have scientifically proven antibacterial qualities, too. In addition, they smell nice, which makes the cleaning process more pleasant. Other herbs, like peppermint and rosemary, have both magickal and mundane applications—for a good list, check out any magickal herbal book, such as the ones written by Scott Cunningham or Ellen Dugan.

The easiest way to use most herbs or other plants in cleaning is in the form of essential oils. A few drops of an individual oil can be placed into the wash water or onto a cleaning rag. I like to combine a few that smell good together into a "spiritual cleaning" magickal oil that I can keep on hand for whenever I need it. Just be sure to dilute the oils and test any new mixtures on surfaces before you use them on a wide scale.

And don't forget the humble sage smudge stick. I like to start or end a serious housecleaning session by smudging the whole house, like when I do spiritual spring cleaning at the end of the winter.

Spiritual Spring Cleaning

Whether or not you add magickal cleansing to your everyday cleaning, it is a good idea to give your entire home a thorough spiritual housecleaning at least once a year. I do mine in the spring, both because it is a traditional time to do a major cleanup and because after a long, cold upstate New York winter, it feels good to throw open the windows and let in some fresh energy.

Depending on where you live and your own personal circumstances, you may decide to do your yearly "deep clean" at a different time—in September, when the kids go back to school and you finally have your house back, for instance, or on the day before your birthday so you can start the next year fresh. Whenever you choose to do it, here are some simple spiritual "spring" cleaning tips. Keep in mind that you can use some or all of these, and alter them to fit your needs.

• Start by opening up a window in every room. If it is too cold to do that, open at least one window at the top of the house (or farthest room into an apartment).

- Gather whatever magickal tools you are going to use: a sage smudge stick, salt, water, a container to put them in, and anything else that suits you. If desired, you can bless these on your altar or under a Full Moon before you use them.

- Say a small prayer or spell for cleansing, protection, and/or positive energy. I use this simple blessing: *Bless this home where I reside, keep it safe from woe and harm. Watch over those who here reside, I make it so by will and charm.* If you want, light a candle on your altar or some other place where it is safe to leave it burning unattended while you finish your cleansing.

- Light the smudge stick and walk from room to room, wafting the fragrant smoke into every corner. Pay special attention to energetic entrances and exits: doors, windows, chimneys, etc. As you walk through the house, keep your focus on your intention to clear and cleanse all the energy of anything negative or harmful.

- Repeat this with either salt and water separately or a mix of both in a bowl. Sprinkle the water from your fingertips in the same way you wafted the smoke of the sage stick, and make sure you get salt on the windowsills and doorways. (This will create a bit of mess, but you can clean up when you do physical spring cleaning afterward.)

- Put those rags, brooms, and polishes to good use!

- When you have finished, go through the house again, closing the windows behind you. Be sure to visualize anything unhealthy going out the windows before you close them. Your home is now clean and clear and ready for another year of living.

In Times of Crisis

All this basic clearing and cleansing work is great for keeping your home clean under normal circumstances. But what about when circumstances aren't normal? Everyone has been through bad times, when it seems like everything around you is tainted by fear, or anger, or grief. At times like these—either during, if you are up to it, or afterward—it is a good idea to pull out a few additional spiritual housecleaning tools.

Depending on what issues you are dealing with, there are a few more dynamic approaches to take. One simple way to add more power is to add more people; if you have a coven or even a few witchy friends, a group can really add to the "oomph" of a spiritual cleansing. A group cleansing is nice when you move into a new home, as well.

If you are feeling threatened or vulnerable, you can do some protection magick. I like to use a mixture of sea salt, dried rosemary, dried basil, and dried peppermint. I mix the herbs together in a bag and consecrate them for magickal use. Then I walk around the outside of my home and property line, scattering the mixture (if you live in an apartment, you can do this inside—just be sure to leave it for a day or so before vacuuming it back up again) and saying repeatedly: "This house is protected, this land is protected, all those who reside here are protected from harm, both natural and man-made, intentional or accidental."

Alternatively, you can add any of these or other protective herbs to your mop water or window-cleaning water, or soak rosemary in water overnight and then sprinkle the water on your broom as you sweep.

To deal with anger issues, substitute calming herbs, such as lavender, chamomile, or lemon balm. (Again, using essential oils can be easier than using the fresh or dried herbs, but it is up to you. You can always soak the herbs in water, then strain them out and use the water that has been infused with the magickal essence of the plants.)

And don't forget to say a prayer or cast a spell to help dissipate the unwanted energy or emotions. After all, spells and prayers are among the most powerful tools a Witch has at his or her disposal.

Maintaining the Magic

All the tools we've talked about are easy to use, relatively cheap, and not hard to find. But let's not forget about the most basic tool a Witch has: faith.

One of the tenets of witchcraft is that we can use magick to create positive changes in the world around us and in ourselves. By adding a dash of magick to everyday chores like mopping, dusting, or sweeping, we are not only cleansing the energy of our homes; each swipe of a cloth or swish of a broom reinforces our faith in our gods and in our own ability to create positive change through the smallest of actions.

Repeated daily or weekly, such actions strengthen our power as Witches and demonstrate our intention to integrate our spiritual beliefs into every aspect of our lives. We truly become Everyday Witches.

And hopefully, our houses are a little bit cleaner.

Lessons From the East:
The Rituals of Everyday Life

by Marcus F. Griffin

In the often all-too-hurried pace of our everyday lives, we look to the East for inspiration and a new beginning—the Far East, a land steeped in ceremony, tradition, and ritual. Let us visit the Land of the Rising Sun. Close your eyes and see a vision of the Goddess before you . . .

You see the goddess of mercy and compassion, the timeless Quan Yin. She smiles at you and extends her hand, beckoning you to come away with her and journey for a time.

You reach for her, and like a vision from a dream, the two of you rise into the air together, sailing, flying high above the world. You pass over fields and forests, mountains and rivers. The land finally gives way to the blue-green waters of a vast ocean, and you are awed by its scope and beauty. You soon see a hazy tracing of coastline far ahead in the distance. You realize that in a matter of moments, you have traveled thousands of

71

miles from your home. The outline becomes clearer, and you recognize that it is an island, one of the islands of Japan. Led by the guiding hand of Quan Yin, you race inland. Soon you see signs of civilization below. You begin to descend, and in the blink of an eye, you find yourself standing in a beautiful Buddhist garden. You look at the goddess as if to question what has happened, but she is no longer there. Instead, you find yourself standing next to a young Japanese woman dressed in a kimono. She smiles and bows to you, and bids you to accompany her deeper into the garden.

You follow her, and you soon see that she is leading you to an area of the garden that has been prepared for a special ceremony. A straw mat has been laid on the ground. Placed neatly on the mat are a bowl, a scoop, and a whisk. The young woman kneels on the mat, and you realize that you have been invited to participate in a traditional Japanese tea ceremony . . .

~

I have always been fascinated by the Japanese culture and the habit of the Japanese people to ritualize seemingly mundane events and tasks. In fact, it was this very fascination that led me to study magick and Paganism, thus helping to create the person I am today. Although the majority of modern-day Westerners find little reason to celebrate or ritualize everyday events and tasks, such as inviting someone into our homes or serving liquid refreshments, adding even a little ritual and ceremony to our mundane lives and situations can make a huge difference in the amount of enjoyment we reap from our day-to-day existence. This is the gift of the Japanese people, a gift from the East.

Magick is all around us, and we must use our magickal eyes to see it, for the mundane world often clouds such vision. I have heard many Pagans complain about never having enough time to practice ritual and magick in their everyday lives. Even worse, I have heard members of the magickal community say they feel like "bad Pagans" or "lousy Witches" simply because they don't have or can't make enough time in their lives for ritual and magick. This is both sad and unnecessary. As modern-day practitioners, it is not only our right but also our responsibility to find the magick in the mundane and set an example for those who would follow in our footsteps.

Being a truly magickal individual means putting magick into everything we say and do. To live a truly magickal life, we must ritualize even seemingly mundane events and tasks. We must rediscover the sacred ceremony of everyday life and learn to draw magick from the mundane. Let's take a look at a few mundane tasks and situations most of us experience on a regular basis. Let's gain some understanding of how much or how little magick we have allowed to permeate our everyday lives.

In my early years, I was formally trained as a chef, so I naturally learned to appreciate the ritual of preparing and serving great food. While there are many good books available on kitchen witchery, I have yet to find one that offers in-depth study into the art of ritualizing the everyday mundane meal. Since the preparation and consumption of food is such an integral and necessary part of our daily lives, it's a good place to start. To discover how much magick and ritual you have been putting into your daily meals, visualize yourself preparing a meal in your home. What is your attitude as you go about the task of preparing the meal? Are you putting love and joy into your work or are you just haphazardly tossing ingredients into a pan? Are you grumbling about having to cook after a long day of work, or are you taking pleasure in the escape from your long hard day? Are you envisioning the enjoyment that you and your family will receive from the meal, or are you thinking about the dirty dishes you'll have to wash? Are you taking pleasure in serving the meal, or are you just happy the whole ordeal is over with?

Now that you have gained some understanding of how you have been approaching the task of preparing a meal on a daily basis, imagine how the mealtime would be different if you were preparing the meal for a very special guest you invited into your home for dinner. Would you have put a little extra time and care into selecting the ingredients for the meal than you would if the meal were for you alone? Why or why not? Would you have taken the time to create a special recipe and a unique dining atmosphere for you and your guest to enjoy? Now imagine that *you* are the guest . . . does it make you feel special when someone takes the time to create something fantastic, just for you?

More than anything else, it is our awareness and attitude toward everyday tasks and events that are key to making them either magickal or mundane. Something as simple as sweeping the floor can become a ritual. We not only clean our homes when

we sweep, but we also clean our spirits by symbolically sweeping away what is no longer useful and opening the door to change.

It has been suggested by the six degrees of separation theory that as humans, we are only six people away from everyone else on the planet. The people we interact with ultimately create a chain of acquaintances with no more than five intermediaries. In other words, you and I and everyone we have ever interacted with are only five people away from having interacted with everyone else on Earth! If this theory is correct, then the amount of responsibility we hold as practitioners of the magickal arts must be taken to a whole new level. If we truly influence that many lives, then we need to look at even casual interactions and mundane acquaintances with our magickal eyes to be able to see the scope of our influence.

Imagine yourself making a trip to the grocery store … how many people will you interact with while doing this mundane task? What is your mental attitude while you are doing your shopping? Are you happy to be shopping or do you view it as a burdensome chore? To what degree do you think your attitude will affect the people you interact with? Are you influencing the people you come into contact with in a negative or positive way? How much of your attitude will other people pass on to people they know? Do you see how even a slight adjustment in your outlook or in the way you handle mundane situations can affect yourself and everyone you come into contact with?

Now imagine how it would be different if your trip to the grocery store were a planned-out ritual. Imagine that everything you put in your shopping cart was an important ingredient for a spell. Imagine that every motion you make and every word you speak to the people you come into contact with is spiritually symbolic of the outcome you wish to achieve by performing your ritual.

By taking the time to ritualize even one mundane task every day, you can greatly increase the amount of enjoyment you and everyone around you experiences in your day-to-day lives. The next time someone knocks on your door, make him or her feel welcome, whether they are intruding on your time or not. Honor their visit to your home with a special greeting or a cup of freshly brewed tea. The next time someone treats you rudely, send a little positive energy their way or give them a kind word. By doing so, you just may positively impact the lives of thousands of people you will never meet. The next time you are driving home from the grocery store, ritualize your trip by trying to see the beauty that exists within all things. Honor that beauty by making it a part of your day and sharing it with another person. Honor yourself with the ritual of everyday life.

When you arrive back home from the store with sacks full of the choices you have made, you have decided whether your shelves will be stocked with joy or sadness—that is, the magickal or the ordinary. The sacred ceremony of everyday life is yours for the taking. Only you can decide if you will see the world with your magickal eyes, or if you will close them and turn away. Only you can find the magick in the mundane . . .

～

Close your eyes and find yourself kneeling on a straw mat on which has been placed a bowl, a scoop, and a whisk. You see that the bowl has been filled with fresh tea leaves waiting to be ground into a fine powder. Looking up, you see Quan Yin sitting across the mat from you. The look of anticipation and pleasure shines clearly in her eyes. You see that you are dressed in a kimono, and you realize that somehow you have replaced the young Japanese woman in the tea ceremony.

But you have never performed the Japanese tea ceremony before, and you look to the goddess for guidance. She smiles at you and says, "All life is a ritual. Every moment a chance for celebration. Every breath a ceremony. Always the hard part is deciding where to begin. There is no right or wrong way . . . show me only what is in your heart and you can do no wrong." You pick up the scoop and begin your ceremony—the ritual of everyday life.

Air Magic

A Little Bird Told Me:
The Art of Ornithomancy

by Mickie Mueller

"Birds are often the messengers of the gods," I explained. Autumn was a friend who had come to me for advice. She had been seeing hawks a lot lately, sitting on a signpost, buzzing her car while she was driving, and that afternoon she had come home from work to find a flock of them in her yard.

"A flock! Are you sure? How many are we talking?" I asked, very surprised.

"Oh, there were at least ten of them," she said. I was silent for a moment.

"Hawks don't usually flock," I said in a measured tone. "I would say they have a message for you that you've been ignoring, and now they are really trying to get your attention by acting out of character." Now Autumn was silent for a minute, thinking, searching.

"You know, every other time that I noticed them over the past week, I was thinking about applying for a job at a different company that I heard was hiring. I'm really not happy where I am, but I'm nervous to try switching careers. I don't know if they would even hire me."

"Well, I would say you'd better get your resume together and get on it!" I laughed. "The hawks are telling you that you'll succeed."

Since ancient times, birds have been revered as messengers of the spirit realm. Flitting among the tree-tops and dancing through the air at will, they seemed like they must be aware of the plans of the very gods themselves, privy to the things in the universe that we were unaware of. Therefore, it makes sense that we can learn a lot from their appearances, behavior, and habits. It was believed that the gods would even send messages through the birds, as denizens of both the land and the air, a mystical go-between of sorts. The Greeks called this the art of ornithomancy, and the Romans called it auspicy, but many other civilizations used this form of divination as well.

We can still use this ancient art today. It's a wonderful form of divination for people who want to get in touch with nature, and receiving omens through feathered messengers can be quite rewarding. Orni-

thomancy isn't difficult to learn, and it truly makes you slow down and pay attention to the natural world.

We see birds every day, but it's when they really catch your eye or you feel as if they are there for a reason that it's a good idea to sit up and take notice, and ask, "What do you have to tell me, my friend?" But remember, sometimes a bird is just a bird. How do you know when it's more? When you feel riveted upon seeing it, or feel a pull on your solar plexus or a soaring in your heart. If you see a bird that's unusual for the area, or acting in an unusual way, chances are it is trying to get your attention. Sometimes if you are thinking of a life situation or need an answer, a bird will simply appear in your line of sight. Watching the bird's actions and even noting what kind of bird it is may give you clues to your best course of action.

Some specific bird actions have specific meanings. When a bird flies from right to left, it's a good sign that you will achieve your goals with ease. If the bird flies from left to right, be prepared for some delays or obstacles—you may need to rethink things or seek advice. A bird flying straight toward you means things are quickly improving, and happy days are ahead. A bird flying high and fast—or even better, flying straight up—means great and quick success! A bird flying quickly away from you warns you to proceed with caution and delay plans for a short time to get your bearings. If a bird flies horizontally, you will reach your goal, but the going will probably get tough. If you see a bird land and take off several times, or flying erratically, you need to go back to the drawing board because there are unseen problems to be resolved before you proceed. If the bird in question takes off and then changes direction mid-flight, you'll need to be flexible because a change of heart may lie ahead. Have you ever seen a bird flying against the wind? They kind of hover and seem to stand still. This is an indicator that someone you're dealing with is not what they appear to be, so beware: someone you think is a friend may not have your best interests at heart.

There are also different meanings behind what kinds of birds you see. Birds come in many colors. If you can't identify the exact species, the color of a bird can be used as an indicator. Use these color correspondences if you can't identify the bird.

Red: a sign of good luck
Orange: excitement and bliss
Yellow: keep your guard up
Green: an adventure is ahead
Blue: love and joy
White: happiness and joy, a good omen
Gray: peace and contentment
Black and white: you will avoid trouble
Brown: good health, healing
Brown and white: happy hearth and home
Black: a warning of danger or a show of the unseen

If you *can* identify the bird in question, you have a more accurate oracle because each bird species has its own personal message. Here is a short list of common birds and the themes of the messages they bring us. Of course, some birds have personal significance to individuals, so interpretations may differ. As with any form of divination, listen to your heart and spirit.

Bluebird: happiness, spiritual awakening
Cardinal: life-changing events, take care of your health

Crane: use all the wisdom at your disposal

Crow: cawing means you may have enemies working against you, so it's time to bump up your shields; a crow in flight foretells of upcoming travel

Dove: peace and joy, a goddess bird, promise for the future

Duck: everything is stable in a relationship, whether romance or business; a quacking duck is lucky

Eagle: using your skills wisely will bring success

Hawk: soaring above your head means you will be victorious

Hummingbird: faithfulness, prosperity, joy

Jays: success through perseverance, being tough when you need to

Owl: hooting three times foretells an impending death or a big change in status; otherwise, its appearance can mean wisdom and magic

Raven: if met before going up against an obstacle, you will be victorious

Robin (North American): if you see one in the morning, you may have guests later in the day; if one nests near your home, it's very good luck

Sparrow: a peaceful and happy home; a nest near your window may mean strife in your love life

Woodpecker: your work will be a success

Wren: current situations are improving

A great way to use this knowledge is by simply noticing these birds and their actions during a pivotal time in your life, as they will often voluntarily come along with a message for you. If you have the need for a quick answer and want to take your cues from the birds, here is a great ornithomancy spell.

Messenger Bird Spell

You'll need: a plain white paper plate, a pen, birdseed, and small pieces of bread.

Write your question for the birds on the bottom of the paper plate, then turn it over and fill the paper plate with some birdseed and bread pieces. Sitting with the plate of seed and bread before you, meditate upon your question, then repeat this charm over the seed:

My feathered friends, hear my request,
Of the gods' intentions you stay abreast.
Please join me for this humble meal
And share your news, let none conceal.

Your most wise counsel do I seek,
By wing and feather, tail and beak.

Put the plate outside where birds are likely to gather. Grab a pen and paper to jot down quick notes, and then wait patiently to see who comes for a visit. Pay attention to which direction the first birds come from, and also how they depart. Note what kind of bird arrives first, and if any birds show up that you don't normally see in the area, or if a bird makes a big show upon arrival or departure. With patience and a keen eye, you should get some great insight into the situation. When you feel your question has been answered, leave the rest of the seed for the birds to finish.

Keeping birdseed and fresh water out for the birds all year long will not only keep your garden view beautiful and help nature, but it can also help you gain insight into life's many questions.

For Further Study

Telesco, Patricia, and Rowan Hall. *Animal Spirit: Spells, Sorcery, and Symbols From the Wild.* Franklin Lakes, NJ: New Page Books, 2002.

VonCripps, Saywood. "Auspicy." *Witchcraft & Wicca Magazine* June, Beltane to Lammas 2001: 26–27.

Sayahda. "Cycle of Power: Animal Totems." http://www.sayahda.com/cycle.htm (accessed August 5, 2009).

Magickal Education Today

by Susan "Moonwriter" Pesznecker

The magickal community thirsts for enlightenment. Whether seeking to expand our craft focus, communicate with like-minded practitioners, establish groups, or engage in study, we reach deeply into the mundane and magickal realms to understand and educate ourselves. In today's digital world, the Internet provides an ever-increasing level of access to all things magickal, and today's pointy-hatted folks share their knowledge through blogs, social networks, zines, online audio/video, open source texts and libraries, and entire sites devoted to online education. Cyber-learning is egalitarian in its availability to all, but comes with its own pros, cons, and "yeah . . . but" issues. These issues are worth exploring, for online learning provides an extraordinary opportunity to develop knowledge, expand community, and bring education to all types of magickal practitioners.

What is education? It's the process of giving or receiving systematic instruction in one or more subjects. The student (springing from the Latin verb *studere*, literally, "to take pains") receives the instruction, while the teacher (from the Old English *tǣcan*, "show") is the one who shows, explains, or demonstrates. Education is tricky enough in person, with differing learning styles, interest levels, curricula, and the challenges of reaching individual students; when you place student and teacher on opposite sides of a computer screen with no face time, things become even trickier. Let's consider the issues.

The Advantages of Online Learning

It's safe to say that most who gravitate toward online education do so because of the perceived convenience. Going to school online means the ability to access classes at any time and from any place. It means studying at a time of day that works best for each individual rather than having to bend and stretch one's schedule around a classroom appointment. With online education, there are no commutes and no worries about parking or catching the right bus. With electronic texts and assignment submission, the online classroom can also be almost paperless, which makes it greener and more sustainable than the traditional setting. There's no need for the supervisory institution to identify or maintain a physical classroom, library, or janitorial network. Faculty and student services can likewise be established and maintained online.

From an educator's perspective, a key plus for online education is its availability. All a student needs is a computer and Internet access and he or she can, literally, attend school from any location. Most of our largest magickal communities are found in big cities, meaning that in-person access to those resources is limited to those within a reasonable travel distance. Put those same services online and anyone can reach them—even those living hundreds or thousands of miles away. Many of today's four-year and graduate universities offer classes—and in many cases degrees—that are fully online, and today's schools of magick are increasingly doing the same.

Another big plus for the online community is privacy. Although Paganism, Wicca, and other New Age or Earth-based practices are exploding in popularity and becoming more commonplace, there remain bastions of conservatism that ostracize or discredit those practicing outside of the mainstream. I teach in the online Grey School of Wizardry and recently launched a survey asking several hundred students to describe how private or public their practices were. Only 50 percent claimed to be fully "out" with their magick; the remainder were studying and practicing with some degree of secrecy. Sadly, fully 10 percent worked their magick in *total* secrecy, with all aspects hidden from friends, family, and employers. For those who feel the need to guard and protect their magickal practices, online work may provide one option.

The Disadvantages of Online Learning

Online learning also comes with challenges, and first among these is the issue of access. Even in today's über-connected world, some people still lack fast, reliable online access. While free-use computers and wireless connections can be found in libraries and Internet cafés, many students of magick prefer to study in a quiet setting or may be uncomfortable with others peering over their shoulders. In rural communities, connection speed can also be an issue; without access to high-speed wireless, pages may load with terrible slowness and large-bandwidth goodies such as online videos or podcasts may be inaccessible.

Online education may pose special challenges for specific students. Students thirty years old and younger have grown up in the electronic era and can immerse themselves in the online classroom, quickly mastering the details of accessing lessons, communicating with teachers and fellow students, and exchanging information. They're quick to see the "cyber-magick" that connects the online world to the face-to-face version; indeed, many magick students view the quantum realities of cyberspace as every bit as real as the three-dimensional world around us, embracing  the Internet as something akin to a new dimension or realm. But for students fifty years and older, the process isn't as intuitive, and additional support and guidance may be needed to bring them up to speed. Students with certain physical challenges may also have difficulty working online. Others, regardless of age or ability, simply can't function well in an online classroom. Learning styles differ greatly, and these students need direct teacher interaction and can't succeed with what feels to them like a faceless computer screen.

Plagiarism is another problem in online education. Plagiarism occurs when a student uses someone else's work, writing, or ideas but fails to give that person proper credit. This use creates the false appearance that the material is the student's own creation. It's a tricky area, for in today's digital world, information is at our fingertips, and the easy access blurs the lines between material that's freely available and material that is still owned and protected (or copyrighted) by someone else. It's all too easy for a student to respond to an assignment by simply visiting several Web sites and cutting and pasting "borrowed" information from the sites into an assignment response. Without proper citations to credit the information's owner, this is plagiarism, pure and simple. This is a serious form of academic dishonesty and an ethical issue as well—not to mention that while it shows how effectively a student can assemble a pieced-together essay of source material, it shows nothing about how well he has internalized his studies and synthesized a personal understanding of the ideas presented.

Another important drawback of cyberlearning is its two-dimensionality. Most online schools focus on three methods of teaching and learning: reading (including watching video and listening to podcasts), written assignments, and discussions. These methods work, at least to a point. But the unadorned, flat online fit isn't perfect for all magickal subjects. Asking students to research and write a simple essay about the history of the runic alphabet or the development of the telescope is an acceptable approach. But asking a student to write about her use of a magickal chant doesn't work well and isn't as effective as watching a bit of video or hearing a recording of her actually performing the chant.

Successful online education means keeping abreast of the latest and greatest technologies—podcasting, digital video, YouTube, Skype, etc.—and using these resources to enhance lessons and assignments to their fullest. Some schools use a "hybrid" approach, integrating online lessons with face-to-face time via Skype, adding in audio or video tutorials, or even hosting in-person learning sessions.

The Challenges of Teaching

One of the biggest enemies of online learning is a student's tendency to procrastinate. In a face-to-face classroom, students are required to show up in class with assignments in hand, and receive the teacher's constant reminders about schedules and due dates. These students may still put off tasks until the last minute, but because of the constant real-time reminders, they're likely to complete the work. It's different for online students. The Hermione Granger types (tremendously self-motivated) will have no problem taking charge of their own assignments and schedules. But many others lack this kind of motivation and will struggle and founder in the less-structured online setting. This can have dire consequences in certain types of magickal education, where it becomes important for students to master one concept before moving on to the next. The teacher is left to decide whether he has extra time to devote to helping a struggling student or whether the student must be left to sink or swim on her own.

Time is another important issue in online learning. Many people have a false vision of the "ease" of online classes, and sign up for too much, too soon, confident that it'll be a breeze. In truth, taking (or teaching) a subject through the online medium is typically much more time-consuming than approaching the same subject in a face-to-face setting. In my experience, teachers must give lots more feedback in the online classroom, both as a way of reinforcing work done well and of redirecting work that's gone awry. In a physical class, teachers can host a review that addresses the entire class simultaneously; in the online setting, most work is done individually and feedback is typically given to one student at a time. Some online magick schools solve this time crunch by not giving individual feedback at all and by creating assignments that are mostly multiple choice. While this eases the teacher's load, it also deprives the student of feedback from a magickal mentor, which is often more valuable than the class material itself. Other schools ease the load by capping the number of classes or credits a student is allowed to take at one time.

Community is another critical issue. Learning can't occur— or at least not easily—in a vacuum, and online students thirst for the same social opportunities that in-person students have. The community setting can be created through online forums, chat rooms, Skype, and other venues. Some online schools also sponsor face-to-face activities, allowing students and faculty to occasionally meet in real space.

Student Success in the Online Classroom

As a college writing teacher, I can assess a student's success with apostrophes or allegory by simply reading her essays. But as a teacher of magick, it's much harder to judge a student's work. How can I assess her success with energy, her ability to lay out a ritual circle, or her skill in brewing an infusion of the correct density simply by reading an essay?

Online classrooms must also consider the issue of learning styles. The auditory learner learns by listening and will perform best if he can listen to lectures via Skype or podcast rather than (or in addition to) reading them. The visual learner learns best by seeing and processing; this student may do okay with an online written lecture but will do even better if she can also watch the teacher in action via digital video or if she has access to vivid online images, animations, and so on. The kinesthetic learner learns by touch and doing, and needs to actually handle and work with materials. This student will thrive in an online setting of visual and animated instruction, after which he puts his hands on real materials and creates a physical result, rather than a written one.

In considering the above issues, it seems clear that the successful online classroom is one that supports students in their ability to access the online community, uses a wide variety of approaches to present course materials and generate assignments, and maximizes interaction between students and teachers.

Online Schools of Magick

Ask a magickal practitioner about online magickal education and chances are she'll say, "You mean like Witch School?" **Witch**

School, founded in 2001, is a for-profit online religious school teaching the precepts of Correllian Wicca. A curriculum of required classes and electives leads to completion of degrees and potential ordination. Classes are presented via written online format; assignments and tests are automated, and student-teacher interaction is minimal. Witch School supplements its online classes with its own YouTube channel, available to the general Internet community. http://www.witchschool.com/

The **Grey School of Wizardry**, founded in 2004, is a non-profit educational institution teaching magick and arcane lore and welcoming students of all religions, magickal and mundane. The curriculum, organized in seven levels of required and elective classes, leads to a certificate of Journeyman Wizardry. Classes are presented via written online format and supplemented with online forums; homework may require anything from writing essays to taking photos to creating podcasts, videos, Web pages, or blogs. Student-teacher interaction is significant, with all assignments and most tests graded by hand and featuring individual teacher-student response. The GSW also teaches face-to-face via summer Conclaves—weekend or longer outdoor gatherings—and year-round Moots—daylong meetings for magickal study. http://www.greyschool.com/

Cherry Hill Seminary is a fully online religious graduate school providing distance education for professional Pagan ministry. The Seminary confers master's degrees in disciplines of ministry and counseling. Classrooms are administered through Moodle (an open-source education software package) with student-teacher interaction via Skype. http://www.cherryhill seminary.org/index.html

The **Order of Bards, Ovates, and Druids** (OBOD) is an online school teaching revival Druidism. First level (Bard) students receive a by-mail home study course that follows a year-long curriculum. One course option provides audio CDs as well. Each student works alone but has access to community forums and a personal tutor. http://www.druidry.org/

∼

As magickal folks continue to embrace their spiritual revolution, this new style of learning is important to us all, and it's likely here to stay. Try your hand: the future is now!

Wind

by Harmony Usher

The magic of wind has long been revered. Invisible, powerful, and unpredictable, wind has inspired poetry, music, and prayer. Wind stokes fires, rips away rooftops, and dries flooded fields. An invisible force in our everyday lives, wind can awaken awe and wonder.

I became fascinated with the wind when I was invited to go sailing with a friend. Being silently spirited across the bay with nothing but air powering us, I found myself curious about humankind's relationship with wind and realized I hadn't fully appreciated its complexity. I also realized that my daily practice of honoring the Earth had neglected to include this beautiful natural force.

Waking to the Wind

I am indebted to the art of sailing for awakening my senses to the wonder of wind. At the top of the mast of most sailboats is a small swiveling arrow that points in the direction from which the wind is coming. This, I discovered, was essential information to navigate the boat. I became fascinated with trying to "feel" where the wind was coming from before I looked to the arrow and soon became conscious of sudden shifts in wind direction. I learned that wind in our little bay typically comes from the west, and drops in strength around dusk. When the wind shifts to come from the east, stormy weather is on its way.

I noticed that despite the invisibility of wind, it could paint its course upon the water and you could

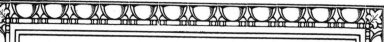

see gusts of wind in the waves before it filled your sails. I learned that for centuries, sailors have used ritual, prayer, and song to invoke the winds. Knots would be ritualistically untied to unleash winds when ships floated motionless on still oceans. Offerings would be given to the sea in hopes that damaging gales would be averted. It wasn't long before my adventures in sailing led to further musings about the wind.

Winds Personified

Wind has long been seen as having spiritual, supernatural, and human attributes. In Greek mythology, winds originated from each of the cardinal directions (north, south, east, and west) and each was believed to have a distinct personality. These winds were called the Anemoi, and they were also associated with the season they most often appeared in. Sometimes they were personified as gods or goddesses. In Roman mythology, the gods of the wind were called the Venti. Although they had different names, they were similar in attributes to the Greek gods.

The west wind was referred to as **Zephyrus** and was associated with gentleness, spring breezes, and mild weather. Sometimes the word *zephyr* is used as a synonym for *gentle breeze*. The north wind was known as **Boreas**. He was the god of winter and was said to reside in the cold mountains of Thrake. The ancient Greeks were fond of stories in which Boreas and Zephyrus coupled with mares in early spring, coming to them in the form of wind-formed stallions. The offspring of these couplings were believed to be the fastest of all horses. Boreas was usually depicted in Greek art as a strong winged god, sometimes with ice in his hair or beard. Sometimes he is shown as a face with puffed up cheeks, blowing air into the clouds. **Notus** was the south wind, associated with summer and autumn rains. **Eurus** was the east wind. He was usually associated with the autumn, and thought to live in the east, near the Sun god Helios.

Wind Attributes

From a practical magic perspective, it is helpful to look to the attributes of wind as you explore ways to integrate wind magic into your daily spiritual practice. As each wind has associations with a direction and a season (which sometimes varied depending on a culture's location and weather patterns), pairing wind

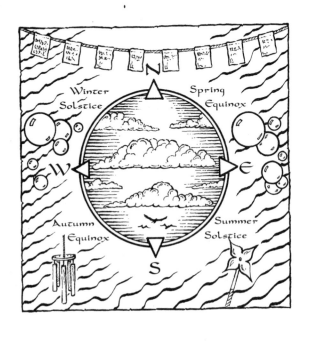

ritual with the attributes of the cardinal direction makes magical sense.

Prayers or rituals honoring the east wind are helpful when you wish to embrace rebirth, change, or problem solving. This is because the east wind is associated with spring and the arrival of cleansing rains. Use east wind magic from the Spring Equinox until the Summer Solstice.

The west wind is associated with autumn and with the period of time from the Autumn Equinox until the Winter Solstice. This is a time of fruition and harvest, and wind magic during this period is particularly useful for addressing love and friendship.

The north wind is an active force from the Winter Solstice until the Spring Equinox. North winds herald winter, a perfect time to retreat to the inner world, to work on issues that have been presenting themselves through the year, and to banish bad habits and ways of thinking that have not been useful or fruitful for you.

The south wind heralds summer and is active from the Summer Solstice until the Autumn Equinox. This is a wonderful time for rituals related to growth, realization, and action. It is also a time of abundance, so money rituals are recommended.

Everyday Wind Magic

You don't need to be a scholar of Greek mythology or a skilled sailor to practice wind magic. There are countless ways to bring the power of the wind into your everyday life. If your magical rituals involve invocation of the cardinal directions, simply begin by including reference to the winds of each direction as well. This will raise your consciousness and enhance your ritual.

If you practice outdoors, consider the location of your altar or circle. Is it in an open area where wind direction and speed are easily felt? If you prefer a more sheltered area for your rituals, perhaps you could find a separate location for wind rituals and venture there on special occasions. Hilltops and open fields clear of buildings or groves are excellent locations to commune with the winds. Stand for a moment in your special location and feel the wind on your face and in your hair. Close your eyes and listen for the wind in nearby trees or passing over the water. Note the rustling of leaves, the whistling of wind through branches, and the lapping of waves— all signs that trees and water have been kissed by the wind. If you are able to tell the wind direction, call it by name and thank it for its presence. Reflect on what is happening in your life and in your inner world, and ask for assistance with meeting the challenges you are facing. Some people find it rewarding to wear flowing clothing that moves in the wind during such rituals.

Consider, too, everyday tasks that might require wind, such as laundry. If you are not already taking advantage of Mother Nature's clothes dryer, consider putting up a clothesline. I didn't realize the beautiful scent of the wind until I began hanging clothes on a line. Don't be shy about asking the wind to bless articles of clothing you plan to wear for special occasions. For instance, hang clothes you are wearing to a job interview in a strong east wind (before the rain comes!) and ask the power of change to infuse the clothing.

Seeing the Wind

Flags and windsocks are wonderful additions to your practice and can be a visible reminder of the presence of a wind spirit. Any purchased flag or windsock will do, but creating your own can add magical meaning. They can be painted or decorated using colors or symbols that are meaningful to you and your magical tradition. If you have a flagpole in your outdoor ritual space, you may design a flag for each wind direction, and hang them as appropriate to weather or ritual.

The addition of flags or windsocks to your outdoor ritual space (or simply in your garden, on your balcony, or in your yard) will remind you of the constant movement of wind around you and the many ways it can bless your life. You can even enjoy such reminders when you are on the road by tying a small piece of cloth (about four inches long and the thickness of a piece of tape) to the antenna of your car. When parked, it will serve as subtle indicator of the winds that are blowing. If you live in an apartment, or if health or mobility keeps you indoors, you can also fashion a small flag and use a household fan to move air from the desired direction!

Wind chimes, whirl-a-gigs, and simple bubble blowers (the kind that children play with) can also be incorporated into ritual to bring the power of wind into your consciousness. Bubbles carrying loving wishes to friends and family can be blown into a west wind, or into an east wind if we have a desire for change.

Prayer flags have been used for centuries throughout Tibet, China, Persia, and India. These flags were hung, usually along long pieces of rope strung between trees, over doorways, or in sacred places. They were often fashioned in colors corresponding to the elements, or healing words or mantras were written upon them. The flag's energy was awakened as the wind passed over it, and healing vibrations were carried through the area. Some prayer flags were made with materials designed to disintegrate as the wind and other elements touched them over time. The slow disappearance of the words on the flag and the eventual wearing away of the material symbolized the way in which our intentions become one with the world around us.

May the healing winds of change bless you as you find ways to honor this force in your everyday life!

Ancient Egyptian Air Deities

by Denise Dumars

In metaphysical terms, air is the element of intellect, and no other deity so typifies the qualities of the intellect as the ibis-headed Egyptian god Thoth. Thoth (his Greek name) is called Tehuti or Djehuti in Egyptian, and he is believed to be thought and reason incarnate. He is the antithesis of rage and chaos, and so he is often depicted as the only Egyptian god other than the creator Ra himself who can control the god of chaos, Set.

The scribes of ancient Egypt declared Thoth their patron, for he was thought to be the god who invented the alphabet and devised a system of writing for mankind, and who, in the afterlife, recorded the answers to the forty-two questions that were posed to the deceased by the goddess of truth, Ma'at. As a deity of wisdom and intellect, Thoth was and still is considered a patron of all academics, writers, scientists, doctors, and those who teach medicine. He is often depicted with a clay tablet and stylus in his hand, writing, or with a caduceus, indicating the practice of medicine. His symbol is the ibis, a water bird that is common in Egypt. Birds are a symbol of the air element and indicate wisdom. Thoth also has another animal as his symbol: the cynocephalus (dog-headed) baboon, which was regarded as a "wise ape" and was therefore called "the ape of Thoth." Thoth was also the god of the Moon, which gave off a "cold light," as in the cold light of intellect, the opposite of the fiery light of the Sun. Thoth was self-created, though some stories say he was born "from the lips of Ra" literally as "the Word."

Because of the aid he gave to the sky goddess Nut and the earth god Geb in their wish to procreate, he is sometimes considered "Uncle Thoth" by the five gods who are Nut and Geb's children: Isis, Osiris, Nephthys, Set, and Horus the Elder. Many Moon deities in the Middle East were considered male, whereas many solar deities were female, unlike the deities of the Pagan Europeans, who tended to see solar traits as male and lunar traits as female.

The goddess Ma'at, whose name means "truth" or "justice" or "right order," is also a deity of air, and she is portrayed as a woman with a feather in her headdress. In the afterlife, one's heart would be weighed on the divine scales against the feather of Ma'at. If one's heart was heavy and one's answers to the forty-two negative confessions were unsatisfactory, then instead of passing on into the Kingdom of Osiris (the afterlife), one's heart would be eaten by a monster called Ammit and that person would cease to exist.

In some parts of Egypt, Ma'at was considered the consort of Thoth, but in others his wife was believed to be the goddess Seshat, another air deity, called "Lady of the House of Books." This "librarian goddess" is also sometimes credited with devising the alphabet for humankind, and she is the patron of librarians, bookkeepers, warehouse workers, and others who "keep" or care for books. She is depicted as a woman with a strange blossom on her head. Some feel it is a type of feather, and others feel it may be a lily of the Nile, or more likely, a papyrus frond; the papyrus reed was used to make writing material for the Egyptians, and is the origin of the word *paper*.

Horus, the son of Isis and Osiris and the defender of the gods, is usually portrayed as a falcon or hawk. Horus is often called "the avenger," for he sought justice for his father who had been killed by Set, who had then usurped the throne. Today we call someone a "hawk" if they are militaristic or pro-war, and this is appropriate when applied to the symbolism of Horus as a bird of prey. But showing Horus as a hawk also has another meaning—it indicates kingship, for Amen Ra (Ra, Re, Amun, Ra-Horakte), ancient Egypt's supreme being, is sometimes portrayed with a hawk's head and a solar disk as a crown.

Isis and her sister Nephthys are also sometimes drawn as kites, small Egyptian birds. Birds were believed to be symbols of the soul, and so the two goddesses were often shown as kites hovering over the sarcophagus of Osiris as mourners. The soul had two parts in Egyptian beliefs: the *ba*, one's personality or ego; and the *ka*, or oversoul, a part of universal consciousness that could be depicted as a bird leaving the body. In many cultures the world over, it was believed that while a person was sleeping, his or her soul could travel the Earth in the body of a bird, and many cultures have folklore about birds as harbingers of death; for example, even today when a bird flies inside a home, some cultures believe that someone in the house will die, and the bird is there to take his or her soul to heaven.

The parents of Isis, Osiris, Nephthys, Set, and Horus the Elder are Nut, the sky goddess—shown as a woman arching over the Earth, her body made of stars and the blackness of space, and Geb, the earth god. Geb lay on the ground, sexually aroused but unable to reach Nut. The space between the two of them gave rise to the element of air and the atmosphere of the Earth that makes life possible . . . consider for example the evidence of water and minerals on our nearest Earth-like planet. Without the addition of an atmosphere there is (currently, anyway) no life on Mars, and the planet as we know it is just a red desert.

Nut and Geb wanted to marry and have children and populate the Earth, but Ra said no. He felt the cosmos was overpopulated already. So Nut and Geb appealed to Uncle Thoth, for they knew he was the only god who had the superior intellect and the good critical-thinking skills to possibly convince Ra to change his mind, or to trick him into doing so. Thoth's first attempt at convincing Ra was not successful, so he challenged Ra to a game

of draughts (checkers). He bet Ra that if he, Thoth, won the game, then Ra would allow Nut and Geb to have children. Needless to say, Thoth won, and the Earth became populated. Ever after, Thoth has been saddled with another attribute—patron of gamblers!

The vulture was an important bird in Egypt and there were several minor goddesses portrayed as vultures or as women with a vulture for a head or headdress. Queens in Egypt also wore vulture-shaped headdresses, and one of the most ancient goddesses of Egypt, Mut, was sometimes shown with a vulture's head. In Thebes she was considered the consort of Amun-Ra and the mother of the Moon god Khonsu, a deity often portrayed as a young man with a sidelock, whom I think of as "Thoth as a teenager." The name Mut means "mother," and in some parts of Egypt she was considered the mother of all the gods. Mut was also often portrayed as a cat or with a cat or lioness head, a patron of fertility and also a ferocious enemy when provoked. The most frightening form of Mut had wings and three heads— human, lioness, and vulture—and was the symbol of the wrath of Ra and the punisher of those who would try to harm him.

Nekhbet was the vulture goddess of Upper Egypt, considered a protector and sometimes paired with Wadjet, the snake goddess of Lower Egypt, or as a combination goddess Nehebka, a snake with the head of the vulture or a winged cobra. These goddesses protected the pharaoh and the royal family, and amulets depicting them were worn by the common people as protection against contagious diseases, which not surprisingly were usually airborne. One of Wadjet's titles was "Lady of the Papyrus," perhaps another association of an air deity and writing.

The Nubian goddess Anuket, considered a daughter of Ra, wore a large feather headdress and was considered the softer side of the "eye of Ra," whereas the fierce lioness goddess Sekhmet sprang from Ra's avenging eye. Anuket was a goddess of beauty and was considered a foster mother or a godmother of Egyptian pharaohs. She was present for the joyous yearly occasion of the inundation of the Nile.

The attributes of the air deities of ancient Egypt are multitudinous, but they by and large converge in a positive grouping of characteristics denoting intellect, wisdom, truth, clear thinking, protection, prudence, and respect for knowledge and teaching. And since Thoth is thought to have written and hidden documents detailing all the secrets of magic, a legend about forty-two books supposedly containing all the secret magical teachings of Thoth has been passed down through many generations. This "book" came to be known as the *Hermetica*, from the Greek identification of Thoth with their god Hermes and the melding of the two into a composite deity known as Thoth/Hermes. The *Hermetica* was supposedly authored by a mysterious adept called Hermes Trismegistus, "Hermes Thrice Blessed." To this day, some of this secret knowledge is said to exist in medieval alchemical and hermetic texts and in more modern books of magical wisdom by famous magicians said to be inspired by Thoth/Hermes, including Dr. John Dee and Aleister Crowley. Ceremonial magicians to this very day rely on "hermetic knowledge" to help them understand magic and the mysteries of the universe, and the word *hermetic* has even gained a popular meaning indicating something that is "secret," "unknowable," or "incorruptible;" for example, a vessel that is "hermetically sealed" is one that is impregnable to contamination.

One practitioner of Egyptian magic tells a funny story about an experience involving Thoth. She was enrolled in college one semester and could not afford the books for her classes, so she made an altar to Thoth and prayed to him in the hopes of getting money to pay for her textbooks. The next day she found a pile of textbooks on her doorstep . . . however, they weren't the ones required for her classes! She didn't know what to think until she looked over the books and realized that they might be even more appropriate to her academic goals than the ones she was assigned. Sometimes Thoth knows best.

For Further Study

Hope, Murry. *Practical Egyptian Magic*. New York: St. Martin's Griffin, 1984.

Pinch, Geraldine. *Handbook of Egyptian Mythology*. Santa Barbara, CA: ABC-CLIO, 2002.

Reed, Ellen Cannon. *Circle of Isis: Ancient Egyptian Magic for Modern Witches*. Franklin Lakes, NJ: New Page, 2002.

Fabric Magick

by Emyme

According to a quaint calendar I own, January 22 is "visit your local fabric store" day. Fabric is a necessity in my magick workings. The variety and combinations of textures and colors are infinite: cotton, silk, satin, velvet, muslin, burlap, and fleece are just a few of the types of fabrics available. A fabric store is a feast for the senses—material delights for not only sight and touch, but also smell and sound. Fabrics make different sounds when rubbed together or drawn through the hands. Silks swish like air and canvas swooshes like water, satins warm like fire and burlap crunches like earth. No matter what your experience with fabric, take some time and visit a fabric store on January 22 (or any old day you'd like!). Should you feel completely intimidated by "raw" fabric, ask a friend with some sewing or crafting experience to accompany you.

Take with you a small notepad or index cards and seek out a store specializing in selling fabric by the yard. Plan to spend some time taking in all of the sensual charms. As you enter, stop for a moment and breathe in the aroma. You are literally on the threshold of future creative energy. Welcome that promise. A short, silent plea to Vesta/Hestia is a good idea at this point. Something along the lines of "Lady of the hearth and home, allow this everpresent creative energy to inspire me as I embark on this quest" would be appropriate.

Quickly scan the store and let your eye settle on a color and/or pattern that calls you. As you make your way to that spot, be sure to reach out and touch the fabrics you pass along the way. Lightly run your fingertips over folds, occasionally stop and press your entire palm into piles, and rub samples between your finger and thumb. If

the feel of a certain fabric gives you pause, examine that. What about the color or texture may be special to you? How might you be inspired to use this particular fabric in your practice and spells? Write down your thoughts.

After you have wandered the store and recorded some ideas—this calico for an altar cloth or that corduroy for a Samhain robe—go to the discount section, usually located in the rear of the store. I always find much magick here! Peruse the leftover rolls, stacks, and bolts of cloth. These are the remnants of once-beloved fabrics and may hold powerful energy. This is also the place to look for off-season bargains. You will almost certainly uncover Yule patterns in July and Ostara designs in October.

Relax your mind and let your thoughts drift as you examine the textiles and allow a project to come to you. Perhaps you do indeed need a new robe, or robes for different seasons. Could your personal space or group space use a new altar cloth? If your supply of drawstring pouches is getting low, why not purchase several different fabric types for different spells? Velvet or satin, say, for those small pouches that lie close to the skin, and open-weave muslin or tulle that allows the scent of herbs to waft about. Does your sacred space need fresh, sturdy floor coverings, billowy curtains, or comfy pillows? Heavy canvas is a fine choice upon which to draw a pentagram or labyrinth; it can be rolled up and stored when not in use.

Establishments that sell fabric by the yard almost always sell all of the extras needed to complete any project. You will find thread in every tone and hue, ribbons and laces of every width and texture, and elastic for every sort of gathering need. Also to be had are buttons in sizes and shapes too numerous to mention, and scissors with dozens of diverse blades. Taken all together, these are called "notions." I find that when I have a particular sewing task in mind, it is a good practice to gather all of the necessary notions when I buy the fabric. On the other hand, when I am simply open to inventiveness, a separate trip just for notions works best, so as not to become distracted by the pull of fabric. Buttons and ribbons are particularly attractive, and attracted, to me.

If fabric art is not new to you, you will know what you need to give life to something special. You may already have an undertaking plotted out. For those inexperienced in the fabric arts, do not become overwhelmed—permit me to assign a task. I suggest you make four fabric choices by color, texture, or even price, and purchase one yard of each. (If you have ventured into the store for the first time alone, find a helpful salesperson. Your request of the goddess upon entering the store will likely cause them to appear when you most need them.) An example: choose inexpensive calico quilting cotton by color for each of the four directions: forest greens for north, desert yellows for east, mountain reds for south and aquatic blues for west. Fray the edges and use as simple altar cloths or furniture covers.

Back in your sacred space, ritually cleanse and bless the fabrics to remove any negative energy. Set the folded bundles in a place of honor and allow the material to soak up your own personal and magickal power. Once again, call on Vesta/Hestia, or any goddess or god with whom you personally identify. If you have no project in mind, ask for inspiration; for those who know exactly what they will create, ask for skill. The following covers all levels of proficiency and may be adapted as you like. My personal goddess of choice is Demeter. Again, please feel free to place any name in this incantation, and take joy in the creating.

> *Lady Demeter, goddess of the seasons, representing the*
> *mother—*
> *Bless me as I begin this project*
> *My mind and sight: to see the steps and the completed article*
> *My hands: to work magic and positive energy into the cloth*
> *My heart: to instill love in every stitch and seam*
> *As I say, so mote it be.*

Elder Futhark Runes

by Graham Miller

I ween that I hung / on the windy tree,
Hung there for nights full nine;
With the spear I was wounded, / and offered I was
To Othin, myself to myself,
On the tree that none / may ever know
What root beneath it runs.

None made me happy / with loaf or horn,
And there below I looked;
I took up the runes, / shrieking I took them,
And forthwith back I fell.

These words, taken from the *Hovamol*, part of the Norse *Poetic Edda*, reveal why the runes of the Vikings are regarded as one of the most powerful and respected magical systems. Odin, Father of the Gods, subjected himself to a shamanic trial to gain access to the secrets of the runes. This raised him to a higher state, after which he fell back to the normal world. The runes have a further layer of meaning given in several rune poems. The poems contain a cryptic couplet for each rune and would have been learned by rote and passed down orally through the generations, from teacher to student.

In addition, runes were used by the Vikings as a system of writing. There are many examples of runes carved on objects from all over the Viking world. The Elder Futhark runes were mainly used in Scandinavia to make charms and amulets. The word *Futhark* comes from the first six runes in order, F, U, Th, A, R, and K. All the runes are arranged in their own particular order. Unlike the Roman alphabet, they are also split into three groups of eight letters, called ætts.

The runes are a magical system, and therefore each rune has a host of symbols and meanings attached to it. For example, the first rune of the Futhark, F, has a symbol and a Roman letter, in this case F. It also has a runic name (Fehu), a number (1), and an English name (Cattle). The meaning then goes beyond this simple word *cattle* to encompass everything that means. In the Viking world, the number of cattle you had was an indicator of your wealth. Cattle are a type of wealth that can be traded, moved from one place to another, and can easily change. Thus, in the modern world, this rune represents the mobile, fluid wealth that is in your bank account or the money in your wallet, rather than assets like your house and land. Fehu is also the beginning of the first ætt, which is ascribed to the goddess Freya, whose symbol is gold. So that gives us another confirmation of the meaning of this rune, associated with money and coinage.

If you wanted to delve even deeper into the meaning of the runes, you could consider numerology. By adding together the digits of each number over 10, the number of each rune can be reduced to a single digit. To continue our example, Fehu, number 1, has links to Nauthis, which is number 10. This is the rune of hunger, or need-fire. It's fairly easy to see how ideas of hunger and growth link in to ideas of wealth and cattle.

When the runes are written in order with the ætts placed one above the other, the vertical links between the runes provide additional illumination to their meaning.

ᚠ ᚢ ᚦ ᚨ ᚱ ᚲ ᚷ ᚹ
ᚺ ᚾ ᛁ ᛃ ᛇ ᛈ ᛉ ᛊ
ᛏ ᛒ ᛖ ᛗ ᛚ ᛜ ᛞ ᛟ

In this way, they act as a web of knowledge. Each of the three ætts is ruled by one of the deities of the Norse pantheon. Many of the individual runes are also associated with a god or goddess.

One of the easiest ways to work with the runes is to meditate with them. If you have a set of runes, pick one at random to work with. Try sounding out the letter. Get a good book about runes or hop on the Internet to look up alternative versions and meanings. Meditate on the shape of the rune. Try to visualize it in red, as this is a color commonly used for writing runes. Think about the English name of the rune and the qualities it symbolizes. Work out the numerology and where it fits in its ætt. Just let your mind wander and see what occurs to you about the rune. Look back at the example for Fehu and build up all that information for yourself. If you work through the runes one at

a time, you'll probably spend several days on each rune. The runes are experiential—the best knowledge comes from working with them and meditating on them. When you have finished, it will be very helpful to write out your thoughts. In this way, as you work through the set of runes, you will probably start to see links between your interpretation of different runes.

The other way to use the runes is as a tool for divination. Historically there is reference to casting runes on a white sheet. Read only the runes that land face up, with those closest to the caster representing the past and those farthest away representing the future. My preferred technique, however, is to use a tarot-style reading spread with runes. To do this I draw seven runes, one at a time, from a closed bag and lay them from left to right in an ellipse. The reading then can be read from left to right as past, present, future, what to do now, outside influences, hopes and fears, and final outcome.

The most powerful rune sets are those that the worker makes for him- or herself. I make mine by taking a tree branch (once I've asked permission, of course) and cutting twenty-four thin slices from it. Then I stain one side and carve and paint the rune on the other before varnishing the whole. If this doesn't appeal to you, you could collect twenty-four pebbles, or buy twenty-four crystals. Or you could use a form of modeling clay to make runes. It really is up to you and what you would feel happiest doing.

Talismans can be made by using several runes together in what is known as a bind rune. These runes are usually combined into one symbol. Numerology is also important—most historical examples of bind runes add up to a multiple of 9 or 24. Nine is a very special number in Norse myth; for example, there are 9 worlds arranged around Yggdrasil, the World Tree.

Freya's Ætt

The first eight runes of the Elder Futhark run from Fehu to Wunjo and are ruled by the goddess Freya, the personification of nature. She loved Odur, the god of the summer Sun, but in a classic tale of winter and the return of spring, she wept when he left and traveled the Earth searching for him. When she found him again, all was fruitful.

In different realms, these eight runes refer to how we interact with the natural world.

1 • F • Fehu • Cattle

This represents money and wealth, as well as cattle, implying that all wealth comes from nature. It also contains the concept that money should be allowed to flow and not stagnate. The higher meaning is that you need a secure material base before you start on a spiritual journey.

2 • U • Uruz • Aurochs

The auroch was a giant wild ox that died out in the seventeenth century. In the creation myth, a block of ice was licked into shape by a giant cow, so this rune represents the ordering creative force of the universe. In readings, Uruz means manifestation. Like all second runes, it is in direct contrast with the first rune in the ætt, Fehu.

3 • Th • Thurisaz • Thorn

This is the rune of the god Thor and his hammer Mjolnir. It is about raw, primal energy that comes from the synthesis of opposites, such as frost and fire in the creation myth. It represents the more primal forces of nature that we can harness but never own. The thorn is blackthorn, which was grown to protect livestock, so it is also a defensive rune.

4 • A • Ansuz • A God

Ansuz represents the higher realms, those the shaman travels to talk to the spirits and return with wisdom. It is the rune for Odin, who is shaman, poet, and warrior. In a reading, Ansuz is about receiving guidance and wisdom from other people.

5 • R • Raidho • Riding

Raidho is the symbol for all types of journeys, from the shamanic to the mundane. Depending on the surrounding runes, it can be a good or a difficult journey. It also relates to natural cycles, as the Sun is drawn across the sky on Thor's chariot. At its highest level, Raidho relates to a student on the right spiritual path, and those forces of the universe that act to return him to the path if he strays.

6 • K • Kenaz • A Torch

Kenaz is a symbol of fire harnessed in a torch, another force of nature brought under our control. This also covers smiths and forges, creativity (whether artistic or fertilizing), and now technology. This rune gives us two word groups in English. Firstly, *canny* or *knowing*, and the Scottish verb *to ken* also means to know or understand. Secondly, *kin* are the family who gather around the hearth.

7 • G • Gebo • Gift

Gebo represents the giving of gifts to seal a bond or agreement. This was common in Viking times and still occurs now, with wedding rings, for example. On a high level, it is about the gift of life given to man from Odin when he gave us breath. This brings us around to sacrifice, giving something back to the gods out of thanks for the life they gave us. Overall, Gebo symbolizes the give and take principle that characterizes our relationship with natural forces.

8 • W • Wunjo • Joy

Wunjo, the final rune in the first ætt, is the state of joy in which it is possible to live if we are in harmony with the forces around us. It is quite a complex idea, because it is bound up with the joy of belonging to a clan and giving up individual freedoms so you can belong to something bigger. It is also the force that binds together guilds and societies.

Heimdall's Ætt

Heimdall rules the second eight runes, from Hagalaz to Sowihlo. Heimdall is the watcher of the Æsir, the principle group of Norse gods. He lives at the top of Bifrost, the rainbow bridge, and guards against invasion by frost giants. He is possessed of extraordinary sight and hearing and hardly ever sleeps. Compared to Freya, he is less concerned with mankind and more with protecting the gods.

Taken together, these eight runes refer to the pattern, order, and machinery of the universe. Heimdall was both wise and good, and these attributes can also be found in his runes.

9 • H • Hagalaz • Hailstone

Hagalaz begins the ætt and represents the pattern and seed for all things. It is numbered 9, which makes it a very important rune. One of its earlier forms was a hexagon around a snowflake, a pattern that includes all other runes. In this way it represents a seed that has the DNA inside it to build a whole new plant or creature. In a mundane reading, Hagalaz represents a bolt from the blue, an influx of energy to jolt us out of the happiness of Wunjo and get us on our way again.

10 • N • Nauthis • Need

Nauthis is the need for forward movement that drives creation. It represents the fire-bow that uses friction to create fire. It is about awkward situations where the universe is driving us forward to higher levels of spiritual growth. This idea of destiny and struggle is because this rune is also connected to the three Norns, who sit around a spring at the base of Yggdrasil and weave the fate of mankind.

11 • I • Isa • Ice

Isa is the opposite of the preceding rune and represents inwardness and a time of stillness. In the Viking creation myth, everything came out of a gap between fire and ice. This rune represents that fundamental ice, one of the primal creative forces of nature. In a reading, it can represent blockages that can be overcome by finding a balanced viewpoint.

12 • J • Jera • Harvest

Jera represents the turning forces in the universe and all forms of cycles, in particular, the seasons and the turning of the wheel. It is the principle that if you sow, then food will grow. Together with Eihwaz, the next rune, these two lie at the center of all the runes, and the other twenty-two runes can be said to turn around them. Jera can also indicate summer, as it follows Isa, which is winter.

13 • Ei • Eihwaz • Yew

Where Jera represents the turning force, Eihwaz is the axis about which everything turns. From this it also represents Yggdrasil, the World Tree, and the pathways that exist between the different realms of existence. The yew tree lives for thousands of years and is evergreen, making it a symbol of life, but it is also found in graveyards and has always been associated with death. This reconciling of opposites to find a middle ground is the mundane interpretation of the rune.

14 • P • Perthro • Fate

Perthro is the secret of cause and effect, determinism versus free will. Rather than being linked to a fixed, deterministic fate, this rune is instead about the interconnectedness of all things in a web—*wyrd*. It is about the three Norns—"what has been," "what is becoming," and "that which should become"—who weave the lives of men and decide when to cut the thread. On a mundane level, Perthro can be about secrets, hidden knowledge, good luck, and sometimes birth.

15 • Z • Elhaz • Elk

Elhaz is Heimdall's rune and represents protection and the connection of all with the gods. Where Eihwaz is the trunk of the yew tree, this rune is the branches. It is named after the elk sedge plant, whose leaves look like swords. It is concerned with man's connection with his gods as well as the link between your mundane personality and your spiritual one.

16 • S • Sowilho • Sun

The ætt ends with Sowihlo, the Sun, the benign force that lights and powers creation. Sowilho refers to the light of the Sun and its life-giving properties. It is also about finding your way. On a higher level, this corresponds to being on the right spiritual path. It is also linked to the concept of the will. Sowilho's mundane meaning is honor and fame.

Tyr's Ætt

Tyr is a god of courage, war, and honor. He represents the sacrifice that is a necessary part of kingship. He let the wolf Fenris bite off his right hand so that Fenris could be bound and prevented from harming the rest of the gods. Tyr had a magical sword, which is another of his symbols.

The eight runes ruled by Tyr run from Tiwaz to Orthala and are about the partnerships man makes with his gods, goddesses, and other spirits.

17 • T • Tiwaz • Tyr

The ætt begins with Tyr's own rune, Tiwaz, representing the sovereign order, with subjects paying homage to a king who had responsibilities to them. It is about the noble sacrifice that Tyr made to keep the gods safe from Fenrir. In a mundane

sense, it is about doing the right thing for the greater good. It can also relate to love and passion.

18 • B • Berkano • Birch

Berkano is, in contrast to Tiwaz, the goddess principle and embodies a more motherly approach. The birch goddess is probably one of the oldest mother goddess symbols in Europe. This rune is about the process of growth, of moving through life's stages, becoming an adult, marrying, birthing, and dying. In a reading, Berkano can refer to family gatherings and celebrations.

19 • E • Ehwaz • Horse

Ehwaz is about any spiritual or mundane partnership that helps all parties. Initially this is about the relationship between man and horse, which allows both parties to achieve more than they would alone. But it is also about power animals that help a worker travel farther between the worlds. In readings, it can be about travel, communication, or new, mutually beneficial relationships.

20 • M • Mannaz • A Man

Mannaz symbolizes the divine spark within all men. This is Odin's gift of life to us, the divine plan for each member of the human race. It can represent the caster in a reading and can indicate that you have to proceed with caution.

21 • L • Laguz • Lake

Laguz is about the power of water and represents passions and subconscious desires. The sea in Viking times would have been a source of food, a way to travel, and something to fear, as it could take life. The sea is connected to female archetypes—birth, death, and creativity. In a reading, Laguz would be information from the subconscious.

22 • Ng • Ingwaz • Ing

Ingwaz is about the male force and the realization of potentials. It is the inrush of male fertilizing energy that then dies or departs when it has done its job. It can represent the completion of projects, often with a sudden burst of new energy.

23 • D • Dagaz • Day

Dagaz is about the day as a twenty-four-hour period that's split into daytime and nighttime. This means it represents the synthesis of opposites into one force. This rune is about looking at two opposing concepts and moving beyond them to recognize the concept that embraces them both. It is also about the dawning of inspiration, and the periods of dawn and dusk when it is neither day nor night.

24 • O • Orthala • Homestead

Orthala is the final rune of the Futhark and symbolizes the clan, the fact that one person is the sum of his ancestors and his environment. It is about the fence that keeps the clan safe, and everyone else outside. It is also about fixed wealth, in contrast and harmony with Fehu, which is about mobile wealth.

Rune	Number	Letter	Name	Word
ᚠ	1	F	Fehu	Cattle
ᚢ	2	U	Uruz	Aurochs
ᚦ	3	Th	Thurisaz	Thorn
ᚨ	4	A	Ansuz	A God
ᚱ	5	R	Raidho	Riding
ᚲ	6	K	Kenaz	A Torch
ᚷ	7	G	Gebo	Gift
ᚹ	8	W	Wunjo	Joy
ᚺ	9	H	Hagalaz	Hailstone
ᚾ	10	N	Nauthis	Need
ᛁ	11	I	Isa	Ice
ᛃ	12	J	Jera	Harvest
ᛇ	13	Ei	Eihwaz	Yew
ᛈ	14	P	Perthro	Fate
ᛉ	15	Z	Elhaz	Elk
ᛊ	16	S	Sowilho	Sun
ᛏ	17	T	Tiwaz	Tyr
ᛒ	18	B	Berkano	Birch
ᛖ	19	E	Ehwaz	Horse
ᛗ	20	M	Mannaz	A Man
ᛚ	21	L	Laguz	Lake
◊	22	Ng	Ingwaz	Ing
ᛞ	23	D	Dagaz	Day
ᛟ	24	O	Orthala	Homestead

Voice Magic:
The Power of Your Words
by Michelle Skye

The voice is a tricky thing. It's something we all have yet rarely use to its full potential. Even in magical circles, voice magic, known as incantation, is underutilized. It is often glossed over in favor of more exciting forms of magic, such as candle magic, symbolic magic, or physical magic. Personally, I blame Hollywood for the general bias against incantation. After all, movies and television shows almost exclusively use voice magic when a spell is needed, and they make it look so easy! Anyone can spout an incantation and destroy an evil demon or create a glamour or teleport to another dimension. So why bother getting proficient at it? Why spend the time honing vocal skills when there are so many more obscure magical techniques to pursue? Voice magic has become passé, overused, underappreciated, and boring. Who wants those kinds of vibes mixed with their spellwork?

Well, I'm here to reawaken the mystique of voice magic. Used since ancient times, voice magic has intrinsic power due to its connection to the breath. Breath is life. It sustains all living things on planet Earth. If we don't breathe, we die. Our words, uttered from the caverns of our mouths, from the depths of our psyches, push out on the exhalation of our breath, mingling with the air and the breaths of others. Our words become one with the breath and the air of all those people and animals and plants around us, connecting our solitary existence with their solitary existence. The voice, as one of our most powerful communication tools, is the great connector. It allows us to express our needs, our wants, and our desires. It gives us the opportunity to state them to other beings that inhabit our planet. And, once our words are heard, we in turn are more fully able to listen to the words of others, creating a lovely ebb and flow, a give and take paradigm that functions for the benefit of everyone.

This paradigm not only functions on a mundane level but on a spiritual, magical level as well. If we agree that the entire natural world, including ourselves, is representative of and connected to the Divine, then it follows that air, which sustains us, is also sacred. Throughout many mythologies, air, wind, and breezes are considered to be the breath of the Divine. When we expel our breath into the air around us, we are mixing our human energies with the sacred energies of the divine. This occurs no matter what mundane sentence we are uttering, from "please take out the trash" to "I'm off to work today." Along with the actual words used, all of these utterances express emotion, tone, and mood. These vibrate upon the wind and scatter up and out to the world at large, affecting, on a minute scale, the words, emotions, and moods of others. Your words have immense power, more than you've probably considered.

The power of your words can be harnessed to connect with the energies of the Divine and to manifest your wishes and desires. That's right, folks, I'm talking about voice magic or incantation. Viewed from this perspective, it doesn't seem so boring any more, does it? By adding intent, you shift your mundane words into the realm of magic, allowing you access to the spiritual energies all around us. Your words allow you to manifest your deepest wishes, heal troublesome wounds, and remove overwhelming obstacles. In short, your voice can create the life you want—all you have to do is say the word!

Incantations

Incantation magic has been around since the time of the ancient Egyptians. Egyptian magicians used incantations to bless the dead, cajole babies into the world, obtain visions, purify one's body, and, basically, to better the life of anyone who could leave them a decent offering. To the ancient Egyptians, words of power created a foundation onto which other magical forms could be added in order to craft powerful spellwork. So while amulets were made and drawings painted, creating a physical manifestation of the need or want, the magical chant droned in the background, infusing the magic with the power of the voice.

In fact, the mouth and the voice were so important to the ancients that they included an "Opening of the Eyes and Mouth" ceremony in the preparation of the dead. This ceremony was designed to allow the deceased soul to be able to walk, talk, and see in the afterlife. The ability to talk was especially important, as the dead needed to be able to explain themselves to the gods upon arrival in the afterworld. A dying person depended upon his or her relatives to ensure that he or she was provided with the "words of power, which were necessary for him in the next world, but without a mouth it was impossible for him to utter them. Now that the mouth, or rather the use of it, was restored to the deceased, it was all important to give him not only the words of power, but also the ability to utter them correctly and in such wise that the gods and other beings would harken to them . . ."[1]

Words of power, and especially names, could not only help the dead but also the soon-to-be-born as well. In the 1500 BCE story "Khufu and the Magician," four goddesses attend the birthing of triplets who are destined to be kings of Egypt. The wife of a priest of Ra, Raddjedet, begins to experience difficulty bringing her children into the world. Ra requests the aid of deities of childbirth and creativity: the great goddess Isis, her sister Nephthys, the birthing brick goddess Meskhenet, and the frog goddess Heqet. The goddesses travel under the guise of musicians and dancers, with the god Khnum as their manager. When they arrive at the house, they are immediately ushered into the birthing chamber.

1 E.A. Wallis Budge, *Egyptian Magic* (New York: Wings Books, 1991) pp. 196–197.

Isis and Nephthys flank the birthing woman, at her head and feet, while Heqet hastens the birth. Before each child is born, Isis commands he leave the womb and enter the room. She calls each child by name, drawing him out of the mother with the power of her voice.[2] It is Isis who, as a goddess of fertility and of magical incantations, literally pulls the child from the transitory life of the womb into the warmth of Ra's light here in the mundane world. All three boys are born healthy and strong, ready to grow up and rule Egypt.

The examples of voice magic and incantations in ancient Egypt go on and on. Isis uses her voice to draw scorpion poison out of a wound and even to stop time in order to heal her son, Horus. As she states to the grieving woman whose son has been stung by the scorpion, "Come to me! Come to me! For my word is a talisman which beareth life. I am a daughter well known in the city also, and I will do away the evil by means of the word of my mouth which my father hath taught me, for I am the daughter of his own body."[3] We are all daughters and sons of the Divine (exemplified by Isis' father Ra) and we, too, can follow Isis' lead, touching the Divine through our own words of power.

Mantras

Mantras are important spiritual tools of the Hindu and Buddhist religions. They are used to connect to the Divine through the mind (meditation, vibration) and through the body (words and sounds). They are repetitive sounds and words that are said (usually, although not always) aloud to honor a specific deity. Often the characteristics of the deity are considered when choosing a mantra to say. So, for instance, if you wish to increase your prosperity, you might intone the mantra "Om Shreem Om," which is the mantra for Lakshmi, the goddess of abundance and prosperity. A mantra differs from a prayer because you are seeking to welcome the energy and guidance of the Divine into your life by actually connecting to their energetic presence. In other words, the mantra helps to lift you out of mundane reality and into the

---

2 Caroline Seawright, "Tales of Magic in Ancient Egypt," *Egyptology*, April 24, 2001, http://www.thekeep.org/~kuniochio/kuniochi/themestream/egypt_magic.html (accessed September 2009).

3 Budge, *Egyptian Magic*, p. 131.

reality of the universe and of the spirit. By chanting the mantras continually, you access a frequency and vibration higher than that of the earthly plane. You become more than the words; you connect with universal energy. In short, your life changes because you no longer are the same person.

Mantras can be chanted as many times in a row as you would like, although they generally follow a particular pattern, based on your spirituality. This pattern manifests in the physical embodiment of mala beads. In traditional Eastern religions, mantras are counted out with the aid of mala beads. Mala beads generally consist of 108 beads strung together, with a larger *mother/parent*, *guru*, or *Buddha* bead serving as the place to begin the recitations. The number 108 is significant and has been broken down to explain numerous spiritual truths. For Tibetan Buddhists, the number 108 is divided into the numbers 6×3×3×2 = 108, with each number having a corresponding meaning in relation to Buddhist spirituality. The number 6 represents the six senses of a human being: sight, sound, smell, taste, touch, and thought. The first 3 represents past, present, and future and the second 3 signifies the three disturbing states of emotion: like, dislike, and indifference. The 2 corresponds to the two states of the mind, heart, and soul: pure or impure. In the Japanese culture, the number of beads also equals 108 but their number corresponds to the 108 worldly desires, confused thoughts, and passions that the follower works to relinquish in the course of spiritual discipline.[4] In India, a predominantly Hindu country, there are fifty-four letters in the Sanskrit alphabet and each letter has a masculine and feminine quality, thus bringing the total to 108 (54×2 =108). It is said that 108 energy lines converge on the heart chakra, the energy center of the body related to relationships, love, and self-love. If so, perhaps each bead represents one of these energy lines.[5] In short, the number 108 fits into numerous spiritual pursuits and religious philosophies around the world.

No matter how many times you chant your mantra, the repetition of it allows you to access the Divine and shift your percep-

4. Sakura Designs, "What is a Mala?," http://www.buddhistmala.com/store/mantra .html (accessed September 2009).
5. Swami Jnaneshvara Bharati, "Meaning of 108 Beads on a Mala," http://www.wamij .com/108.htm (accessed September 2009).

tion of reality. You are not pleading with the Divine (as in prayer) or cajoling it (as in incantation). Rather, you are merging with an energy that is ancient and modern and universal. You are becoming one with Goddess energy, worshipped in distant lands, across oceans and deserts, and right around the corner. Mantras are much more intimate than prayer, incantation, or affirmation because the goal is a side-benefit of the connection with the Divine. So, while the goal is still important, the focus is on the sacred, both within and without.

Galdr

Galdr comes to us from the lands of snowy fields and icy evergreens, far to the north. It is a chanting part of the magical practice of the Norse, a term used to describe the ancient and medieval culture of Scandinavia, Holland, Iceland, Greenland, and Anglo-Saxon England. Rather than connecting to the power and might of the Divine, galdr works on accessing and harnessing the sacred power of the runes, a magical divination alphabet. Although the runes can be used to spell things out and to see into the future, they are actually much more than just an alphabet or a divination tool. The runes connect the *vitki* (rune master) to universal energies that shape our current lives and connect us to cultural concepts held sacred by the Norse peoples. The runes are a part of the world's creation and our own creation. They help us to understand the weather; the past, present, and future; and all aspects of life on this planet. Galdr is one way to connect to and utilize the latent power held in these mysterious symbols.

In Norse stories, the runes were granted to the god Odin after he hung upside down on a tree for nine days and nine nights, and so working with the runes often necessitates a sacrifice of some kind or another. The knowledge of the world order; of past, present, and future; and of our role in the cosmic balance is not to be taken lightly and not to be granted to everyone. Galdr is the Norse magic associated with the runes and, thus, with Odin. It is most often described as having a masculine polarity because of its connection with Odin and its connection with the voice. Galdr is the chanting of the runes in order to connect with their essence and might through the voice.

Typically, you would not chant all twenty-four runes in a row, one after the other. Rather, you would choose a few runes that would aid you in accomplishing your magical or mundane goal. You would then chant them to bring your consciousness into direct connection with the consciousness of the runes. You can infuse an object with the power of the galdr or you can simply chant the runes in order to have their magic in your life. One of my favorite uses of galdr is to chant a rune over a cup or horn of sacred drink. (Wine, mead, or stout works well when working with the Norse deities.) After chanting the rune over the drink, you can drink a small amount in order to literally imbibe the rune, bringing it inside you. The rest of the drink is then given in offering to the gods so that the rune can fortify and honor them as well. In this way, you are connecting to the gods and the Divine through the sacred power of the runes, as expressed through your voice and your breath, the very essence that gives you life.

Affirmations

Affirmations were made popular by an icon in the self-help industry, Louise Hay. Louise's premise in her seminal work, *You Can Heal Your Life*, is that all of our emotional and physical wounds can be traced back to thoughtforms that are hindering our life's work. These "old stories" hold us back from progressing forward in life and achieving our goals. Her book offers tools and guidelines for removing these blocks. One of her favorite tools is the use of affirmations.

Affirmations are statements that are said in order to change negative thoughts into positive ones. So, say you are mired in self-doubt, which is making you question your ability to perform and even apply for a new job. Recognizing this blockage, you would then craft a simple, one-sentence affirmation that you would repeat throughout your day, whenever you remembered it. Your affirmation might say: "My power is limitless as I am a child of the Divine." As you repeated this statement over a period of time (perhaps a week, perhaps a month, perhaps longer), these words would begin to change your own mental view of yourself. Your new perspective would, in turn, transform your emotional and physical self as well, allowing you to remove or ignore the old negativity and fear. The actual words themselves would alter your world, simply because they helped you see yourself in a more positive light.

As probably the purest example of voice magic, affirmations do not connect to any particular divinity or even the divinity in the world around us. Rather, they work on recognizing and accessing the Divine within. When using affirmation, your words and your voice alter your world for the better. You hold the power; it is intrinsic to you and your body. It is inherent to your voice

and a part of your true self. You simply have to open your mouth and begin the healing process.

~

With incantations and mantras, galdr chants and affirmations, voice magic is a diverse and exciting area of spellcraft. It is a way to tap into the primal power within and without. It allows us to access the Divine in nature, in divinity, and in ourselves. Although it is relatively simple and easy, voice magic can shift worlds and change lives. So, give it a try! Don't let the accessibility and availability of this magic keep you from achieving your goals and living your life. Voice magic is powerful and transformative and wonderful. Boring? Never.

Native American Legends of the White Spirit Deer

by Katherine Weber-Turcotte

The white deer is a predominant creature in the mythology of many cultures. Legend has it that Diomedes consecrated a white hart to the goddess Diana and placed a collar of gold around its neck. The Celts considered the white stag to be a messenger from the otherworld. Arthurian legend states that the white deer or hind had the perennial ability to evade capture, thus the pursuit of it represents man's spiritual quest. This can be seen in the adventures of Sir Gawain and King Arthur and his Knights of the Round Table. In Christianity, the white stag was the vision responsible for the conversion of the martyr Saint Eustace, who saw a vision of Christ between the antlers of the great white stag.

The most numerous legends of the white deer are from Native Americans. To the Native Americans, the white deer was a symbol of the Great Spirit. They were usually encountered on soul quests and journeys. Various legends of the white deer exist among the tribes of the Lenape, Seneca, Chickasaw, Roanoke, Algonquin, Nanticoke, and Pocomoke nations.

Native American Legends

The Chickasaw people tell a tale of Blue Jay, a young warrior who fell in love with the tribal chief's daughter, Bright Moon. Bright Moon's father was against the pairing and knew he had to come up with something to stop them. He requested that Blue Jay bring him the hide of the magical and rare white deer, knowing full well that this was a task nearly impossible.

Blue Jay loved Bright Moon and accepted the offer. But fate had other plans for Blue Jay, and three weeks later, under the light of the Full Moon, he shot his sharpest arrow at the magnificent white deer. And although the arrow hit the deer straight in the heart, the deer did not drop. Instead it charged ferociously toward Blue Jay. No one ever saw Blue Jay again.

Bright Moon mourned her loss greatly and never married. Legend has it that when the Full Moon shines brightly in the night sky, Bright Moon would see in the smoke of the campfire visions of the tragically wounded white deer, still running the forest with an arrow piercing its heart.

The Seneca tribe had a similar legend. The brave hunter Joninedah became unlucky in providing food for his wife Mona-sha-sha and their baby. Mona-sha-sha felt so badly for her husband that she would go fishing in an attempt to bring home food. When Joninedah would return empty-handed, Mona-sha-sha tried to make him smile, but Joninedah felt like the evil eye had been cast upon him. He could not bring himself to smile.

Feeling shunned and ignored, Mona-sha-sha thought her husband no longer loved her. She stole away during the dark of night with her baby while Joninedah slept. In her bark canoe, she and the baby disappeared over a waterfall.

The next morning, Joninedah woke to find his beloved and their baby gone. He followed what trail they had left down to the water's edge, where he found the missing bark canoe, but no Mona-sha-sha and no baby. Grief struck deeply into Joninedah's heart. It was at this time that a white doe and her baby fawn darted across his path. Seeing this as an omen from the spirit world, he knew that he would never see Mona-sha-sha and their baby again. Joninedah took his knife and plunged it deep into his heart so that he could join his wife and child in the otherworld.

Among the vast majority of Native American cultures, the white deer was regarded as a spirit of a deceased ancestor or other soul. The piebald deer (white with brown spots), however, was regarded as a spirit in the process of transferring to or from the spirit world. If the deer were to be mortally wounded while in this intermediate form, the Lenape strongly believed that it would die in the mortal form it had taken and not be able to cross over to the otherworld. Hunting the albino deer was taboo, as it was protected by most customs of the Native Americans. Those who did kill a white deer would surely suffer an untimely death, their spirit to be taken over by the white deer. Many tribes believe that there is high spiritual activity in areas where the white deer are prominent.

The white animal was seen by the Native Americans as a great symbol of prophesy, a sign that a major change was on the horizon. The Lenni Lenape tribe predicted that when a white stag and doe were seen together, it would be a message of hope and peace, a sign to the people to come together. The legend of the white deer is not just a story but a spiritual truth that has been passed down through generations of the Lenape people.

The color white represented purity and holiness and was considered to have protective properties. White also indicates wisdom and ancient knowledge of a spiritual nature. Thus the white stag was held in awe and was sacred not only in mythology but in various religions as well.

According to Avia Venifica, the message of a white animal includes higher thoughts, ideals, purity of the

soul, spirit cleansing, and attainment of greater/higher knowledge. To break this down further, the white doe was associated with benevolence, kindness, creativity, spirituality, renewal, and connectedness; the white stag represented longevity, virility, abundance, and endurance.

Myth or Reality?

Is the white spirit deer a legend, or does it really exist? A true albino deer is indeed a rarity and they seldom live beyond three to four years, as their lack of camouflage makes them easy prey. They have pink eyes, pink skin under their white hair, a pink nose, and pink hooves. Albino deer are known for genetic disorders, including problems with their hearing and eyesight as well as deformities of the legs and feet.

There are, however, quite a few white deer with leucism. Leucism is a rare genetic pattern that causes a loss of pigment in the animal's hair and skin. It's not just the lack of melanin—leucism is a variation in pigment cell activity that can be caused by a variety of reasons, ranging from genetic to inbreeding to nutritional changes. These animals are not true albinos, as they don't have the pink eyes or other albino traits. So, a white deer or stag is not albino, but is actually a red deer with a condition that causes the hair and skin to lose their color.

Seneca County, New York, contains the largest herd of white deer (white-pigmented white-tailed deer) in the conservation area formerly known as the Seneca Army Depot. I can also tell you that on my property, I am blessed with the companionship of several white spirit deer as well as a few piebald deer. I may very well have the second largest herd. They are magnificent to look upon and every time I see them, I am held in awe of their beauty.

So, what is the message of the white spirit deer? My personal belief is the same as that of many Native Americans: a white deer is a good omen, but also a powerful warning of coming change. We have entered a time of profound prophecy, a time when we must reconnect to the Earth. We must unite as a people if mankind is to survive. Perhaps most of all, I think we need to believe that magic does exist if only we will stop long enough to see and appreciate it.

For Further Studay

Andrews, Ted. *Animal Speak*. St. Paul, MN: Llewellyn Worldwide Ltd., 2003.

Dugan, Ellen. *Autumn Equinox: The Enchantment of Mabon*. St. Paul, MN: Llewellyn Worldwide Ltd., 2005.

Knowles, Sir James. *King Arthur and His Knights*. New York: Long Meadow Press, 1986.

Scully, Nicki. *PowerAnimal Meditations*. Rochester, VT: Bear & Co., 2001.

Recommended Web Sites

King, Scott Alexander. "The Sacred White Animals Prophecy." www.animaldreaming.com/whitebuffalo.php (accessed August 27, 2009).

Seneca White Deer Inc. "White Deer Prophecy." http://senecawhitedeer.org/history/prophesy.php (accessed August 27, 2009).

Sugar Loaf Historical Society, NY. "White and Piebald Deer." http://www.orangecountyweb.org/legends.html (accessed August 27, 2009).

Venefica, Avia. "Symbolic Meaning of a White Deer." http://www.symbolic-meanings.com/2007/11/02/symbolic-meaning-of-a-white-deer/ (accessed August 28, 2009).

Dowsing for Custom Tarot Spells

by Calantirniel

As a tarot diviner, when I learned I could use tarot cards to do spellwork, I thought it was genius! After all, a compact deck of tarot cards contains every expression of energy in the Universe, and I always carried one with me. As much as I love candles, oils, and other props, it was so appealing to me as a busy single mother to be able to do any kind of spell with the cards. It did not take me long to decide to have at least two decks—one for divination and one for magical work.

I loved my well-used *Tarot Spells* book when I first started. Even without the recommended candles and colored cloth for layouts, the spells worked, and worked in a hurry. The more I used the format, the more I felt comfortable with the process, including the focusing of intention and even feeling how the energies worked together. However, there were a few situations that needed great alterations to the spells in the book, and even some that required their own tarot spell created from scratch. These situations were often very urgent in nature, and I didn't have time to do more research on an effective tarot spell. What to do?

Dowsing with a Pendulum

I highly recommend learning dowsing with a pendulum, which is just as portable as a tarot deck. Only beginner's skills are necessary for this process. If you do not have a pendulum, use something that is weighted and swings freely in all directions (a pendant on a chain, or even a key on a string). You may wish to smudge the item with sage smoke or perform another cleansing to remove any residual energies that could affect results. Get used to how the swinging feels, and then ask to see a "yes" response. For me, the pendulum swings forward and backward to indicate yes, but for you it may turn clockwise, or counterclockwise. Use what works for you, and be patient.

Then, ask to see a "no" response. For me, the pendulum swings left to right for a negative, but you may again have a different swing. Honor your wiring and your way of connecting to Spirit. If you have trouble getting your pendulum to move, intend a certain form of response and then get some practice with yes and no. After you've established the yes and no answers, ask to see a "restate the question" response, and then an "ask later" response. These go in varying diagonal directions for me, but again, do what works for you.

Before dowsing with your pendulum, ask if you are aligned with the highest good, with no harm to yourself or to others, and without interfering with another's free will, and wait for a yes response before you proceed. Know that the Universe is wise. If you receive a no, this may not be a good time for you to perform divination.

Choosing the Right Cards for Your Spell

There's not room here to cover every tarot card in creating a spell. This information can easily be learned from other sources (see For Further Study). What we will concentrate on is the ability to use the pendulum to choose the cards that you need for a spell. This process can work even if you have no other tarot spell books available, making this technique very handy.

There are two ways to choose the cards with your pendulum's help. One way is to think or write out the "story" of your spell—what happened as well as what you wish to accomplish, who is involved, and so on—then lay out card choices for particular elements in this story. You then use your pendulum to dowse for which card(s)

would best fit the different elements of your story. For instance, if you are attempting to choose a card that represents a person who stole something from you, it is a good idea to know the person's motives, so that the energy of the spellwork is consistent with the energies of the mundane. Maybe the person is a drug addict and stole things randomly to sell or trade to support their negative habit, in which case you will likely use the Devil card, as well as the Justice or the Emperor card to represent the law catching up to this person. You would lay out these cards and ask if they are the best ones to use in your spell. However, maybe the reason for the theft was more personal—the person is young and jealous and wished to receive your energy or some type of attention from you. In this case, perhaps a Page of Cups reversed, mixed with the Seven of Disks (here meaning theft) can be used, and the Star, Sun, or World card might be used for resolution, in order to instill confidence into that person, so they realize their act of theft was counterproductive and feel they must correct it.

Sometimes, we won't know the energies we need from the cards, but the Universe does. Dowsing is the way the Universe communicates this with you; in fact, dowsing can be viewed as a spiritual communication, and your pendulum is the telephone. This procedure can be done with every portion of the spell, and if there are more than two choices, just lay the cards side by side, hold the pendulum back from these cards and centered, and ask it to swing to the right card. Remember to write down which cards the pendulum "chooses" for future spellwork.

A faster way to pick cards for the spell is to think or write out the story, but to go through the deck and choose cards that represent any portion of the energies you are looking for. Ask the pendulum to make sure you've pulled all cards needed for your spell. When in doubt, pull a card and put it in the pile for consideration. Stack the cards face down so you cannot see them. Then, wave the pendulum over each card, separating the cards into yes, no, and maybe piles. When done, look at the yes cards and see if you can figure out what Spirit is telling you. Then, come up with an spell arrangement that makes sense. Perhaps an inspired design will pop into your head, which can be really fun! Good examples are a cross for a protective action, a heart shape for love or clearing a broken heart, and a star for fame or recognition.

Then, go through your "maybe" cards and ask the pendulum if any will add to the effectiveness of the spell or fill out the symbolic layout. Trust Spirit.

If some of the cards that really felt right and strong to you ended up in the no pile, ask the pendulum afterward if there was already a better card to represent that energy. Almost every time, the answer is yes, and then I need to go through my yes cards again to see which card is already filling that purpose. However, if you do not see the logic of the pendulum and use a rejected card anyway, be prepared for some unforeseen trouble with your spell-work—not working in the highest good for you and/or others, for example. Let your mistakes and missteps be lessons to guide you to stronger dowsing skills.

Extras

Although not necessary, don't be afraid to integrate other items into your tarot spellwork if they are available. For instance, when my son's video game was stolen, I used an unwanted CD to rep-

resent his game, which he recovered immediately and in perfect condition.

As a side note, CDs make excellent substitutes for mirrors, so if you don't have any mirrors, CDs are often more available. Kitchen herbs and spices are often available no matter where you go, and their influences can also be integrated in your tarot spell—cinnamon attracts, pepper repels, salt grounds. You can use coins or jewelry along with tarot cards that represent money, or use them for their energy-conducting qualities. I have also used seeds from apples or oranges to represent new projects, and I would bring dirt and grass on a plate from outside for symbolic planting. Once, when I wanted badly to visit California, I took sand from a nearby sandbox, added water, sea salt, and kelp powder, and then added a seashell I had obtained from the Pacific Ocean. I kept these items in a clear glass overnight, surrounded by my dowsed-for tarot cards. The next day, I dumped the sandy water outside and rinsed the shell to dry. Adding creative touches to your tarot spells can definitely increase their effectiveness. Do whatever works and whatever feels right for you.

Tarot Spell Example

Once long ago, I purchased concert tickets for a friend and I. The friend was to meet me there and pay me back the night of the show. Due to a strange string of events, I misplaced the tickets in a spot I later discovered, where I would have never put them (and I do not rule out other spiritual activity playing a trick on me to teach me a lesson). I couldn't find the tickets in time for the concert and thus spent all that money yet again for replacement tickets. Not exactly rolling in the dough at the time, I didn't know what to do.

So I dowsed for cards to create a tarot spell. I used the Hermit card to find the tickets I purchased the first time, then I used the Temperance card to work with delicate balanced energies to recover my money, or to at least receive compensation in whatever way the Universe wished it to be so. I used the Star card to give me hope, since I knew I would need a miracle, and then the Sun card to bring everything to fruition. After the spell was cast, I found the original tickets and was inspired to write a letter to the promoter of the concert, and though I could not explain the paranormal stuff, I was inspired with a story that was believable and did not cause harm and would gently tug heartstrings. I wrote that if they wished for the original tickets to be turned in for new ones for a future show, this would be fantastic, though I knew not to expect anything; after all, they owed me nothing. I waited, and waited. I was about to write the whole thing off when, two months later, I received in the mail, with no note, two complimentary tickets to another show! I didn't want to attend that particular show, but I learned it was sold out and so went to the venue that night and sold the tickets!

When Finished Casting

When you feel you are ready, release your spell in the most comfortable way for you (for many, just saying "so mote it be" is plenty). Then, when clearing up your cards and items, use your breath to blow the spell's energies off each card before returning it to the deck. Also, periodically smudging your deck with sage smoke keeps your cards in top shape for energy work, and I recommend doing this for your divination deck and tools as well. Then, get ready to reap the rewards of the focused tarot card spell that you created with Spirit.

For Further Study

Cunningham, Scott, *Cunningham's Encyclopedia of Magical Herbs*. St. Paul, MN: Llewellyn, 1985, 2nd Edition 2005.

Donaldson, Terry. *The Tarot Spellcaster*. London: Barron's/Quarto Publishing, 2001.

"Free Dowsing Lessons." www.lettertorobin.org

Morrison, Dorothy. *Everyday Tarot Magic*. St. Paul, MN: Llewellyn, 2002.

Renée, Janina. *Tarot Spells*. St. Paul, MN: Llewellyn, 1998.

Tyson, Donald. *Portable Magic*. St. Paul, MN: Llewellyn, 2006.

Palm Reading Sunday

by Ellen Dugan

About astrology and palmistry:
they are good because they make people vivid
and full of possibilities.

—Kurt Vonnegut

What snarky, twisted individual came up with the "Palm Reading Sunday" idea? (Ellen proudly raises her hand in the air.) Yes, that would be me.

My coven started this little get-together about five years ago. One of our Full Moon celebrations had fallen on a Palm Sunday and I, with my quirky sense of humor, said, "Hey, I know. Let's make it Palm *Reading* Sunday. We'll get together, do divination, and read each others palms!" We all thought it was hilarious, and we had such a great time with the palm reading and other various divinations that it's become a yearly tradition.

The reaction to our little "holiday" is interesting. My friend Mary, a high priestess from Pennsylvania, covered her mouth, started to giggle, and then totally lost it. Once she composed herself, she finally managed to get out in a strangled voice. "That's hysterical! I have to start doing that with my coven, too!" One of my covenmates told a magickal friend about our themed get-together and her friend responded with very big eyes and said quietly with a chuckle, "Oh, my. You guys are so bad." And apparently it is catching on. Nice! I posted a blog about Palm Reading Sunday last year and the reaction was overwhelming.

Aww come on, you gotta admit, it is pretty funny. I think it's only fair. After all, Christians took a bunch of our holidays and adapted them to their celebrations, so why not turn the tables on the situation a bit and have some fun? Wearing flowing black is entirely optional. I promise you don't have to play Stevie Nicks music or the soundtrack from *Practical Magic*—unless you really want to.

Start Your Own Palm Reading Sunday Tradition

Decide ahead of time who will host this event. Then each of the coven members or study group members should choose a type of divination that they can teach to others. Since the gathering was my idea, I offered to read up on palmistry and teach the basics to the group.

I never claimed to be a walking encyclopedia of the occult. Ask me a question about magickal plants or gardens and I'll dazzle you. But palmistry? Well . . . I had some studying to do.

Many people assume I can read palms because I'm clairvoyant and read tarot cards. It still surprises me when people stick their hand in my face and ask me to read their palm. It must be the whole mentality of, "Well, you are a Witch. Don't you guys all read palms?" I think they may have us confused with the storybook version of Gypsies. (Not every Gypsy reads palms, either, and to assume so would be rude.) When I hold a person's hand for a reading, I'm actually reading them psychically, not physically through their palm. In a pickle after coming up with the whole Palm Reading Sunday idea, I tried to learn some of the palm reading basics, and that's what I taught my coven sisters. It worked out great and we all had a fantastic time.

A Few Rules of Etiquette

I should take a moment here to point out a few basic rules when it comes to reading people. Whether you read the tarot, runes, or palms, the rules of etiquette and ethical magick still apply.

1. Never predict death. Why? Because honestly, you could be wrong. You are not a god and you shouldn't frighten or upset anyone on purpose. Don't even do it as a joke or by accident. To do so would be cruel. Remember: "Harm none."

2. If you don't know the answer, say, "I don't know." Also remind the person whose palm you are reading that this is for *fun*, so you can learn more about the topic together, not for hard and fast answers.

3. Break out the ball-point pens and mark the palm lines you are reading so the person knows what you are referring to. When my coven gets together, we all mark our own palms, then compare and try to figure out what it all means. We have a blast, plus it's funny to watch everyone walk around with lines drawn and highlighted on their hand.

4. Don't ignore your gut instincts when it comes to reading palms. The shape and the "feel" of the person's hand is very important as well.

Palm Reading Basics

Often the first thing that is studied is the shape of the hand itself. This is broken down into four basic categories: the conical hand, the spatulate hand, the pointed hand, and the square hand. Interestingly enough, these four types coordinate with the four magickal elements, which makes it easy to remember, especially since the personality traits match right up to the Witch's classic elemental personality qualities.

The Air Hand (Conical) = square palm + long fingers

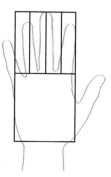

Just as the name implies, the conical hand is wider at the base of the palm than at the top of the fingers. Fingers tend to be long and tapered, with a fine texture to the skin. This type of hand is sometimes called a "feminine hand" because of its shape and texture. These folks are full of thoughts, dreams, and inspiration. A person who possesses an air hand may be a worrier, or may have problems dealing with stress in healthy ways. They may also spend a little too much time in their own mind. However, they possess a real hunger for knowledge and have a wonderful imagination, and are witty, romantic, and intellectual. These folks love tranquility and are family oriented.

The Fire Hand (Spatulate) = oblong palm + short fingers

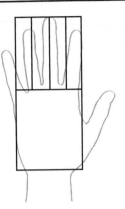

The spatulate hand is narrower at the base of the palm and the wrist and wider at the top where it meets with the fingers. The fingers themselves are shorter and fan out in the form of a spatula. People who possess a fire type of palm are strong, vibrant, and outgoing. These folks are one of a kind, confident, and independent. They are active and impulsive and like a lot of variety in their lives. They may be prone to bad tempers and get bored very quickly. But they are sexy, warm, and outgoing, so it all balances out. Fire hand individuals are adventurous, creative, sensual, energetic, and passionate.

The Water Hand (Pointed) = oblong palm + long fingers

This elemental type of hand has a wide, rounded base that tapers up to slender, pointed fingers. This is the beautiful and graceful hand of a natural psychic or empath. This shape is classically known as the psychic hand. These perceptive individuals are insightful, compassionate, and artistic. These folks do not hide their feelings and are proud of all of their emotions. Because of this, they can be easily overwhelmed by negative thoughts and bad energy. They truly dislike confrontations and try to avoid them if at all possible, which may make them appear aloof or withdrawn. Water hand people may be artists, poets, or musicians, but they have a deeply emotional side and are happiest when their world is calm.

The Earth Hand (Square) = square palm + short fingers

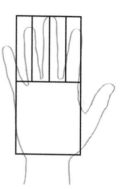

An earth hand is square-shaped with palms and fingers being of equal length and size. These hands are sturdy and strong and are sometimes described as a "masculine" hand. Earth hand folks are level-headed, honest, hard-working, and down-to-earth. They tend to be stubborn and can be called a stick in the mud when confronted with something they do not care for. They do not like change, unless they get to think about it and prepare for it first. These individuals love structure and order. They are practical and reliable, love the outdoors, and are physical, fun, and lusty. They love their family, their pets, and the natural world and are probably into gardening and plants.

The Four Major Lines

When reading palms, the right hand is thought to show the present and the probable future, while the left hand shows potential. You should look at both hands when doing a reading and remember: the lines on the hands do change as time passes. These are the four main lines on the palm.

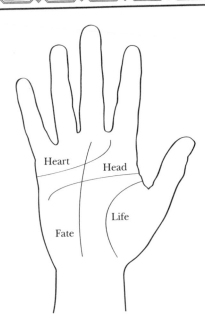

Heart Line

The heart line is the highest horizontal line on the palm. It can be curved or straight, and it starts somewhere between the first and second fingers. This line represents the emotional side of your personality. The more of a curve the heart line has, the more poignant and sensual its owner is thought to be. This line commonly describes the emotions, temperament, and love life in general.

Head Line

This is the second horizontal line on the palm. It travels from between the thumb and index finger directly across the palm toward the outer edge. This line shows your working capabilities, how you deal with problems, and the attitude you possess toward your career. The head line also shows your mental qualities, such as concentration and ambition.

Life Line

This is the most well-known line on the hand. It starts close to the head line and is the third of the main lines on the hand. This line starts between the index finger and the thumb, curves out, and then travels down toward the wrist. This line indicates the quality of life, home, and major changes. If the line swoops out far into the hand, it indicates a person who loves to travel. If it hugs closer to the thumb, it represents a homebody.

Fate Line

The fate line begins its journey at the wrist and moves vertically toward the middle finger. The deeper the line, the more fate will play a role in your life. If the fate line is separate from the life line, it shows an independent spirit. This line indicates the general pattern one's life will take and the relationship you have with your parents.

Have Fun

Divination is the theme of the day, so have fun! For more information, I suggest you check out a few books from the library and read up on palmistry. Bring the book along with you to your own Palm Reading Sunday get-together. Don't forget to include other forms of divination as well. Make it a real party atmosphere. I even went so far as to print up little handouts with an old illustration of the lines of the hand. I printed these out on parchment paper and used an old-style font to give it some drama. Everyone loved them and added them to their Book of Shadows.

One clever covener, the hostess for the day, opened up a program on her computer, then got each of our birth dates and printed out astrological charts for each member of the group. Pretty snazzy. Now, if only I could figure out what all of that astrological information really means . . .

For Further Study

Altman, Nathaniel. *Palmistry*. New York: Sterling Publishing Company, 1999.

Siden, Jan. *The Handbook of Palmistry*. Rozelle, AU: Sally Milner Publishing, 1993.

Whitaker, Hazel. *Palmistry: Your Highway to Life*. New York: Barnes & Noble Books, 1997.

Almanac Section

Calendar

Time Changes

Lunar Phases

Moon Signs

Full Moons

Sabbats

World Holidays

Incense of the Day

Color of the Day

Almanac Listings

In these listings you will find the date, day, lunar phase, Moon sign, color, and incense for the day, and festivals from around the world.

The Date

The date is used in numerological calculations that govern magical rites.

The Day

Each day is ruled by a planet that possesses specific magical influences:

MONDAY (MOON): Peace, sleep, healing, compassion, friends, psychic awareness, purification, and fertility.

TUESDAY (MARS): Passion, sex, courage, aggression, and protection.

WEDNESDAY (MERCURY): The conscious mind, study, travel, divination, and wisdom.

THURSDAY (JUPITER): Expansion, money, prosperity, and generosity.

FRIDAY (VENUS): Love, friendship, reconciliation, and beauty.

SATURDAY (SATURN): Longevity, exorcism, endings, homes, and houses.

SUNDAY (SUN): Healing, spirituality, success, strength, and protection.

The Lunar Phase

The lunar phase is important in determining the best times for magic.

THE WAXING MOON (from the New Moon to the Full) is the ideal time for magic to draw things toward you.

THE FULL MOON is the time of greatest power.

THE WANING MOON (from the Full Moon to the New) is a time for study, meditation, and little magical work (except magic designed to banish harmful energies).

The Moon's Sign

The Moon continuously "moves" through the zodiac, from Aries to Pisces. Each sign possesses its own significance.

ARIES: Good for starting things, but lacks staying power. Things occur rapidly, but quickly pass. People tend to be argumentative and assertive.

TAURUS: Things begun now last the longest, tend to increase in value, and become hard to alter. Brings out appreciation for beauty and sensory experience.

GEMINI: Things begun now are easily changed by outside influence. Time for shortcuts, communication, games, and fun.

CANCER: Stimulates emotional rapport between people. Pinpoints need, supports growth and nurturance. Tends to domestic concerns.

LEO: Draws emphasis to the self, central ideas or institutions, away from connections with others and other emotional needs. People tend to be melodramatic.

VIRGO: Favors accomplishment of details and commands from higher up. Focuses on health, hygiene, and daily schedules.

LIBRA: Favors cooperation, social activities, beautification of surroundings, balance, and partnership.

SCORPIO: Increases awareness of psychic power. Precipitates psychic crises and ends connections thoroughly. People tend to brood and become secretive.

SAGITTARIUS: Encourages flights of imagination and confidence. This is an adventurous, philosophical, and athletic Moon sign. Favors expansion and growth.

CAPRICORN: Develops strong structure. Focus on traditions, responsibilities, and obligations. A good time to set boundaries and rules.

AQUARIUS: Rebellious energy. Time to break habits and make abrupt changes. Personal freedom and individuality is the focus.

PISCES: The focus is on dreaming, nostalgia, intuition, and psychic impressions. A good time for spiritual or philanthropic activities.

Color and Incense

The color and incense for the day are based on information from *Personal Alchemy* by Amber Wolfe, and relate to the planet that rules each day. This information can be taken into consideration along with other factors when planning works of magic or when blending magic into mundane life. Please note that the incense selections listed are not hard and fast. If you cannot find or do not like the incense listed for the day, choose a similar scent that appeals to you.

Festivals and Holidays

Festivals are listed throughout the year. The exact dates of many of these ancient festivals are difficult to determine; prevailing data has been used.

Time Changes

The times and dates of all astrological phenomena in this almanac are based on **Eastern Standard Time (EST)**. If you live outside of the Eastern time zone, you will need to make the following changes:

PACIFIC STANDARD TIME: Subtract three hours.

MOUNTAIN STANDARD TIME: Subtract two hours.

CENTRAL STANDARD TIME: Subtract one hour.

ALASKA: Subtract four hours.

HAWAII: Subtract five hours.

DAYLIGHT SAVING TIME (ALL ZONES): Add one hour.

Daylight Saving Time begins at 2 am on March 13, 2011, and ends at 2 am on November 6, 2011.

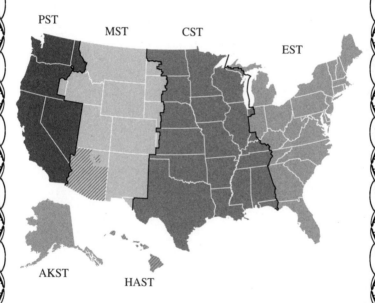

Please refer to a world time zone resource for time adjustments for locations outside the United States.

2011 Sabbats
and Full Moons

January 19	Cancer Full Moon 4:21 pm
February 2	Imbolc
February 18	Leo Full Moon 3:36 am
March 19	Virgo Full Moon 2:10 pm
March 20	Ostara (Spring Equinox)
April 17	Libra Full Moon 10:44 pm
May 1	Beltane
May 17	Scorpio Full Moon 7:09 am
June 15	Sagittarius Full Moon 4:14 pm
June 21	Midsummer (Summer Solstice)
July 15	Capricorn Full Moon 2:40 am
August 1	Lammas
August 13	Aquarius Full Moon 2:58 pm
September 12	Pisces Full Moon 5:27 am
September 23	Mabon (Fall Equinox)
October 11	Aries Full Moon 10:06 pm
October 31	Samhain
November 10	Taurus Full Moon 3:16 pm
December 10	Gemini Full Moon 9:36 am
December 22	Yule (Winter Solstice)

All times are Eastern Standard Time (EST)
or Eastern Daylight Time (EDT)

2011 Sabbats in
the Southern Hemisphere

Because Earth's Northern and Southern Hemispheres experience opposite seasons at any given time, the season-based Sabbats listed on the previous page and in this almanac section are not correct for those residing south of the equator. Listed here are the Southern Hemisphere sabbat dates for 2011:

February 2	Lammas
March 20	Mabon (Fall Equinox)
May 1	Samhain
June 21	Yule (Winter Solstice)
August 2	Imbolc
September 23	Ostara (Spring Equinox)
November 1	Beltane
December 22	Midsummer (Summer Solstice)

Birthstone poetry reprinted from
The Occult and Curative Powers of Precious Stones
by William T. Fernie, M.D.
Harper & Row (1981)

Originally printed in 1907 as
Precious Stones:
For Curative Wear; and Other Remedial Uses;
Likewise the Nobler Metals

January

1 Saturday
New Year's Day • Kwanzaa ends
Waning Moon
Moon phase: Fourth Quarter
Color: Gray

Moon Sign: Sagittarius
Incense: Patchouli

2 Sunday
First Writing Day (Japanese)
Waning Moon
Moon phase: Fourth Quarter
Color: Gold

Moon Sign: Sagittarius
Incense: Frankincense

3 Monday
St. Genevieve's Day
Waning Moon
Moon phase: Fourth Quarter
Color: Silver

Moon Sign: Sagittarius
Moon enters Capricorn 2:39 am
Incense: Clary Sage

4 Tuesday
Frost Fairs on the Thames
Waning Moon
Moon phase: New Moon 4:03 am
Color: Red

Moon Sign: Capricorn
Incense: Geranium

5 Wednesday
Epiphany Eve
Waxing Moon
Moon phase: First Quarter
Color: Brown

Moon Sign: Capricorn
Moon enters Aquarius 11:08 am
Incense: Marjoram

6 Thursday
Epiphany
Waxing Moon
Moon phase: First Quarter
Color: Turquoise

Moon Sign: Aquarius
Incense: Clove

7 Friday
Rizdvo (Ukrainian)
Waxing Moon
Moon phase: First Quarter
Color: White

Moon Sign: Aquarius
Moon enters Pisces 9:57 pm
Incense: Violet

January

8   Saturday
Midwives' Day
Waxing Moon
Moon phase: First Quarter
Color: Blue

Moon Sign: Pisces
Incense: Sage

9   Sunday
Feast of the Black Nazarene (Filipino)
Waxing Moon
Moon phase: First Quarter
Color: Yellow

Moon Sign: Pisces
Incense: Eucalyptus

10   Monday
Business God's Day (Japanese)
Waxing Moon
Moon phase: First Quarter
Color: Gray

Moon Sign: Pisces
Moon enters Aries 10:24 am
Incense: Lily

11   Tuesday
Carmentalia (Roman)
Waxing Moon
Moon phase: First Quarter
Color: White

Moon Sign: Aries
Incense: Bayberry

☽   Wednesday
Revolution Day (Tanzanian)
Waxing Moon
Moon phase: Second Quarter 6:31 am
Color: Yellow

Moon Sign: Aries
Moon enters Taurus 10:37 pm
Incense: Lavender

13   Thursday
Twentieth Day (Norwegian)
Waxing Moon
Moon phase: Second Quarter
Color: White

Moon Sign: Taurus
Incense: Apricot

14   Friday
Feast of the Ass (French)
Waxing Moon
Moon phase: Second Quarter
Color: Coral

Moon Sign: Taurus
Incense: Thyme

January

15 Saturday
Birthday of Martin Luther King, Jr. (actual)
Waxing Moon
Moon phase: Second Quarter
Color: Gray

Moon Sign: Taurus
Moon enters Gemini 8:23 am
Incense: Sandalwood

16 Sunday
Apprentices' Day
Waxing Moon
Moon phase: Second Quarter
Color: Gold

Moon Sign: Gemini
Incense: Juniper

17 Monday
Birthday of Martin Luther King, Jr. (observed)
Waxing Moon
Moon phase: Second Quarter
Color: Ivory

Moon Sign: Gemini
Moon enters Cancer 2:29 pm
Incense: Hyssop

18 Tuesday
Assumption Day
Waxing Moon
Moon phase: Second Quarter
Color: Black

Moon Sign: Cancer
Incense: Cedar

☺ Wednesday
Kitchen God Feast (Chinese)
Waxing Moon
Moon phase: Full Moon 4:21 pm
Color: White

Moon Sign: Cancer
Moon enters Leo 5:16 pm
Incense: Lilac

20 Thursday
Breadbasket Festival (Portuguese)
Waning Moon
Moon phase: Third Quarter
Color: Green

Moon Sign: Leo
Incense: Nutmeg
Sun enters Aquarius 5:19 am

21 Friday
St. Agnes' Day
Waning Moon
Moon phase: Third Quarter
Color: Purple

Moon Sign: Leo
Moon enters Virgo 6:10 pm
Incense: Alder

January

22 Saturday
Saint Vincent's Day (French)
Waning Moon
Moon phase: Third Quarter
Color: Brown

Moon Sign: Virgo
Incense: Magnolia

23 Sunday
St. Ildefonso's Day
Waning Moon
Moon phase: Third Quarter
Color: Orange

Moon Sign: Virgo
Moon enters Libra 6:59 pm
Incense: Heliotrope

24 Monday
Alasitas Fair (Bolivian)
Waning Moon
Moon phase: Third Quarter
Color: Gray

Moon Sign: Libra
Incense: Neroli

25 Tuesday
Burns' Night (Scottish)
Waning Moon
Moon phase: Third Quarter
Color: Scarlet

Moon Sign: Libra
Moon enters Scorpio 9:15 pm
Incense: Ginger

◑ Wednesday
Republic Day (Indian)
Waning Moon
Moon phase: Fourth Quarter 7:57 am
Color: Topaz

Moon Sign: Scorpio
Incense: Marjoram

27 Thursday
Vogelgruff (Swiss)
Waning Moon
Moon phase: Fourth Quarter
Color: Purple

Moon Sign: Scorpio
Incense: Balsam

28 Friday
St. Charlemange's Day
Waning Moon
Moon phase: Fourth Quarter
Color: White

Moon Sign: Scorpio
Moon enters Sagittarius 1:55 am
Incense: Mint

January

29 Saturday
Australia Day
Waning Moon
Moon phase: Fourth Quarter
Color: Blue

Moon Sign: Sagittarius
Incense: Rue

---

30 Sunday
Three Hierarch's Day (Eastern Orthodox)
Waning Moon
Moon phase: Fourth Quarter
Color: Amber

Moon Sign: Sagittarius
Moon enters Capricorn 9:04 am
Incense: Almond

---

31 Monday
Independence Day (Nauru)
Waning Moon
Moon phase: Fourth Quarter
Color: White

Moon Sign: Capricorn
Incense: Rosemary

January Birthstones

By her in January born
No gem save Garnets should be worn;
They will ensure her constancy,
True friendship, and fidelity.

Modern: Garnet   Zodiac (Capricorn): Ruby

February Birthstones

The February-born shall find
Sincerity, and peace of mind,
Freedom from passion and from care,
If they the Amethyst will wear.

Modern: Amethyst   Zodiac (Aquarius): Garnet

February

1 **Tuesday**
St. Brigid's Day (Irish)
Waning Moon
Moon phase: Fourth Quarter
Color: Red

Moon Sign: Capricorn
Moon enters Aquarius 6:21 pm
Incense: Basil

 **Wednesday**
Imbolc • Groundhog Day
Waning Moon
Moon phase: New Moon 9:31 pm
Color: White

Moon Sign: Aquarius
Incense: Honeysuckle

---

3 **Thursday**
Chinese New Year (rabbit)
Waxing Moon
Moon phase: First Quarter
Color: White

Moon Sign: Aquarius
Incense: Clove

---

4 **Friday**
Independence Day (Sri Lankan)
Waxing Moon
Moon phase: First Quarter
Color: Rose

Moon Sign: Aquarius
Moon enters Pisces 5:24 am
Incense: Cypress

---

5 **Saturday**
Festival de la Alcaldesa (Italian)
Waxing Moon
Moon phase: First Quarter
Color: Brown

Moon Sign: Pisces
Incense: Patchouli

---

6 **Sunday**
Bob Marley's Birthday (Jamaican)
Waxing Moon
Moon phase: First Quarter
Color: Gold

Moon Sign: Pisces
Moon enters Aries 5:45 pm
Incense: Hyacinth

---

7 **Monday**
Ful Moon Poya (Sri Lankan)
Waxing Moon
Moon phase: First Quarter
Color: Silver

Moon Sign: Aries
Incense: Lily

February

8 Tuesday
Mass for Broken Needles (Japanese)
Waxing Moon
Moon phase: First Quarter
Color: Gray

Moon Sign: Aries
Incense: Cedar

---

9 Wednesday
St. Marion's Day (Lebanese)
Waxing Moon
Moon phase: First Quarter
Color: Brown

Moon Sign: Aries
Moon enters Taurus 6:22 am
Incense: Bay laurel

---

10 Thursday
Gasparilla Day (Floridian)
Waxing Moon
Moon phase: First Quarter
Color: Green

Moon Sign: Taurus
Incense: Mulberry

☾ Friday
Foundation Day (Japanese)
Waxing Moon
Moon phase: Second Quarter 2:18 am
Color: Purple

Moon Sign: Taurus
Moon enters Gemini 5:20 pm
Incense: Vanilla

---

12 Saturday
Lincoln's Birthday (actual)
Waxing Moon
Moon phase: Second Quarter
Color: Gray

Moon Sign: Gemini
Incense: Ivy

---

13 Sunday
Parentalia (Roman)
Waxing Moon
Moon phase: Second Quarter
Color: Yellow

Moon Sign: Gemini
Incense: Almond

---

14 Monday
Valentine's Day
Waxing Moon
Moon phase: Second Quarter
Color: Gray

Moon Sign: Gemini
Moon enters Cancer 12:48 am
Incense: Narcissus

February

15	Tuesday	
	Lupercalia (Roman)	Moon Sign: Cancer
	Waxing Moon	Incense: Ylang-ylang
	Moon phase: Second Quarter	
	Color: White	

16	Wednesday	
	Fumi-e (Japanese)	Moon Sign: Cancer
	Waxing Moon	Moon enters Leo 4:14 am
	Moon phase: Second Quarter	Incense: Lilac
	Color: Yellow	

17	Thursday	
	Quirinalia (Roman)	Moon Sign: Leo
	Waxing Moon	Incense: Myrrh
	Moon phase: Second Quarter	
	Color: Purple	

☺	Friday	
	Saint Bernadette's Second Vision	Moon Sign: Leo
	Waxing Moon	Moon enters Virgo 4:39 am
	Moon phase: Full Moon 3:36 am	Incense: Orchid
	Color: Pink	Sun enters Pisces 7:25 pm

19	Saturday	
	Pero Palo's Trial (Spanish)	Moon Sign: Virgo
	Waning Moon	Incense: Pine
	Moon phase: Third Quarter	
	Color: Indigo	

20	Sunday	
	Installation of the New Lama (Tibetan)	Moon Sign: Virgo
	Waning Moon	Moon enters Libra 4:01 am
	Moon phase: Third Quarter	Incense: Eucalyptus
	Color: Amber	

21	Monday	
	Presidents' Day (observed)	Moon Sign: Libra
	Waning Moon	Incense: Neroli
	Moon phase: Third Quarter	
	Color: White	

February

22 Tuesday
Caristia (Roman)
Waning Moon
Moon phase: Third Quarter
Color: Maroon

Moon Sign: Libra
Moon enters Scorpio 4:29 am
Incense: Bayberry

23 Wednesday
Terminalia (Roman)
Waning Moon
Moon phase: Third Quarter
Color: Topaz

Moon Sign: Scorpio
Incense: Lavender

Thursday
Regifugium (Roman)
Waning Moon
Moon phase: Fourth Quarter 6:26 pm
Color: Crimson

Moon Sign: Scorpio
Moon enters Sagittarius 7:46 am
Incense: Carnation

25 Friday
Saint Walburga's Day (German)
Waning Moon
Moon phase: Fourth Quarter
Color: Rose

Moon Sign: Sagittarius
Incense: Thyme

26 Saturday
Zamboanga Festival (Filipino)
Waning Moon
Moon phase: Fourth Quarter
Color: Black

Moon Sign: Sagittarius
Moon enters Capricorn 2:32 pm
Incense: Sage

27 Sunday
Threepenny Day
Waning Moon
Moon phase: Fourth Quarter
Color: Orange

Moon Sign: Capricorn
Incense: Marigold

28 Monday
Kalevala Day (Finnish)
Waning Moon
Moon phase: Fourth Quarter
Color: Ivory

Moon Sign: Capricorn
Incense: Clary sage

March

1   Tuesday
Matronalia (Roman)
Waning Moon
Moon phase: Fourth Quarter
Color: Scarlet

Moon Sign: Capricorn
Moon enters Aquarius 12:14 am
Incense: Cinnamon

---

2   Wednesday
St. Chad's Day (English)
Waning Moon
Moon phase: Fourth Quarter
Color: Brown

Moon Sign: Aquarius
Incense: Bay laurel

---

3   Thursday
Doll Festival (Japanese)
Waning Moon
Moon phase: Fourth Quarter
Color: Purple

Moon Sign: Aquarius
Moon enters Pisces 11:47 am
Incense: Myrrh

☽   Friday
St. Casimir's Day (Polish)
Waning Moon
Moon phase: New Moon 3:46 pm
Color: Pink

Moon Sign: Pisces
Incense: Yarrow

---

5   Saturday
Isis Festival (Roman)
Waxing Moon
Moon phase: First Quarter
Color: Blue

Moon Sign: Pisces
Incense: Rue

---

6   Sunday
Alamo Day
Waxing Moon
Moon phase: First Quarter
Color: Amber

Moon Sign: Pisces
Moon enters Aries 12:14 am
Incense: Marigold

---

7   Monday
Bird and Arbor Day
Waxing Moon
Moon phase: First Quarter
Color: Ivory

Moon Sign: Aries
Incense: Hyssop

March

8 Tuesday
Mardi Gras (Fat Tuesday)
Waxing Moon
Moon phase: First Quarter
Color: White

Moon Sign: Aries
Moon enters Taurus 12:52 pm
Incense: Ylang-ylang

---

9 Wednesday
Ash Wednesday
Waxing Moon
Moon phase: First Quarter
Color: Topaz

Moon Sign: Taurus
Incense: Honeysuckle

---

10 Thursday
Tibet Day
Waxing Moon
Moon phase: First Quarter
Color: Turquoise

Moon Sign: Taurus
Incense: Balsam

---

11 Friday
Feast of the Gauri (Hindu)
Waxing Moon
Moon phase: First Quarter
Color: White

Moon Sign: Taurus
Moon enters Gemini 12:31 am
Incense: Orchid

☽ Saturday
Receiving the Water (Buddhist)
Waxing Moon
Moon phase: Second Quarter 6:45 pm
Color: Black

Moon Sign: Gemini
Incense: Magnolia

---

13 Sunday
Daylight Saving Time begins
Waxing Moon
Moon phase: Second Quarter
Color: Gold

Moon Sign: Gemini
Moon enters Cancer 10:29 am
Incense: Heliotrope

---

14 Monday
Mamuralia (Roman)
Waxing Moon
Moon phase: Second Quarter
Color: Silver

Moon Sign: Cancer
Incense: Rosemary

March ♈

15 Tuesday
Phallus Festival (Japanese)
Waxing Moon
Moon phase: Second Quarter
Color: Gray

Moon Sign: Cancer
Moon enters Leo 3:33 pm
Incense: Geranium

16 Wednesday
St. Urho's Day (Finnish)
Waxing Moon
Moon phase: Second Quarter
Color: Yellow

Moon Sign: Leo
Incense: Marjoram

17 Thursday
St. Patrick's Day
Waxing Moon
Moon phase: Second Quarter
Color: Crimson

Moon Sign: Leo
Moon enters Virgo 4:53 pm
Incense: Nutmeg

18 Friday
Sheelah's Day (Irish)
Waxing Moon
Moon phase: Second Quarter
Color: Rose

Moon Sign: Virgo
Incense: Mint

☺ Saturday
St. Joseph's Day (Sicilian)
Waxing Moon
Moon phase: Full Moon 2:10 pm
Color: Gray

Moon Sign: Virgo
Moon enters Libra 4:03 pm
Incense: Sage

20 Sunday
Purim • Ostara • Spring Equinox • Int'l Astrology Day
Waning Moon
Moon phase: Third Quarter
Color: Amber

Moon Sign: Libra
Incense: Hyacinth
Sun enters Aries 7:21 pm

21 Monday
Juarez Day (Mexican)
Waning Moon
Moon phase: Third Quarter
Color: Gray

Moon Sign: Libra
Moon enters Scorpio 3:17 pm
Incense: Lily

22 Tuesday
Hilaria (Roman)
Waning Moon
Moon phase: Third Quarter
Color: Red

Moon Sign: Scorpio
Incense: Ginger

23 Wednesday
Pakistan Day
Waning Moon
Moon phase: Third Quarter
Color: White

Moon Sign: Scorpio
Moon enters Sagittarius 4:45 pm
Incense: Lilac

24 Thursday
Day of Blood (Roman)
Waning Moon
Moon phase: Third Quarter
Color: Green

Moon Sign: Sagittarius
Incense: Clove

25 Friday
Tichborne Dole (English)
Waning Moon
Moon phase: Third Quarter
Color: Purple

Moon Sign: Sagittarius
Moon enters Capricorn 9:57 pm
Incense: Cypress

Saturday
Prince Kuhio Day (Hawaiian)
Waning Moon
Moon phase: Fourth Quarter 8:07 am
Color: Indigo

Moon Sign: Capricorn
Incense: Sandalwood

27 Sunday
Smell the Breezes Day (Egyptian)
Waning Moon
Moon phase: Fourth Quarter
Color: Yellow

Moon Sign: Capricorn
Incense: Juniper

28 Monday
Oranges and Lemons Service (English)
Waning Moon
Moon phase: Fourth Quarter
Color: Lavender

Moon Sign: Capricorn
Moon enters Aquarius 7:00 am
Incense: Narcissus

March

29 Tuesday
Feast of St. Eustace's of Luxeuil
Waning Moon
Moon phase: Fourth Quarter
Color: White

Moon Sign: Aquarius
Incense: Cinnamon

30 Wednesday
Seward's Day (Alaskan)
Waning Moon
Moon phase: Fourth Quarter
Color: Brown

Moon Sign: Aquarius
Moon enters Pisces 6:38 pm
Incense: Lavender

31 Thursday
The Borrowed Days (Ethiopian)
Waning Moon
Moon phase: Fourth Quarter
Color: White

Moon Sign: Pisces
Incense: Apricot

March Birthstones

Who in this world of ours, her eyes
In March first opens, shall be wise.
In days of peril, firm and brave,
And wear a Bloodstone to her grave.

Modern: Aquamarine
Zodiac (Pisces): Amethyst

169

April

♈

1 Friday
April Fools' Day
Waning Moon
Moon phase: Fourth Quarter
Color: Coral

Moon Sign: Pisces
Incense: Mint

---

2 Saturday
The Battle of Flowers (French)
Waning Moon
Moon phase: Fourth Quarter
Color: Gray

Moon Sign: Pisces
Moon enters Aries 7:16 am
Incense: Pine

☽ **Sunday**
Thirteenth Day (Iranian)
Waning Moon
Moon phase: New Moon 10:32 am
Color: Gold

Moon Sign: Aries
Incense: Eucalyptus

---

4 Monday
Megalesia (Roman)
Waxing Moon
Moon phase: First Quarter
Color: Silver

Moon Sign: Aries
Moon enters Taurus 7:46 pm
Incense: Clary sage

---

5 Tuesday
Tomb-Sweeping Day (Chinese)
Waxing Moon
Moon phase: First Quarter
Color: Red

Moon Sign: Taurus
Incense: Bayberry

---

6 Wednesday
Chakri Day (Thai)
Waxing Moon
Moon phase: First Quarter
Color: Brown

Moon Sign: Taurus
Incense: Lilac

---

7 Thursday
Festival of Pure Brightness (Chinese)
Waxing Moon
Moon phase: First Quarter
Color: White

Moon Sign: Taurus
Moon enters Gemini 7:22 am
Incense: Nutmeg

8 **Friday**
Buddha's Birthday   Moon Sign: Gemini
Waxing Moon   Incense: Thyme
Moon phase: First Quarter
Color: Rose

---

9 **Saturday**
Valour Day (Filipino)   Moon Sign: Gemini
Waxing Moon   Moon enters Cancer 5:02 pm
Moon phase: First Quarter   Incense: Ivy
Color: Indigo

---

10 **Sunday**
The Tenth of April (English)   Moon Sign: Cancer
Waxing Moon   Incense: Frankincense
Moon phase: First Quarter
Color: Orange

◐ **Monday**
Heroes Day (Costa Rican)   Moon Sign: Cancer
Waxing Moon   Moon enters Leo 11:37 pm
Moon phase: Second Quarter 8:05 am   Incense: Lily
Color: Gray

---

12 **Tuesday**
Cerealia (Roman)   Moon Sign: Leo
Waxing Moon   Incense: Geranium
Moon phase: Second Quarter
Color: Maroon

---

13 **Wednesday**
Thai New Year   Moon Sign: Leo
Waxing Moon   Incense: Bay laurel
Moon phase: Second Quarter
Color: White

---

14 **Thursday**
Sanno Festival (Japanese)   Moon Sign: Leo
Waxing Moon   Moon enters Virgo 2:40 am
Moon phase: Second Quarter   Incense: Carnation
Color: Green

April

15 Friday
Plowing Festival (Chinese)
Waxing Moon
Moon phase: Second Quarter
Color: White

Moon Sign: Virgo
Incense: Yarrow

16 Saturday
Zurich Spring Festival (Swiss)
Waxing Moon
Moon phase: Second Quarter
Color: Blue

Moon Sign: Virgo
Moon enters Libra 2:59 am
Incense: Patchouli

17 Sunday
Palm Sunday
Waxing Moon
Moon phase: Full Moon 10:44 pm
Color: Yellow

Moon Sign: Libra
Incense: Almond

18 Monday
Flower Festival (Japanese)
Waning Moon
Moon phase: Third Quarter
Color: Lavender

Moon Sign: Libra
Moon enters Scorpio 2:19 am
Incense: Rosemary

19 Tuesday
Passover begins
Waning Moon
Moon phase: Third Quarter
Color: White

Moon Sign: Scorpio
Incense: Cinnamon

20 Wednesday
Drum Festival (Japanese)
Waning Moon
Moon phase: Third Quarter
Color: Yellow

Moon Sign: Scorpio
Moon enters Sagittarius 2:50 am
Incense: Marjoram
Sun enters Taurus 6:17 am

21 Thursday
Tiradentes Day (Brazilian)
Waning Moon
Moon phase: Third Quarter
Color: Purple

Moon Sign: Sagittarius
Incense: Balsam

April

22   **Friday**
Earth Day • Good Friday
Waning Moon
Moon phase: Third Quarter
Color: Pink

Moon Sign: Sagittarius
Moon enters Capricorn 6:24 am
Incense: Vanilla

---

23   **Saturday**
St. George's Day (English)
Waning Moon
Moon phase: Third Quarter
Color: Brown

Moon Sign: Capricorn
Incense: Pine

○   **Sunday**
Easter
Waning Moon
Moon phase: Fourth Quarter 10:47 pm
Color: Gold

Moon Sign: Capricorn
Moon enters Aquarius 1:59 pm
Incense: Heliotrope

---

25   **Monday**
Robigalia (Roman)
Waning Moon
Moon phase: Fourth Quarter
Color: Silver

Moon Sign: Aquarius
Incense: Neroli

---

26   **Tuesday**
Passover ends • Arbor Day
Waning Moon
Moon phase: Fourth Quarter
Color: Gray

Moon Sign: Aquarius
Incense: Ginger

---

27   **Wednesday**
Humabon's Conversion (Filipino)
Waning Moon
Moon phase: Fourth Quarter
Color: White

Moon Sign: Aquarius
Moon enters Pisces 12:57 am
Incense: Honeysuckle

---

28   **Thursday**
Floralia (Roman)
Waning Moon
Moon phase: Fourth Quarter
Color: Crimson

Moon Sign: Pisces
Incense: Mulberry

April

29 Friday
Green Day (Japanese)
Waning Moon
Moon phase: Fourth Quarter
Color: Purple

Moon Sign: Pisces
Moon enters Aries 1:33 pm
Incense: Violet

30 Saturday
Walpurgis Night • May Eve
Waning Moon
Moon phase: Fourth Quarter
Color: Black

Moon Sign: Aries
Incense: Magnolia

April Birthstones

She who from April dates her years,
Diamonds shall wear, lest bitter tears
For vain repentance flow; this stone
Emblem for innocence is known.

Modern: Diamond
Zodiac (Aries): Bloodstone

May

1 Sunday
Beltane • May Day
Waning Moon
Moon phase: Fourth Quarter
Color: Yellow

Moon Sign: Aries
Incense: Juniper

2 Monday
Big Kite Flying (Japanese)
Waning Moon
Moon phase: Fourth Quarter
Color: Lavender

Moon Sign: Aries
Moon enters Taurus 1:58 am
Incense: Lily

☽ Tuesday
Holy Cross Day
Waning Moon
Moon phase: New Moon 2:51 am
Color: Black

Moon Sign: Taurus
Incense: Cinnamon

4 Wednesday
Bona Dea (Roman)
Waxing Moon
Moon phase: First Quarter
Color: White

Moon Sign: Taurus
Moon enters Gemini 1:09 pm
Incense: Bay laurel

5 Thursday
Cinco de Mayo (Mexican)
Waxing Moon
Moon phase: First Quarter
Color: Turquoise

Moon Sign: Gemini
Incense: Jasmine

6 Friday
Martyrs' Day (Lebanese)
Waxing Moon
Moon phase: First Quarter
Color: Rose

Moon Sign: Gemini
Moon enters Cancer 10:32 pm
Incense: Cypress

7 Saturday
Pilgrimage of St. Nicholas (Italian)
Waxing Moon
Moon phase: First Quarter
Color: Indigo

Moon Sign: Cancer
Incense: Magnolia

May

8 Sunday
Mother's Day
Waxing Moon
Moon phase: First Quarter
Color: Gold

Moon Sign: Cancer
Incense: Marigold

9 Monday
Lemuria (Roman)
Waxing Moon
Moon phase: First Quarter
Color: Gray

Moon Sign: Cancer
Moon enters Leo 5:35 am
Incense: Narcissus

☽ Tuesday
Census Day (Canadian)
Waxing Moon
Moon phase: Second Quarter 4:33 pm
Color: White

Moon Sign: Leo
Incense: Basil

11 Wednesday
Ukai Season opens (Japanese)
Waxing Moon
Moon phase: Second Quarter
Color: Yellow

Moon Sign: Leo
Moon enters Virgo 9:59 am
Incense: Lavender

12 Thursday
Florence Nightingale's Birthday
Waxing Moon
Moon phase: Second Quarter
Color: Green

Moon Sign: Virgo
Incense: Carnation

13 Friday
Pilgrimage to Fatima (Portuguese)
Waxing Moon
Moon phase: Second Quarter
Color: Purple

Moon Sign: Virgo
Moon enters Libra 11:56 am
Incense: Rose

14 Saturday
Carabao Festival (Spanish)
Waxing Moon
Moon phase: Second Quarter
Color: Gray

Moon Sign: Libra
Incense: Pine

May

♊

15	Sunday
	Festival of St. Dympna (Belgian)
	Waxing Moon
	Moon phase: Second Quarter
	Color: Yellow

Moon Sign: Libra
Moon enters Scorpio 12:31 pm
Incense: Almond

16	Monday
	St. Honoratus' Day
	Waxing Moon
	Moon phase: Second Quarter
	Color: White

Moon Sign: Scorpio
Incense: Rosemary

☺ Tuesday
Norwegian Independence Day
Waxing Moon
Moon phase: Full Moon 7:09 am
Color: Red

Moon Sign: Scorpio
Moon enters Sagittarius 1:22 pm
Incense: Cedar

18	Wednesday
	Las Piedras Day (Uraguayan)
	Waning Moon
	Moon phase: Third Quarter
	Color: Topaz

Moon Sign: Sagittarius
Incense: Lilac

19	Thursday
	Pilgrimage to Treguier (French)
	Waning Moon
	Moon phase: Third Quarter
	Color: White

Moon Sign: Sagittarius
Moon enters Capricorn 4:16 pm
Incense: Clove

20	Friday
	Pardon of the Singers (British)
	Waning Moon
	Moon phase: Third Quarter
	Color: Coral

Moon Sign: Capricorn
Incense: Violet

21	Saturday
	Victoria Day (Canadian)
	Waning Moon
	Moon phase: Third Quarter
	Color: Blue

Moon Sign: Capricorn
Moon enters Aquarius 10:32 pm
Incense: Patchouli
Sun enters Gemini 5:21 am

May

♊

---

22 **Sunday**
Heroes' Day (Sri Lankan)
Waning Moon
Moon phase: Third Quarter
Color: Amber

Moon Sign: Aquarius
Incense: Frankincense

---

23 **Monday**
Tubilustrium (Roman)
Waning Moon
Moon phase: Third Quarter
Color: Ivory

Moon Sign: Aquarius
Incense: Hyssop

☾ **Tuesday**
Culture Day (Bulgarian)
Waning Moon
Moon phase: Fourth Quarter 2:52 pm
Color: Black

Moon Sign: Aquarius
Moon enters Pisces 8:24 am
Incense: Geranium

---

25 **Wednesday**
Urbanas Diena (Latvian)
Waning Moon
Moon phase: Fourth Quarter
Color: Brown

Moon Sign: Pisces
Incense: Marjoram

---

26 **Thursday**
Pepys' Commemoration (English)
Waning Moon
Moon phase: Fourth Quarter
Color: Purple

Moon Sign: Pisces
Moon enters Aries 8:36 pm
Incense: Nutmeg

---

27 **Friday**
St. Augustine of Canterbury's Day
Waning Moon
Moon phase: Fourth Quarter
Color: White

Moon Sign: Aries
Incense: Orchid

---

28 **Saturday**
St. German's Day
Waning Moon
Moon phase: Fourth Quarter
Color: Black

Moon Sign: Aries
Incense: Ivy

May

29 Sunday
Royal Oak Day (English)
Waning Moon
Moon phase: Fourth Quarter
Color: Gold

Moon Sign: Aries
Moon enters Taurus 9:02 am
Incense: Eucalyptus

---

30 Monday
Memorial Day (observed and actual)
Waning Moon
Moon phase: Fourth Quarter
Color: Lavender

Moon Sign: Taurus
Incense: Narcissus

---

31 Tuesday
Flowers of May
Waning Moon
Moon phase: Fourth Quarter
Color: Scarlet

Moon Sign: Taurus
Moon enters Gemini 7:56 pm
Incense: Ginger

May Birthstones

Who first beholds the light of day,
In spring's sweet flowery month of May,
And wears an Emerald all her life,
Shall be a loved, and happy wife.

Modern: Emerald
Zodiac (Taurus): Sapphire

June
♊

☽ **Wednesday**
National Day (Tunisian)
Waning Moon
Moon phase: New Moon 5:03 pm
Color: Topaz

Moon Sign: Gemini
Incense: Lavender

2 **Thursday**
Rice Harvest Festival (Malaysian)
Waxing Moon
Moon phase: First Quarter
Color: Green

Moon Sign: Gemini
Incense: Mulberry

3 **Friday**
Memorial to Broken Dolls (Japanese)
Waxing Moon
Moon phase: First Quarter
Color: Pink

Moon Sign: Gemini
Moon enters Cancer 4:36 am
Incense: Thyme

4 **Saturday**
Full Moon Day (Burmese)
Waxing Moon
Moon phase: First Quarter
Color: Black

Moon Sign: Cancer
Incense: Rue

5 **Sunday**
Constitution Day (Danish)
Waxing Moon
Moon phase: First Quarter
Color: Amber

Moon Sign: Cancer
Moon enters Leo 11:03 am
Incense: Heliotrope

6 **Monday**
Swedish Flag Day
Waxing Moon
Moon phase: First Quarter
Color: Lavender

Moon Sign: Leo
Incense: Rosemary

7 **Tuesday**
St. Robert of Newminster's Day
Waxing Moon
Moon phase: First Quarter
Color: Scarlet

Moon Sign: Leo
Moon enters Virgo 3:33 pm
Incense: Cedar

June

♊

☽ **Wednesday**
Shavuot
Waxing Moon
Moon phase: Second Quarter 10:11 pm
Color: White

Moon Sign: Virgo
Incense: Honeysuckle

---

9 **Thursday**
Vestalia (Roman)
Waxing Moon
Moon phase: Second Quarter
Color: Turquoise

Moon Sign: Virgo
Moon enters Libra 6:31 pm
Incense: Myrrh

---

10 **Friday**
Time-Observance Day (Chinese)
Waxing Moon
Moon phase: Second Quarter
Color: White

Moon Sign: Libra
Incense: Alder

---

11 **Saturday**
Kamehameha Day (Hawaiian)
Waxing Moon
Moon phase: Second Quarter
Color: Blue

Moon Sign: Libra
Moon enters Scorpio 8:33 pm
Incense: Sandalwood

---

12 **Sunday**
Independence Day (Filipino)
Waxing Moon
Moon phase: Second Quarter
Color: Gold

Moon Sign: Scorpio
Incense: Hyacinth

---

13 **Monday**
St. Anthony of Padua's Day
Waxing Moon
Moon phase: Second Quarter
Color: White

Moon Sign: Scorpio
Moon enters Sagittarius 10:38 pm
Incense: Hyssop

---

14 **Tuesday**
Flag Day
Waxing Moon
Moon phase: Second Quarter
Color: Black

Moon Sign: Sagittarius
Incense: Geranium

June

☺ **Wednesday**
St. Vitus' Day Fires
Waxing Moon
Moon phase: Full Moon 4:14 pm
Color: Brown

Moon Sign: Sagittarius
Incense: Lilac

16 **Thursday**
Bloomsday (Irish)
Waning Moon
Moon phase: Third Quarter
Color: Purple

Moon Sign: Sagittarius
Moon enters Capricorn 1:59 am
Incense: Nutmeg

17 **Friday**
Bunker Hill Day
Waning Moon
Moon phase: Third Quarter
Color: Coral

Moon Sign: Capricorn
Incense: Mint

18 **Saturday**
Independence Day (Egyptian)
Waning Moon
Moon phase: Third Quarter
Color: Gray

Moon Sign: Capricorn
Moon enters Aquarius 7:47 am
Incense: Sage

19 **Sunday**
Father's Day
Waning Moon
Moon phase: Third Quarter
Color: Yellow

Moon Sign: Aquarius
Incense: Marigold

20 **Monday**
Argentinian Flag Day
Waning Moon
Moon phase: Third Quarter
Color: Lavender

Moon Sign: Aquarius
Moon enters Pisces 4:45 pm
Incense: Clary sage

21 **Tuesday**
Midsummer • Summer Solstice
Waning Moon
Moon phase: Third Quarter
Color: Gray

Moon Sign: Pisces
Incense: Basil
Sun enters Cancer 1:16 pm

June

22 Wednesday
Rose Festival (English)
Waning Moon
Moon phase: Third Quarter
Color: Topaz

Moon Sign: Pisces
Incense: Bay laurel

○ Thursday
St. John's Eve
Waning Moon
Moon phase: Fourth Quarter 7:48 am
Color: White

Moon Sign: Pisces
Moon enters Aries 4:24 am
Incense: Balsam

24 Friday
St. John's Day
Waning Moon
Moon phase: Fourth Quarter
Color: Rose

Moon Sign: Aries
Incense: Vanilla

25 Saturday
Fiesta of Santa Orosia (Spanish)
Waning Moon
Moon phase: Fourth Quarter
Color: Brown

Moon Sign: Aries
Moon enters Taurus 4:53 pm
Incense: Rue

26 Sunday
Pied Piper Day (German)
Waning Moon
Moon phase: Fourth Quarter
Color: Orange

Moon Sign: Taurus
Incense: Almond

27 Monday
Day of the Seven Sleepers (Islamic)
Waning Moon
Moon phase: Fourth Quarter
Color: Gray

Moon Sign: Taurus
Incense: Clary sage

28 Tuesday
Paul Bunyan Day
Waning Moon
Moon phase: Fourth Quarter
Color: White

Moon Sign: Taurus
Moon enters Gemini 3:56 am
Incense: Ylang-ylang

June

29 Wednesday
Feast of Saints Peter and Paul
Waning Moon
Moon phase: Fourth Quarter
Color: Yellow

Moon Sign: Gemini
Incense: Marjoram

---

30 Thursday
The Burning of the Three Firs (French)
Waning Moon
Moon phase: Fourth Quarter
Color: Green

Moon Sign: Gemini
Moon enters Cancer 12:13 pm
Incense: Apricot

June Birthstones

Who comes with summer to this earth,
And owes to June her hour of birth,
With ring of Agate on her hand,
Can health, wealth, and long life command.

Modern: Moonstone or Pearl
Zodiac (Gemini): Agate

July

🌙 **Friday**
Climbing Mount Fuji (Japanese)
Waning Moon
Moon phase: New Moon 4:54 am
Color: White

Moon Sign: Cancer
Incense: Rose

2 Saturday
Heroes' Day (Zambian)
Waxing Moon
Moon phase: First Quarter
Color: Indigo

Moon Sign: Cancer
Moon enters Leo 5:43 pm
Incense: Ivy

3 Sunday
Indian Sun Dance (Native American)
Waxing Moon
Moon phase: First Quarter
Color: Orange

Moon Sign: Leo
Incense: Frankincense

4 Monday
Independence Day
Waxing Moon
Moon phase: First Quarter
Color: Ivory

Moon Sign: Leo
Moon enters Virgo 9:15 pm
Incense: Lily

5 Tuesday
Tynwald (Nordic)
Waxing Moon
Moon phase: First Quarter
Color: Scarlet

Moon Sign: Virgo
Incense: Basil

6 Wednesday
Khao Phansa Day (Thai)
Waxing Moon
Moon phase: First Quarter
Color: White

Moon Sign: Virgo
Moon enters Libra 11:54 pm
Incense: Lavender

7 Thursday
Weaver's Festival (Japanese)
Waxing Moon
Moon phase: First Quarter
Color: Purple

Moon Sign: Libra
Incense: Clove

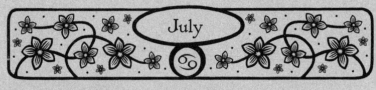

July

◐ Friday
St. Elizabeth's Day (Portuguese)
Waxing Moon
Moon phase: Second Quarter 2:29 am
Color: Coral

Moon Sign: Libra
Incense: Vanilla

---

9 Saturday
Battle of Sempach Day (Swiss)
Waxing Moon
Moon phase: Second Quarter
Color: Brown

Moon Sign: Libra
Moon enters Scorpio 2:31 am
Incense: Sage

---

10 Sunday
Lady Godiva Day (English)
Waxing Moon
Moon phase: Second Quarter
Color: Gold

Moon Sign: Scorpio
Incense: Heliotrope

---

11 Monday
Revolution Day (Mongolian)
Waxing Moon
Moon phase: Second Quarter
Color: White

Moon Sign: Scorpio
Moon enters Sagittarius 5:47 am
Incense: Neroli

---

12 Tuesday
Lobster Carnival (Nova Scotian)
Waxing Moon
Moon phase: Second Quarter
Color: Red

Moon Sign: Sagittarius
Incense: Ginger

---

13 Wednesday
Festival of the Three Cows (Spanish)
Waxing Moon
Moon phase: Second Quarter
Color: Yellow

Moon Sign: Sagittarius
Moon enters Capricorn 10:14 am
Incense: Marjoram

---

14 Thursday
Bastille Day (French)
Waxing Moon
Moon phase: Second Quarter
Color: Green

Moon Sign: Capricorn
Incense: Myrrh

July

Friday
St. Swithin's Day
Waxing Moon
Moon phase: Full Moon 2:40 am
Color: Rose

Moon Sign: Capricorn
Moon enters Aquarius 4:30 pm
Incense: Thyme

16 Saturday
Our Lady of Carmel
Waning Moon
Moon phase: Third Quarter
Color: Blue

Moon Sign: Aquarius
Incense: Patchouli

17 Sunday
Rivera Day (Puerto Rican)
Waning Moon
Moon phase: Third Quarter
Color: Orange

Moon Sign: Aquarius
Incense: Eucalyptus

18 Monday
Gion Matsuri Festival (Japanese)
Waning Moon
Moon phase: Third Quarter
Color: Lavender

Moon Sign: Aquarius
Moon enters Pisces 1:13 am
Incense: Narcissus

19 Tuesday
Flitch Day (English)
Waning Moon
Moon phase: Third Quarter
Color: Gray

Moon Sign: Pisces
Incense: Cinnamon

20 Wednesday
Binding of Wreaths (Lithuanian)
Waning Moon
Moon phase: Third Quarter
Color: Brown

Moon Sign: Pisces
Moon enters Aries 12:25 pm
Incense: Lavender

21 Thursday
National Day (Belgian)
Waning Moon
Moon phase: Third Quarter
Color: White

Moon Sign: Aries
Incense: Jasmine

July

22 Friday
St. Mary Magdalene's Day
Waning Moon
Moon phase: Third Quarter
Color: Purple

Moon Sign: Aries
Incense: Yarrow

Saturday
Mysteries of Santa Cristina (Italian)
Waning Moon
Moon phase: Fourth Quarter 1:02 am
Color: Black

Moon Sign: Aries
Moon enters Taurus 12:58 am
Incense: Magnolia
Sun enters Leo 12:12 am

24 Sunday
Pioneer Day (Mormon)
Waning Moon
Moon phase: Fourth Quarter
Color: Yellow

Moon Sign: Taurus
Incense: Juniper

25 Monday
St. James' Day
Waning Moon
Moon phase: Fourth Quarter
Color: Ivory

Moon Sign: Taurus
Moon enters Gemini 12:34 pm
Incense: Rosemary

26 Tuesday
St. Anne's Day
Waning Moon
Moon phase: Fourth Quarter
Color: Maroon

Moon Sign: Gemini
Incense: Geranium

27 Wednesday
Sleepyhead Day (Finnish)
Waning Moon
Moon phase: Fourth Quarter
Color: Brown

Moon Sign: Gemini
Moon enters Cancer 9:11 pm
Incense: Lilac

28 Thursday
Independence Day (Peruvian)
Waning Moon
Moon phase: Fourth Quarter
Color: Crimson

Moon Sign: Cancer
Incense: Balsam

29 Friday
Pardon of the Birds (French)
Waning Moon
Moon phase: Fourth Quarter
Color: White

Moon Sign: Cancer
Incense: Cypress

 Saturday
Micman Festival of St. Ann
Waning Moon
Moon phase: New Moon 2:40 pm
Color: Gray

Moon Sign: Cancer
Moon enters Leo 2:16 am
Incense: Rue

---

31 Sunday
Weighing of the Aga Kahn
Waxing Moon
Moon phase: First Quarter
Color: Amber

Moon Sign: Leo
Incense: Hyacinth

July Birthstones

The glowing Ruby shall adorn
Those who in warm July are born;
Then will they be exempt and free
From love's doubt, and anxiety.

Modern: Ruby
Zodiac (Cancer): Emerald

August

1 Monday
Lammas • Ramadan begins
Waxing Moon
Moon phase: First Quarter
Color: Gray

Moon Sign: Leo
Moon enters Virgo 4:41 am
Incense: Clary sage

2 Tuesday
Porcingula (Native American)
Waxing Moon
Moon phase: First Quarter
Color: White

Moon Sign: Virgo
Incense: Ylang-ylang

3 Wednesday
Drimes (Greek)
Waxing Moon
Moon phase: First Quarter
Color: White

Moon Sign: Virgo
Moon enters Libra 6:04 am
Incense: Lilac

4 Thursday
Cook Islands Constitution Celebration
Waxing Moon
Moon phase: First Quarter
Color: Turquoise

Moon Sign: Libra
Incense: Carnation

5 Friday
Benediction of the Sea (French)
Waxing Moon
Moon phase: First Quarter
Color: White

Moon Sign: Libra
Moon enters Scorpio 7:57 am
Incense: Orchid

☾ Saturday
Hiroshima Peace Ceremony
Waxing Moon
Moon phase: Second Quarter 7:08 am
Color: Black

Moon Sign: Scorpio
Incense: Sandalwood

7 Sunday
Republic Day (Ivory Coast)
Waxing Moon
Moon phase: Second Quarter
Color: Yellow

Moon Sign: Scorpio
Moon enters Sagittarius 11:21 am
Incense: Heliotrope

August

8 Monday
Dog Days (Japanese)
Waxing Moon
Moon phase: Second Quarter
Color: Silver

Moon Sign: Sagittarius
Incense: Narcissus

9 Tuesday
Nagasaki Peace Ceremony
Waxing Moon
Moon phase: Second Quarter
Color: Maroon

Moon Sign: Sagittarius
Moon enters Capricorn 4:38 pm
Incense: Cinnamon

10 Wednesday
St. Lawrence's Day
Waxing Moon
Moon phase: Second Quarter
Color: Yellow

Moon Sign: Capricorn
Incense: Bay laurel

11 Thursday
Puck Fair (Irish)
Waxing Moon
Moon phase: Second Quarter
Color: White

Moon Sign: Capricorn
Moon enters Aquarius 11:47 pm
Incense: Apricot

12 Friday
Fiesta of Santa Clara
Waxing Moon
Moon phase: Second Quarter
Color: Purple

Moon Sign: Aquarius
Incense: Violet

☻ Saturday
Women's Day (Tunisian)
Waxing Moon
Moon phase: Full Moon 2:58 pm
Color: Gray

Moon Sign: Aquarius
Incense: Magnolia

14 Sunday
Festival at Sassari
Waning Moon
Moon phase: Third Quarter
Color: Amber

Moon Sign: Aquarius
Moon enters Pisces 8:54 am
Incense: Juniper

15 Monday
Assumption Day   Moon Sign: Pisces
Waning Moon   Incense: Lily
Moon phase: Third Quarter
Color: White

---

16 Tuesday
Festival of Minstrels (European)   Moon Sign: Pisces
Waning Moon   Moon enters Aries 8:01 pm
Moon phase: Third Quarter   Incense: Basil
Color: Gray

---

17 Wednesday
Feast of the Hungry Ghosts (Chinese)   Moon Sign: Aries
Waning Moon   Incense: Honeysuckle
Moon phase: Third Quarter
Color: Topaz

---

18 Thursday
St. Helen's Day   Moon Sign: Aries
Waning Moon   Incense: Nutmeg
Moon phase: Third Quarter
Color: Green

---

19 Friday
Rustic Vinalia (Roman)   Moon Sign: Aries
Waning Moon   Moon enters Taurus 8:36 am
Moon phase: Third Quarter   Incense: Alder
Color: Rose

---

20 Saturday
Constitution Day (Hungarian)   Moon Sign: Taurus
Waning Moon   Incense: Ivy
Moon phase: Third Quarter
Color: Indigo

◑ Sunday
Consualia (Roman)   Moon Sign: Taurus
Waning Moon   Moon enters Gemini 8:53 pm
Moon phase: Fourth Quarter 5:54 pm   Incense: Frankincense
Color: Gold

22 Monday
Feast of the Queenship of Mary (English)   Moon Sign: Gemini
Waning Moon   Incense: Neroli
Moon phase: Fourth Quarter
Color: Gray

---

23 Tuesday
National Day (Romanian)   Moon Sign: Gemini
Waning Moon   Incense: Cedar
Moon phase: Fourth Quarter   Sun enters Virgo 7:21 am
Color: Red

---

24 Wednesday
St. Bartholomew's Day   Moon Sign: Gemini
Waning Moon   Moon enters Cancer 6:31 am
Moon phase: Fourth Quarter   Incense: Lavender
Color: White

---

25 Thursday
Feast of the Green Corn (Native American)   Moon Sign: Cancer
Waning Moon   Incense: Clove
Moon phase: Fourth Quarter
Color: Purple

---

26 Friday
Pardon of the Sea (French)   Moon Sign: Cancer
Waning Moon   Moon enters Leo 12:09 pm
Moon phase: Fourth Quarter   Incense: Mint
Color: Coral

---

27 Saturday
Summer Break (English)   Moon Sign: Leo
Waning Moon   Incense: Pine
Moon phase: Fourth Quarter
Color: Blue

☽ Sunday
St. Augustine's Day   Moon Sign: Leo
Waning Moon   Moon enters Virgo 2:13 pm
Moon phase: New Moon 11:04 pm   Incense: Marigold
Color: Gold

29 Monday
St. John's Beheading
Waxing Moon
Moon phase: First Quarter
Color: Ivory

Moon Sign: Virgo
Incense: Hyssop

---

30 Tuesday
Ramadan ends
Waxing Moon
Moon phase: First Quarter
Color: Black

Moon Sign: Virgo
Moon enters Libra 2:25 pm
Incense: Ginger

---

31 Wednesday
Unto These Hills Pageant (Cherokee)
Waxing Moon
Moon phase: First Quarter
Color: Yellow

Moon Sign: Libra
Incense: Marjoram

August Birthstones

Wear Sardonyx, or for thee
No conjugal felicity;
The August-born without this stone,
'Tis said, must live unloved, and lone.

Modern: Peridot
Zodiac (Leo): Onyx

September ♍

1 Thursday
Greek New Year
Waxing Moon
Moon phase: First Quarter
Color: Green

Moon Sign: Libra
Moon enters Scorpio 2:48 pm
Incense: Mulberry

---

2 Friday
St. Mama's Day
Waxing Moon
Moon phase: First Quarter
Color: White

Moon Sign: Scorpio
Incense: Mint

---

3 Saturday
Founder's Day (San Marino)
Waxing Moon
Moon phase: First Quarter
Color: Black

Moon Sign: Scorpio
Moon enters Sagittarius 5:03 pm
Incense: Rue

☾ Sunday
Los Angeles' Birthday
Waxing Moon
Moon phase: Second Quarter 1:39 pm
Color: Orange

Moon Sign: Sagittarius
Incense: Frankincense

---

5 Monday
Labor Day
Waxing Moon
Moon phase: Second Quarter
Color: Lavender

Moon Sign: Sagittarius
Moon enters Capricorn 10:03 pm
Incense: Clary sage

---

6 Tuesday
The Virgin of Remedies (Spanish)
Waxing Moon
Moon phase: Second Quarter
Color: Gray

Moon Sign: Capricorn
Incense: Ginger

---

7 Wednesday
Festival of the Durga (Hindu)
Waxing Moon
Moon phase: Second Quarter
Color: Brown

Moon Sign: Capricorn
Incense: Lavender

September ♍

8 Thursday
Birthday of the Virgin Mary
Waxing Moon
Moon phase: Second Quarter
Color: Turquoise

Moon Sign: Capricorn
Moon enters Aquarius 5:42 am
Incense: Apricot

9 Friday
Chrysanthemum Festival (Japanese)
Waxing Moon
Moon phase: Second Quarter
Color: Purple

Moon Sign: Aquarius
Incense: Rose

10 Saturday
Festival of the Poets (Japanese)
Waxing Moon
Moon phase: Second Quarter
Color: Brown

Moon Sign: Aquarius
Moon enters Pisces 3:26 pm
Incense: Sage

11 Sunday
Coptic New Year
Waxing Moon
Moon phase: Second Quarter
Color: Yellow

Moon Sign: Pisces
Incense: Juniper

☻ **Monday**
National Day (Ethiopian)
Waxing Moon
Moon phase: Full Moon 5:27 am
Color: Gray

Moon Sign: Pisces
Incense: Hyssop

13 Tuesday
The Gods' Banquet (Roman)
Waning Moon
Moon phase: Third Quarter
Color: Black

Moon Sign: Pisces
Moon enters Aries 2:49 am
Incense: Ylang-ylang

14 Wednesday
Holy Cross Day
Waning Moon
Moon phase: Third Quarter
Color: White

Moon Sign: Aries
Incense: Marjoram

15 Thursday
Birthday of the Moon (Chinese)
Waning Moon
Moon phase: Third Quarter
Color: Purple

Moon Sign: Aries
Moon enters Taurus 3:25 pm
Incense: Balsam

16 Friday
Mexican Independence Day
Waning Moon
Moon phase: Third Quarter
Color: Pink

Moon Sign: Taurus
Incense: Violet

17 Saturday
Von Steuben's Day
Waning Moon
Moon phase: Third Quarter
Color: Black

Moon Sign: Taurus
Incense: Ivy

18 Sunday
Dr. Johnson's Birthday
Waning Moon
Moon phase: Third Quarter
Color: Gold

Moon Sign: Taurus
Moon enters Gemini 4:06 am
Incense: Almond

19 Monday
St. Januarius' Day (Italian)
Waning Moon
Moon phase: Third Quarter
Color: Silver

Moon Sign: Gemini
Incense: Neroli

○ Tuesday
St. Eustace's Day
Waning Moon
Moon phase: Fourth Quarter 9:39 am
Color: White

Moon Sign: Gemini
Moon enters Cancer 2:53 pm
Incense: Geranium

21 Wednesday
UN International Day of Peace
Waning Moon
Moon phase: Fourth Quarter
Color: Yellow

Moon Sign: Cancer
Incense: Bay laurel

September ♎

22 **Thursday**
St. Maurice's Day (Swiss)
Waning Moon
Moon phase: Fourth Quarter
Color: White

Moon Sign: Cancer
Moon enters Leo 9:55 pm
Incense: Clove

---

23 **Friday**
Mabon • Fall Equinox
Waning Moon
Moon phase: Fourth Quarter
Color: Rose

Moon Sign: Leo
Incense: Orchid
Sun enters Libra 5:05 am

---

24 **Saturday**
Schwenkenfelder Thanksgiving (German-American)
Waning Moon
Moon phase: Fourth Quarter
Color: Gray

Moon Sign: Leo
Incense: Pine

---

25 **Sunday**
Dolls' Memorial Service (Japanese)
Waning Moon
Moon phase: Fourth Quarter
Color: Orange

Moon Sign: Leo
Moon enters Virgo 12:49 am
Incense: Eucalyptus

---

26 **Monday**
Feast of Santa Justina (Mexican)
Waning Moon
Moon phase: Fourth Quarter
Color: Silver

Moon Sign: Virgo
Incense: Rosemary

☽ **Tuesday**
Saints Cosmas and Damian's Day
Waning Moon
Moon phase: New Moon 7:09 am
Color: Maroon

Moon Sign: Virgo
Moon enters Libra 12:51 am
Incense: Cedar

---

28 **Wednesday**
Confucius' Birthday
Waxing Moon
Moon phase: First Quarter
Color: Topaz

Moon Sign: Libra
Incense: Lilac

29 Thursday
Rosh Hashanah
Waxing Moon
Moon phase: First Quarter
Color: Crimson

Moon Sign: Libra
Moon enters Scorpio 12:05 am
Incense: Nutmeg

30 Friday
St. Jerome's Day
Waxing Moon
Moon phase: First Quarter
Color: Purple

Moon Sign: Scorpio
Incense: Cypress

September Birthstones

A maiden born when autumn leaves
Are rustling in September's breeze,
A Sapphire on her brow should bind;
'Twill cure diseases of the mind.

Modern: Sapphire
Zodiac (Virgo): Carnelian

October ♎

1   **Saturday**
Armed Forces Day (South Korean)
Waxing Moon
Moon phase: First Quarter
Color: Blue

Moon Sign: Scorpio
Moon enters Sagittarius 12:42 am
Incense: Pine

---

2   **Sunday**
Old Man's Day (Virgin Islands)
Waxing Moon
Moon phase: First Quarter
Color: Yellow

Moon Sign: Sagittarius
Incense: Heliotrope

☽   **Monday**
Moroccan New Year's Day
Waxing Moon
Moon phase: Second Quarter 11:15 pm
Color: White

Moon Sign: Sagittarius
Moon enters Capricorn 4:16 am
Incense: Lily

---

4   **Tuesday**
St. Francis' Day
Waxing Moon
Moon phase: Second Quarter
Color: Gray

Moon Sign: Capricorn
Incense: Basil

---

5   **Wednesday**
Republic Day (Portuguese)
Waxing Moon
Moon phase: Second Quarter
Color: Topaz

Moon Sign: Capricorn
Moon enters Aquarius 11:18 am
Incense: Bay laurel

---

6   **Thursday**
Dedication of the Virgin's Crowns (English)
Waxing Moon
Moon phase: Second Quarter
Color: White

Moon Sign: Aquarius
Incense: Balsam

---

7   **Friday**
Kermesse (German)
Waxing Moon
Moon phase: Second Quarter
Color: Pink

Moon Sign: Aquarius
Moon enters Pisces 9:13 pm
Incense: Yarrow

October

8 Saturday
Yom Kippur
Waxing Moon
Moon phase: Second Quarter
Color: Brown

Moon Sign: Pisces
Incense: Patchouli

9 Sunday
Alphabet Day (South Korean)
Waxing Moon
Moon phase: Second Quarter
Color: Amber

Moon Sign: Pisces
Incense: Juniper

10 Monday
Columbus Day (observed)
Waxing Moon
Moon phase: Second Quarter
Color: Lavender

Moon Sign: Pisces
Moon enters Aries 8:57 am
Incense: Clary sage

☺ Tuesday
Medetrinalia (Roman)
Waxing Moon
Moon phase: Full Moon 10:06 pm
Color: White

Moon Sign: Aries
Incense: Cinnamon

12 Wednesday
National Day (Spanish)
Waning Moon
Moon phase: Third Quarter
Color: Brown

Moon Sign: Aries
Moon enters Taurus 9:35 pm
Incense: Honeysuckle

13 Thursday
Sukkot begins
Waning Moon
Moon phase: Third Quarter
Color: Crimson

Moon Sign: Taurus
Incense: Jasmine

14 Friday
Battle Festival (Japanese)
Waning Moon
Moon phase: Third Quarter
Color: White

Moon Sign: Taurus
Incense: Rose

October

♎

15 Saturday
The October Horse (Roman)
Waning Moon
Moon phase: Third Quarter
Color: Gray

Moon Sign: Taurus
Moon enters Gemini 10:15 am
Incense: Rue

16 Sunday
The Lion Sermon (British)
Waning Moon
Moon phase: Third Quarter
Color: Amber

Moon Sign: Gemini
Incense: Eucalyptus

17 Monday
Pilgrimage to Paray-le-Monial
Waning Moon
Moon phase: Third Quarter
Color: Ivory

Moon Sign: Gemini
Moon enters Cancer 9:38 pm
Incense: Rosemary

18 Tuesday
Brooklyn Barbecue
Waning Moon
Moon phase: Third Quarter
Color: Red

Moon Sign: Cancer
Incense: Bayberry

☽ Wednesday
Sukkot ends
Waning Moon
Moon phase: Fourth Quarter 11:30 pm
Color: Yellow

Moon Sign: Cancer
Incense: Lavender

20 Thursday
Colchester Oyster Feast
Waning Moon
Moon phase: Fourth Quarter
Color: Green

Moon Sign: Cancer
Moon enters Leo 6:06 am
Incense: Nutmeg

21 Friday
Feast of the Black Christ
Waning Moon
Moon phase: Fourth Quarter
Color: Pink

Moon Sign: Leo
Incense: Mint

22 Saturday
Goddess of Mercy Day (Chinese)
Waning Moon
Moon phase: Fourth Quarter
Color: Blue

Moon Sign: Leo
Moon enters Virgo 10:40 am
Incense: Sandalwood

23 Sunday
Revolution Day (Hungarian)
Waning Moon
Moon phase: Fourth Quarter
Color: Gold

Moon Sign: Virgo
Incense: Marigold
Sun enters Scorpio 2:30 pm

24 Monday
United Nations Day
Waning Moon
Moon phase: Fourth Quarter
Color: Lavender

Moon Sign: Virgo
Moon enters Libra 11:49 am
Incense: Neroli

25 Tuesday
St. Crispin's Day
Waning Moon
Moon phase: Fourth Quarter
Color: Black

Moon Sign: Libra
Incense: Ylang-ylang

☽ Wednesday
Quit Rent Ceremony (England)
Waning Moon
Moon phase: New Moon 3:56 pm
Color: White

Moon Sign: Libra
Moon enters Scorpio 11:08 am
Incense: Lilac

27 Thursday
Feast of the Holy Souls
Waxing Moon
Moon phase: First Quarter
Color: White

Moon Sign: Scorpio
Incense: Jasmine

28 Friday
Ochi Day (Greek)
Waxing Moon
Moon phase: First Quarter
Color: Coral

Moon Sign: Scorpio
Moon enters Sagittarius 10:45 am
Incense: Thyme

29 Saturday
Iriquois Feast of the Dead
Waxing Moon
Moon phase: First Quarter
Color: Indigo

Moon Sign: Sagittarius
Incense: Sage

30 Sunday
Meiji Festival (Japanese)
Waxing Moon
Moon phase: First Quarter
Color: Orange

Moon Sign: Sagittarius
Moon enters Capricorn 12:39 pm
Incense: Eucalyptus

31 Monday
Halloween • Samhain
Waxing Moon
Moon phase: First Quarter
Color: White

Moon Sign: Capricorn
Incense: Narcissus

October Birthstones

October's child is born for woe,
And life's vicissitudes must know;
But lay an Opal on her breast,
And hope will lull those foes to rest.

Modern: Opal or Tourmaline
Zodiac (Libra): Peridot

November ♏

1	**Tuesday** *All Saints' Day* Waxing Moon Moon phase: First Quarter Color: Scarlet	Moon Sign: Capricorn Moon enters Aquarius 6:08 pm Incense: Cinnamon

○ **Wednesday**
All Souls' Day
Waxing Moon
Moon phase: Second Quarter 12:38 pm
Color: Yellow

Moon Sign: Aquarius
Incense: Lavender

3 **Thursday**
Saint Hubert's Day (Belgian)
Waxing Moon
Moon phase: Second Quarter
Color: Crimson

Moon Sign: Aquarius
Incense: Clove

4 **Friday**
Mischief Night (British)
Waxing Moon
Moon phase: Second Quarter
Color: Coral

Moon Sign: Aquarius
Moon enters Pisces 3:18 am
Incense: Cypress

5 **Saturday**
Guy Fawkes Night (British)
Waxing Moon
Moon phase: Second Quarter
Color: Blue

Moon Sign: Pisces
Incense: Patchouli

6 **Sunday**
Daylight Saving Time ends
Waxing Moon
Moon phase: Second Quarter
Color: Gold

Moon Sign: Pisces
Moon enters Aries 2:02 pm
Incense: Almond

7 **Monday**
Mayan Day of the Dead
Waxing Moon
Moon phase: Second Quarter
Color: White

Moon Sign: Aries
Incense: Neroli

November ♏

8 **Tuesday**
Election Day (general)
Waxing Moon
Moon phase: Second Quarter
Color: Red

Moon Sign: Aries
Incense: Ginger

---

9 **Wednesday**
Lord Mayor's Day (British)
Waxing Moon
Moon phase: Second Quarter
Color: White

Moon Sign: Aries
Moon enters Taurus 2:45 am
Incense: Lilac

☺ **Thursday**
Martin Luther's Birthday
Waxing Moon
Moon phase: Full Moon 3:16 pm
Color: Turquoise

Moon Sign: Taurus
Incense: Carnation

---

11 **Friday**
Veterans Day
Waning Moon
Moon phase: Third Quarter
Color: Purple

Moon Sign: Taurus
Moon enters Gemini 3:10 pm
Incense: Violet

---

12 **Saturday**
Tesuque Feast Day (Native American)
Waning Moon
Moon phase: Third Quarter
Color: Black

Moon Sign: Gemini
Incense: Pine

---

13 **Sunday**
Festival of Jupiter (Roman)
Waning Moon
Moon phase: Third Quarter
Color: Yellow

Moon Sign: Gemini
Incense: Frankincense

---

14 **Monday**
The Little Carnival (Greek)
Waning Moon
Moon phase: Third Quarter
Color: Silver

Moon Sign: Gemini
Moon enters Cancer 2:19 am
Incense: Lily

15 Tuesday
St. Leopold's Day
Waning Moon
Moon phase: Third Quarter
Color: White

Moon Sign: Cancer
Incense: Basil

---

16 Wednesday
St. Margaret of Scotland's Day
Waning Moon
Moon phase: Third Quarter
Color: Brown

Moon Sign: Cancer
Moon enters Leo 11:17 am
Incense: Bay laurel

---

17 Thursday
Queen Elizabeth's Day
Waning Moon
Moon phase: Third Quarter
Color: Green

Moon Sign: Leo
Incense: Apricot

◐ Friday
St. Plato's Day
Waning Moon
Moon phase: Fourth Quarter 10:09 am
Color: White

Moon Sign: Leo
Moon enters Virgo 5:19 pm
Incense: Vanilla

---

19 Saturday
Garifuna Day (Belizian)
Waning Moon
Moon phase: Fourth Quarter
Color: Indigo

Moon Sign: Virgo
Incense: Sage

---

20 Sunday
Revolution Day (Mexican)
Waning Moon
Moon phase: Fourth Quarter
Color: Amber

Moon Sign: Virgo
Moon enters Libra 8:16 pm
Incense: Eucalyptus

---

21 Monday
Repentance Day (German)
Waning Moon
Moon phase: Fourth Quarter
Color: Ivory

Moon Sign: Libra
Incense: Hyssop

November

22 Tuesday
St. Cecilia's Day
Waning Moon
Moon phase: Fourth Quarter
Color: Gray

Moon Sign: Libra
Moon enters Scorpio 8:58 pm
Incense: Ginger
Sun enters Sagittarius 11:08 am

23 Wednesday
St. Clement's Day
Waning Moon
Moon phase: Fourth Quarter
Color: Brown

Moon Sign: Scorpio
Incense: Marjoram

24 Thursday
Thanksgiving Day
Waning Moon
Moon phase: Fourth Quarter
Color: White

Moon Sign: Scorpio
Moon enters Sagittarius 8:57 pm
Incense: Mulberry

☽ Friday
St. Catherine of Alexandria's Day
Waning Moon
Moon phase: New Moon 1:10 am
Color: Rose

Moon Sign: Sagittarius
Incense: Orchid

26 Saturday
Islamic New Year
Waxing Moon
Moon phase: First Quarter
Color: Gray

Moon Sign: Sagittarius
Moon enters Capricorn 10:05 pm
Incense: Ivy

27 Sunday
Saint Maximus' Day
Waxing Moon
Moon phase: First Quarter
Color: Orange

Moon Sign: Capricorn
Incense: Heliotrope

28 Monday
Day of the New Dance (Tibetan)
Waxing Moon
Moon phase: First Quarter
Color: Lavender

Moon Sign: Capricorn
Incense: Narcissus

November

29 Tuesday
Tubman's Birthday (Liberian)
Waxing Moon
Moon phase: First Quarter
Color: Black

Moon Sign: Capricorn
Moon enters Aquarius 2:02 am
Incense: Cedar

30 Wednesday
St. Andrew's Day
Waxing Moon
Moon phase: First Quarter
Color: White

Moon Sign: Aquarius
Incense: Honeysuckle

November Birthstones

Who first come to this world below,
With drear November's fog, and snow,
Should prize the Topaz's amber hue,
Emblem of friends, and lovers true.

Modern: Topaz or Citrine
Zodiac (Scorpio): Beryl

December

1 **Thursday**
Big Tea Party (Japanese)
Waxing Moon
Moon phase: First Quarter
Color: Purple

Moon Sign: Aquarius
Moon enters Pisces 9:45 am
Incense: Balsam

◖ **Friday**
Republic Day (Loatian)
Waxing Moon
Moon phase: Second Quarter 4:52 am
Color: White

Moon Sign: Pisces
Incense: Vanilla

3 **Saturday**
St. Francis Xavier's Day
Waxing Moon
Moon phase: Second Quarter
Color: Gray

Moon Sign: Pisces
Moon enters Aries 8:51 pm
Incense: Ivy

4 **Sunday**
St. Barbara's Day
Waxing Moon
Moon phase: Second Quarter
Color: Amber

Moon Sign: Aries
Incense: Frankincense

5 **Monday**
Eve of St. Nicholas' Day
Waxing Moon
Moon phase: Second Quarter
Color: White

Moon Sign: Aries
Incense: Narcissus

6 **Tuesday**
St. Nicholas' Day
Waxing Moon
Moon phase: Second Quarter
Color: Gray

Moon Sign: Aries
Moon enters Taurus 9:34 am
Incense: Geranium

7 **Wednesday**
Burning the Devil (Guatemalan)
Waxing Moon
Moon phase: Second Quarter
Color: Topaz

Moon Sign: Taurus
Incense: Marjoram

December

8   **Thursday**
Feast of the Immaculate Conception   Moon Sign: Taurus
Waxing Moon   Moon enters Gemini 9:52 pm
Moon phase: Second Quarter   Incense: Mulberry
Color: Green

9   **Friday**
St. Leocadia's Day   Moon Sign: Gemini
Waxing Moon   Incense: Rose
Moon phase: Second Quarter
Color: Purple

☺   **Saturday**
Nobel Day   Moon Sign: Gemini
Waxing Moon   Incense: Rue
Moon phase: Full Moon 9:36 am
Color: Blue

11   **Sunday**
Pilgrimage at Tortugas   Moon Sign: Gemini
Waning Moon   Moon enters Cancer 8:26 am
Moon phase: Third Quarter   Incense: Almond
Color: Orange

12   **Monday**
Fiesta of Our Lady of Guadalupe (Mexican)   Moon Sign: Cancer
Waning Moon   Incense: Rosemary
Moon phase: Third Quarter
Color: Silver

13   **Tuesday**
St. Lucy's Day (Swedish)   Moon Sign: Cancer
Waning Moon   Moon enters Leo 4:48 pm
Moon phase: Third Quarter   Incense: Cinnamon
Color: Black

14   **Wednesday**
Warriors' Memorial (Japanese)   Moon Sign: Leo
Waning Moon   Incense: Bay laurel
Moon phase: Third Quarter
Color: Yellow

15 Thursday
Consualia (Roman)
Waning Moon
Moon phase: Third Quarter
Color: White

Moon Sign: Leo
Moon enters Virgo 10:58 pm
Incense: Carnation

---

16 Friday
Posadas (Mexican)
Waning Moon
Moon phase: Third Quarter
Color: Rose

Moon Sign: Virgo
Incense: Thyme

◖ **Saturday**
Saturnalia (Roman)
Waning Moon
Moon phase: Fourth Quarter 7:48 pm
Color: Brown

Moon Sign: Virgo
Incense: Sandalwood

---

18 Sunday
Feast of the Virgin Solitude
Waning Moon
Moon phase: Fourth Quarter
Color: Yellow

Moon Sign: Virgo
Moon enters Libra 3:06 am
Incense: Eucalyptus

---

19 Monday
Opalia (Roman)
Waning Moon
Moon phase: Fourth Quarter
Color: Gray

Moon Sign: Libra
Incense: Lily

---

20 Tuesday
Commerce God Festival (Japanese)
Waning Moon
Moon phase: Fourth Quarter
Color: Scarlet

Moon Sign: Libra
Moon enters Scorpio 5:33 am
Incense: Ylang-ylang

---

21 Wednesday
Hanukkah begins
Waning Moon
Moon phase: Fourth Quarter
Color: White

Moon Sign: Scorpio
Incense: Lilac

December

22 Thursday
Yule • Winter Solstice
Waning Moon
Moon phase: Fourth Quarter
Color: Turquoise

Moon Sign: Scorpio
Moon enters Sagittarius 7:03 am
Incense: Nutmeg
Sun enters Capricorn 12:30 am

23 Friday
Larentalia (Roman)
Waning Moon
Moon phase: Fourth Quarter
Color: Coral

Moon Sign: Sagittarius
Incense: Yarrow

☽ Saturday
Christmas Eve
Waning Moon
Moon phase: New Moon 1:06 pm
Color: Indigo

Moon Sign: Sagittarius
Moon enters Capricorn 8:47 am
Incense: Patchouli

25 Sunday
Christmas Day
Waxing Moon
Moon phase: First Quarter
Color: Orange

Moon Sign: Capricorn
Incense: Marigold

26 Monday
Kwanzaa begins
Waxing Moon
Moon phase: First Quarter
Color: Lavender

Moon Sign: Capricorn
Moon enters Aquarius 12:14 pm
Incense: Clary sage

27 Tuesday
Boar's Head Supper (English)
Waxing Moon
Moon phase: First Quarter
Color: Red

Moon Sign: Aquarius
Incense: Bayberry

28 Wednesday
Hanukkah ends
Waxing Moon
Moon phase: First Quarter
Color: Brown

Moon Sign: Aquarius
Moon enters Pisces 6:45 pm
Incense: Honeysuckle

December

29 Thursday
Feast of St. Thomas Becket
Waxing Moon
Moon phase: First Quarter
Color: Purple

Moon Sign: Pisces
Incense: Myrrh

30 Friday
Republic Day (Madagascan)
Waxing Moon
Moon phase: First Quarter
Color: White

Moon Sign: Pisces
Incense: Mint

31 Saturday
New Year's Eve
Waxing Moon
Moon phase: First Quarter
Color: Gray

Moon Sign: Pisces
Moon enters Aries 4:48 am
Incense: Magnolia

December Birthstones

If cold December gives you birth,
The month of snow, and ice, and mirth,
Place in your hand a Turquoise blue;
Success will bless whate'er you do.

Modern: Turquoise or Blue Topaz
Zodiac (Sagittarius): Topaz

Fire Magic

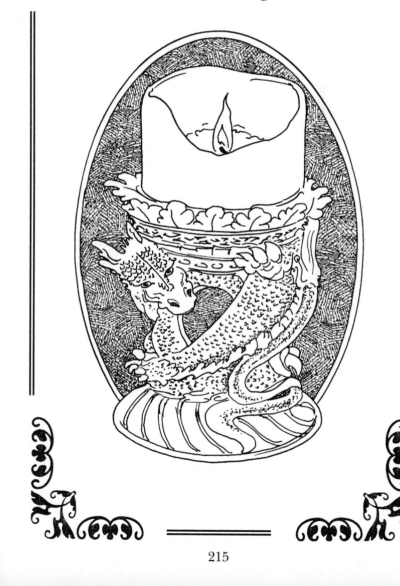

Fire Dancing

by Sybil Fogg

She danced the dance of flames and fire, and the dance of swords and spears; she danced the dance of stars and the dance of space, and then she danced the dance of flowers in the wind.

—Khalil Gibran

Fire dancing is as old as the hills. Many cultures, particularly those in Asia and the South Pacific, have practiced fire dancing in various incarnations. This art form incorporates fire props into a dance, often weaving a spell through the crowd. Fire dancing is growing in popularity in the West, attracting dancers of various styles, including ballet, belly dance, hula hoop, baton or poi spinning, and gymnastics.

The different types of artists each put their own stamp on the ritual of fire dance. Poi (pronounced "poy" rhyming with "toy") finds its beginnings in the Māori people of New Zealand. The translation of *poi* is literally "ball." This ball is made of wicking, on the end of a chain, and is set on fire. Holding on to the chains, the poi spinner manipulates the item by rolling and twisting his or her wrist. This art form can be breathtaking when orchestrated well.

Fire hoopers dance with hula hoops as props that resemble partners. Adult hoops must be made larger than the typical plastic child hoop many of us are familiar with. Often different types of material are used as well, from wood to aluminum. Sometimes, hoopers add the element of fire to create an exotic feel in their performance. Wicks are attached to the end of six- to eight-inch spokes to keep the flames away from the dancer's body. An average fire hoop contains about four to six of these spokes. Over the years, these hoops have been made lighter to keep up with artists' demands for more fluidity and flexibility of movement.

Dancers have used fire in their performances throughout the ages. Props to hold fire include candleholders, candelabras, bowls, knives, swords . . . In other words, fire props are pretty much limited only by the dancer's imagination. These props are balanced on the head, stomach, and palms.

The extent of the fire use is entirely up to the performer. I have seen dancers walk out to the center of their space with a bowl of lit alcohol, lower it to the ground, dance, and then lift the bowl back up and carry it away at the end of the performance. The flame does not become the dancer's partner—instead it is an entity of its own. I myself have choreographed pieces in a similar vein, utilizing a cauldron in which herbs and/or incense are added at different points in the sacred dance. To me, this is not actual "fire dancing" because the fire is separate from the dance. To fully experience the ritual aspect of the fire dancing art form, it is important to incorporate the fire into the performance.

The simplest way to bring the magic of fire into a dance is through candles. The apparatus used to burn candles can be small glass or metal votives purchased at any dollar store or craft store. Many professional belly dancers who do candle dances order their holders direct from Egypt. These holders have a sturdy base beneath a tapered top, which holds the candle. The taper of the holder can be grasped between the pointer and middle fingers, or the base can be balanced in the palm to collect any wax drippings.

When using any sort of flame in a ritual, safety should be of utmost concern. This is especially true in fire dancing, because the dancers also have to be concerned about the safety of their audience. I find that the key to keeping everyone safe is common sense.

• Do not use fire until the routine is memorized and has been practiced extensively without lighting anything.

• Never drink alcohol or do any sort of drug before working with fire. This includes any prescription or over the counter medicine. Read labels first and thoroughly.

• Never use fire in an area that isn't fire-safe, such as outdoors near dry grass, leaves, or places where tree limbs hang low.

• If you are doing a public ritual/dance, make sure you have filed for any permits necessary and are abiding by all laws.

• Be aware of the space around you. This is not limited to nonsentient life forces. Make sure you are aware of the people. Scan the crowd before performing. Are children present? Even those who are attended can break their guardian's grasp long enough to get in your way and cause serious harm to themselves or others.

• Dress appropriately. Long, loose garments may look enchanting, but gauzy sleeves are fire hazards. Choose tight-fitting clothing made of natural fibers, which are less likely to catch on fire than synthetic ones.

• Never dance alone. This is true even in front of crowds. Yes, it may seem as though there are a ton of people surrounding you, but they are the audience. They do not have the training to assist you if something goes terribly wrong. Furthermore, they might not even realize that something is amiss. Make sure you have at least one person on your "crew" who will stand by with a first-aid kit and a fire blanket in case the flames go astray.

~

Before this ritual is attempted with real candles, it is important to have the steps and movements down. Try using empty votives until you are comfortable. When you are ready for fire, be sure to use the stubs of candles that have been burned down for a while. Never do this ritual alone and always be sure to have water available and a smothering blanket at hand.

This ritual—of course—requires dancing. It is not necessary to be a professional dancer or to have ever taken a dance class. However, there are specific ways to hold a candleholder to aid in the movement of fire while you dance. These hand/arm positions are often used by American belly dancers but draw on movements from a Greek dance.

First, balance a candleholder or votive on the palm of each hand.

Practice standing with your hands outstretched to your sides. Try lifting your arms so that your hands are above your head, still holding the candles on your palms (your wrists will need to bend to 90 degrees). You will notice pretty quickly that it is difficult to keep objects balanced. Now try rotating your wrists so that your fingertips meet above your head. This movement keeps the holders balanced. Turn your hands back out away from each other. Repeat this exercise until you feel comfortable.

Once this movement is graceful and easy, try bringing your hands around in front of your chest so that your fingers again are pointing at each other. Do not turn your wrists on this movement! Simply lower your arms and fold them in. Repeat until you are comfortable. Then add the wrist turn to bring your hands above your head. Go over the full rotation as many times as necessary.

Now, lower your hands to waist height and, turning your wrists toward your body, circle your hands 180 degrees away from you. This is one of the trickiest movements, as you have to be careful that the flame does not catch your clothing or your underarms. But with practice, this entire set of arm movements will become flawless. That said, continue the motions until you feel you are ready to add fire.

Before adding fire, try filling your votives with water. That way you know if you are going to spill wax on yourself at any moment and you can run through the motions until not a drop is wasted!

Now you are ready to put together a simple dance. Try walking around the room while you move your arms through the steps. Shake your hips, step side to side, hop, and skip. Now is the time to add any dance moves you normally do when shaking it on the dance floor or that you remember from dance lessons when you were younger. Imagine you are at a drum circle. Put on your favorite music and work with these steps. Once you have a bit of choreography down for the hand movements, you are ready for the ritual.

Fire Dancing Ritual

Correspondences

Goddesses: Pele, Hestia, Brigid, Freya, Sekhmet, Li, Itzpapalotl, Mahuika

Gods: Agni, Ho-Masubi, Hephaestus, Ishum, Mixcoatl, Adranus, Krsnik, Bel

Colors: red, yellow, orange, black

Candles: use white—the wax will dye any material it drips on

Incense: cinnamon, orange, clove

Music: *Fire Dance* by Brian Keane has some wonderful selections as well as Phil Thornton and Hossam Ramzy's *Eternal Egypt*. Siouxsie and the Banshees' "Burn Up" is a favorite of mine. Use any other music that moves you to dance.

Staging and Costuming

This ritual requires a time investment in decoration and costume. Yes, it is possible to perform skyclad if there is enough privacy. Personally, I would be worried about wax landing on sensitive skin, so I would spend some time creating an outfit that is tight-fitting (at least through the arms and torso) and made out of natural fibers. This is another area to work with color.

This ritual does not hold up well outdoors, as the movements, accompanied by the wind, tend to blow out the candles. The flickering has a stronger significance in a dimly lit room. Remember to empty your space of furniture that may inhibit your dancing. Thought should be put into the mood you must create to commune with the fire goddesses and gods.

Keep the staging simple. An elegant oriental rug might be all your dance requires. Perhaps tall candleholders in the corners can add more light and be used to call the quarters before you begin. I have had success with this setup. I have often lit my dance candles from the quarter candles to infuse my movements with the elements.

Once you have decided on your space, costume, and music, consult an almanac and choose a day and time for your ritual. Summer is probably the best season for fire dancing magic. I prefer communing with the fire gods and goddesses on a New Moon in a fire sign. At that time, I feel as though my energy is helping the Moon grow to full and bring my wishes to fruition.

Charge all of your tools on the Full Moon nearest your chosen day. Do this by laying them outside if you have a yard, or inside within view of the Moon. Make sure you include your costume and the candles you will be using. This is a good time to burn your candles, too, as you will want them to be short to avoid any toppling during the dance.

The Dance

On your chosen day, set up your room and smudge it. I like to run my besom through the space to make it sacred. Think of all the things you are asking of the fire gods while you do this cleansing. Try to choose things that work well with fire correspondences. Do you want something to spark and build? Do you want to burn away negativity?

Soaking in a magical bath in tune with your intentions is a good start to the evening. I also enjoy sipping teas aligned with my ritual before slipping into my costume. When I am ready, I will light incense and meditate for a bit, and then do some stretches to stay limber through my ritual work. I then start the music and keep it on a loop if I am not using an entire album.

At this point, cast your circle and call your quarters as you normally do.

Light your candles and begin your dance. From here on out, the ritual is yours to do with as you will. So mote it be.

Animal Totem Primer

by Kelly Proudfoot

Wiccan or atheist, Catholic or Jewish, animals are humans' link to nature as well as to other worlds—which we access in our dreams, in religion and mythology, as well as in understanding our hidden and not so hidden natures. They can represent our animalistic sides, our hidden desires, behaviors, yearnings, dreams, and hopes. Animals invoke our spirituality and can act as guides along our various paths.

In shamanism, an animal totem is necessary to keep the shaman or seeker to the "lower" kingdom, or other worlds, where deeper spiritual knowledge or wisdom is required. In certain tribes, a young warrior or youth going through a rite of passage or initiation will venture out into the wild, find a cave or erect some kind of shelter, and possibly fast for a few days or take some hallucinogenic substance. This process allows for some kind of physical reaction to gain entrance into the spirit world, the void. Once in this trance state, initiates will meet their spirit guide, sometimes in animal form, where they discover their true nature or purpose and cross over to the realm where the journey allows the initiate to gain wisdom and return to the tribe a mature and "evolved" member, bringing with them the gifts of knowledge and wisdom to share.

There are many ancient stories involving animal totems, both mythological (dragons, sphinxes, the Griffin, winged horses like Pegasus, or even half man–half animals such as centaurs and the Minotaur) and animals in the "real" world.

Prehistoric man would dress up as the beast he wanted to hunt, reenacting the whole scene in order to "imprint" a successful hunt to feed the tribe. Cave paintings have been found depicting these kinds of images, with cavemen wearing a headdress, usually with horns, such as bulls or bison. This is called sympathetic magick, where enacting the desired result helps bring about the success of whatever the venture was. Like attracts like, much in the way magick works.

Animals have always represented different human attributes. Ironically, our metaphors for animal-like behavior have been way off the mark in most circumstances, such as "he's a pig"—pigs are usually clean and intelligent; or "stubborn as a mule"—what animal wouldn't be stubborn when forced to do something against their wishes?; or "a snake in the grass," meaning sneaky—first, snakes naturally live and travel in the grass. Also, sneakiness is necessary when fighting for survival; snakes aren't lying or conniving, they're just being good hunters.

When it comes to exploring the associated attributes of each animal (regarding how that animal relates to us), it's important to consider all levels of references, such as historical, mythological, spiritual, and psychological. Also, within those levels are general animal characteristics that we see exhibited in the animal's natural habitats (as well as those exhibited in domestic situations).

Humans have become detached from nature due to industrialization and urbanization. Many humans see the Earth and its inhabitants as an inexhaustible resource that we can use without repercussions. When it comes to animals, we think of them as something to put to use, for work, industry, food, chemicals and pharmaceuticals, or entertainment and companionship. We cage them in zoos, put them in races, dress them up in silly costumes, and mistreat them in arena shows such as rodeos, bull-running, horse jumping/dressage, and so on. Some scientists and biochemists use them in cruel and unnecessary tests in laboratories, caged and denied a natural life. We also hunt them just for sport at times. Some creatures in these situations are treated well, but the fact remains that these are not natural ways of life for animals.

Humans have become far removed from our own animal selves and our links to animals and nature. Then we decide that we want to go on a holiday, doing things such as camping and hiking, disturbing what's left if we're not mindful.

Humans need to see (and redevelop) the whole world as a macrocosm, to consider the delicate balance of nature and modify our existence to replenish the Earth for all of its inhabitants. One way to reestablish our link to nature is to align our-

selves with the animal kingdom by studying animals and the environment they live in. Every creature, no matter how large or small, has a role to play in maintaining the ecosystems on Earth.

When beginning to work with animal totems, the first thing we should study is ourselves. Who are we? Where have we been? What makes us tick? Where are we going? Ask yourself, "Where do I fit in? What am I missing? What messages am I receiving in my dreams and in my waking life?"

Have there been any particular animals that have meant something special to you? Regardless of whether the animals have been wild or domesticated, or even symbolically represented in advertising or mythology, in books or movies, discover what animal images have resonated with you.

You might have had a fascination with dolphins or always adored butterflies or felt a strong bond with cats. You might feel drawn to bats or interested in elephants or have intermittent meetings with snakes. It's important to note what creatures have been a focus in your life. Check out your ancestry and see if there's ever been a link to a particular animal or creature. In my background, the totem of the Aboriginal tribe I belong to is the long-necked turtle! Ever since I was a young child, I've had a fascination with turtles and only discovered my totem as an adult. (However, I've also had connections with snakes, horses, dragonflies, eagles, bats, cats, etc.)

Animals come into our lives at specific times, depending on our circumstances and needs. They come into our lives for different purposes and reasons. Even though you may have one overall totem that stays with you for your whole life, you'll discover that other totems also have their time and place. I remember a time when I was down and depressed for no particular reason and I was living with a friend who had a wonderful Doberman named Lara. I was sitting on my bed with my face in my hands, just weeping, when she came into the doorway and sat, just looking at me, tilting her head one way and then the other. After a few minutes she came up to me and put her head on my lap, her big brown eyes looking up at me as if to say, "What's wrong? Cheer up!" I was so taken aback by her human expression that Lara snapped me out of my funk and we became good friends!

Animal Totem Ritual

If you wish to discover your personal animal totem, you can perform a ritual to welcome it or them into your life. (As we've said, a person can have more than one animal totem throughout the life or during certain time periods.) If you already know your totem animal or animals, you can adjust this ritual to suit and place the related images on your altar.

Preparation

Create a sacred space by clearing the area (or modifying your current space). Clear any unnecessary clutter and make the space as close to nature as you can, with plants, rocks, shells, and so on. Set up the altar with a green or brown cloth (the basic colors of nature) and place a consecrated candle (white, representing your Higher Self) on the altar. During the consecration of your candle, inscribe it with your astrological symbol and your name or your magickal name, and use sandalwood oil, rubbing from the outer ends to the inner, meditating on establishing a link with your Higher Self.

Place items on your altar that represent the elements: a rock or gem for earth (or even a bowl of dirt!), incense or a feather for air, a shell or bowl of water for water, charcoal in your cauldron for fire. Your altar doesn't have to be cluttered with animal images, but a few simple items are okay. If you're inclined to collect animal skulls, bones, feathers, and such, you can place them on your altar.

Gems/Stones

Mercury—topaz, opal, tourmaline, peridot, emerald. *Moon*—silver, moonstone, pearl, amber. The combination of Mercury and Moon influences ensures enhanced psychic receptivity as well as contact with the different realms. Choose one for each to put on the altar or hold in your hand during the ritual. (You can also place them on the edge of the bath/shower when you conduct your ritual cleansing.)

Herbs for the Incense

The purpose of the ritual is based on communication, so Wednesday, the day of communicative Mercury, is a good day for your ritual. The herbs are a combination of Mercury and Moon—for assistance in accessing the subconscious mind, communion with the animal kingdom, and communication. Choose three to five herbs from the following list, but suit yourself if you'd like the incense to be more complicated:

Caraway, celery, cinnamon, coltsfoot, daisy, dittany of Crete, fern, honeysuckle, lavender, lemon, mistletoe, moonwort, nutmeg, parsley, patchouli, poppy hyssop, rosemary, sage, sandalwood, seaweed, valerian, willow, white rose, wormwood.

Ritual Cleansing

A ritual bath or shower before beginning assists in getting you programmed for the meditative process and allows you to focus on dedicating yourself to the purpose. It's also a matter of respect to enter the circle cleansed and in the right mindset. When preparing yourself to meet your totem, don't wear overpowering perfumes—keep it simple. Earthy or natural oils in the bathwater (or used to anoint yourself) are more appropriate. Especially anoint your feet and crown—patchouli oil for your feet and sandalwood for your crown. (You can, of course substitute the oils with what's available, something earthy for your feet and something airy or spiritual for your crown.)

The Ritual

It's preferable to conduct this ritual skyclad or in a simple robe. Cast your circle (clockwise in the Northern Hemisphere and counterclockwise in the Southern) and call the quarters. Move around the circle as you call the quarters, and hold out the corresponding representation for the element as you stop at each direction (starting at north and ending back at north). For example, north/earth—gem, stone, or rock; east/air—feather or incense; south/fire—candle or sword; and west/water—shell or bowl of water.

Call the deities of your choosing to witness the rite and assist you in your purpose. (If you like, you can have a corresponding amulet or symbol for the deity.) Then call on your Higher Self to assist you in your working. The following is a suggested Statement of Purpose:

> *On this night, I seek a meeting and communion with my true Animal Totem (or guide). I enter this circle with pure heart, mind, body, and soul. I ask for your assistance and guidance. Please bestow your wisdom and guidance upon me, so that I can be true to myself and to others and pay homage to the Earth and all its creatures. Hail to the elements who keep the balance! Hail to Mercury/Hermes (or Thoth) who assists me in my communication with my totem! Hail to my Higher Self, who watches over me! So mote it be!*

Next, position yourself to meditate. Focus on imagery regarding a pathway through nature of whatever kind suits you or feels right, such as a field or a beach or a track through a forest. Notice any creatures that come forward. Concentrate on just being—don't think too much or ask too many questions. Don't disregard any creature just because you'd prefer a different creature. If you see a beetle, then that's what is meant for you, at least at this time. Take note of what happens, what creature (or creatures) you see, colors, shapes, textures, and sensations. What memories are being evoked? Whatever creature reveals itself to you, commune with it. Observe it, what it's doing, if it's saying anything to you, or gesturing in a particular manner.

Take mental notes (or write them down if you feel so inclined). Meditate on how the event relates to you. Thank the animals for their presence and ask that they guide you in your life and dreams. After the session is over, thank the totem animal (or animals, if more than one reveals itself to you), the deities, your Higher Self, and the quarters, and then close the circle. Snuff the incense and pour the leftover water on the ground outside as a libation, thanking the elements for their assistance.

Remember to dedicate yourself to honoring your totem(s) by learning all you can about them. Draw pictures of them, hang up images, and collect associated paraphernalia. Look for talismans that match the energies of your totem when you're out and about in nature. Dedicate an altar to them and decorate it with all the items you collect and create. Feel their presence in your life and note any lessons they teach you. Keep a special journal just for your totem and record any dream messages, rituals, emotions, thoughts, and observations.

You can adjust the above ritual to bring about further communication with your totem or to speak to other animals you'd like to connect with, depending on the energies you wish to emulate during particularly trying times.

Refer to the chart here for basic information regarding a selection of creatures and, by all means, research the animals of your choice. There are many books on animal totems out there (see For Further Study), as well as great documentaries and books on the animal kingdom in general.

The correspondences in the chart here are simply suggestions—please feel free to mix it up to suit your particular needs. There is no sense in making the Craft as dogmatic as organized religion. Without spontaneity, magick is dead! Good luck on your journey and Blessed Be!

Animal Totem Correspondences

Purpose	Creature	Deity	Color	Plant	Stone	Element	Day
Contacting Higher Self	Eagle	Isis	White	Sandalwood	Clear Quartz	Spirit	Monday
Personal Power	Horse (or Bull)	Mithras	Red (or Orange)	Dragons-blood	Carnelian	Fire	Tuesday
Transformation	Raven	Morrighan	Black	Yarrow	Obsidian	Earth	Saturday
Love	Dove	Aphrodite	Pink	Rose	Rose Quartz	Water	Friday
Divination	Bat	Odhin	Purple	Frankincense	Moonstone	Water	Monday
Exorcism	Tarantula	Kali	Black	Pepper	Jet	Earth	Saturday
Healing	Turtle	Kuan Yin	Blue	Aloe Vera	Moonstone	Water	Monday
Dreams	Swan	Morpheus	Navy Blue	Valerian	Smoky Quartz	Water	Monday
Grief	Dog	Anubis	Black	Pine	Lapis Lazuli	Earth	Saturday
Mental Powers	Fox	Thoth	Orange	Celery	Amethyst	Air	Wednesday
Communing with Nature	Deer	Cernunnos or Green Man	Green	Fern	Moss Agate	Earth	Any day
Sexuality	Cobra	Eros	Red	Hibiscus	Garnet	Fire	Tuesday
Justice	Scorpion	Maat	Red	Marigold	Agate	Fire	Thursday
Depression	Butterfly	Baldur	Violet	Lavender	Aquamarine	Air	Wednesday
Meditation	Praying Mantis	Buddha	White	Bodhi	Clear Quartz	Air	Monday

Animal Totem Correspondences

Purpose	Creature	Deity	Color	Plant	Stone	Element	Day
Astral Travel	Owl	Arianrhod	Silver	Poplar	Fluorite	Spirit	Monday
Success	Lion	Osiris	Gold	Cinnamon	Pyrite	Fire	Sunday
Protection	Black Panther	Bastet	White	Sandalwood	Tiger Eye	Earth	Monday
Creativity	Platypus	Ptah	Green	Ginseng	Sodalite	Spirit	Wednesday
Crossroads or Decisions	Cerberus	Hecate	Navy Blue	Damiana	Aventurine	Earth	Saturday
Psychic Power	Snake	Brigit	Purple	Mugwort	Moonstone	Water	Monday
Fertility	Rabbit	Inanna	Orange	Peach	Garnet	Earth	Tuesday
Freedom	Wolf	Artemis	White	Sage	Clear Quartz	Air	Wednesday
Harvesting	Squirrel	Ceres	Green	Oak	Moss Agate	Earth	Sunday
Journeys	Kangaroo	Janus	Yellow	Wormwood	Sodalite	Air	Wednesday
Order	Ant	Athena	White	Olive	Clear Quartz	Earth	Thursday
Prosperity	Elephant	Ganesha	Green	Tulip	Tiger Eye	Water	Sunday
Luck	Dragon	Kupala	Green	Bamboo	Jade	Water	Sunday
Rebirth	Phoenix	Horus	Gold	Frankincense	Amber	Fire	Sunday

For Further Study

As this article only scratches the surface of animal totemism, you're encouraged to seek further correspondences, rituals, and animal wisdom in the following books:

Animal Speak by Ted Andrews

Animal Totem by Kristina Benson

Animal Wisdom by Susie Green

The Complete Book of Amulets and Talismans
  by Migene Gonzalez-Wippler

A Dictionary of Symbols by J. E. Cirlot

Magick of the Gods and Goddesses by D.J. Conway

Medicine Cards by Jamie Sams and David Carson

Personal Power Animals by Madonna Gauding

The Masks of God: Primitive Mythology by Joseph Campbell

Sex Magic with Your Clothes On

by Magenta Griffith

Energies of the body, sometimes called *chi* or *ki*, are a fundamental basis of magical workings, and sexual energies can raise a great deal of power. Handled poorly, this energy can wreak havoc; handled correctly, sexual magic can produce amazing results. The following exercises may not seem sexual, but they will allow you to explore and learn to handle the energies used for sex magic.

Before you start, think about the intention you have in mind for using sexual energies. This intention can be healing, charging an object, or other usual magical work.

First, stand or sit in a comfortable position, allowing your hands to hang at your sides if you are standing, or resting your hands on your knees if sitting. Breathe slowly and deeply. As you breathe in and out, notice the energy in your body. Feel energy come in as you inhale and flow out as you exhale. Take ten deep breaths, noticing the energy flow.

Stand, if you can, and imagine a brilliant light above your head, the Divine Radiance in whatever form you conceive it. Imagine this light descending to your throat and pausing a moment, then moving to your heart, where it glows like sunlight. Feel the light spread out to your arms and hands. From your heart, the light goes to your belly, just above your genitals, filling you with energy. Finally the light moves down your legs to your feet, which are planted on the earth.

Next, bring your hands together in front of you, palms facing and fingers up. As you continue to breathe in and out, notice the energy flow around your body. Concentrate

your attention on your hands. Slowly move your hands up and down a few inches, then back and forth a few inches, then around in a small circle. Notice what moving your hands does to the energy flow. Pull your hands apart a few inches, then put them back together. What does that do to the energy flow? Find which movement makes it easier to feel the flow of energy, and do it repeatedly for about a minute. Then feel the energy build between your hands. Put your hands on your heart, and feel the energy return to that area. Imagine the energy moving from your heart, down your left arm, through your hands, up your right arm, and back to your heart. After a while, reverse the flow so that it goes from right to left.

Finally, exhale and drop your hands to your side, letting the energy flow to the earth. Take three deep breaths, and then shake your hands to get rid of the extra energy. Rest for a while, noticing your breath. You may pause here and continue this work another day, or you may move on now.

When you are ready, again pull the energy downward from above your head to your feet, as described previously. Feel the energy in your feet, then pull it back up again, to your belly, to your heart, to your throat, and then to the top of your head and just above. Circulate the energy that way, down and up, three or four times. Do this slowly, taking as much time as you need. Once again, circulate the energy from one arm to the other. Try separating your hands more than a few inches, or holding your hands in different ways. Clasp them together, then pull them a foot apart. Observe what the movement does to the energies.

Go back to keeping your hands near each other but not touching, in whichever position seems to generate the best energy flow for you. Finally, as the energy comes down one arm, instead of letting it go from one hand into the other, exhale and push the energy out toward a previously chosen target. If you are charging an object, it should be close enough to see, and perhaps touch. When you have finished exhaling and the energy has discharged, drop your hands to your sides, shake them three times as if shaking off water, and rest for at least five minutes.

Following these preliminary exercises, you can proceed to working with another person to build sexual energies.

If two people who are in an existing relationship decide to work in this manner, they need to decide on a mutually accepted goal, times to practice, and similar matters. Two people who are not already in a sexual relationship need to decide whether this energy work may lead to one. If two individuals wish to work with these energies outside a physical relationship, they need to be aware that self-control may be called for. Performing this work on a regular basis will affect them; attraction may arise between the participants where none previously existed. Regardless of relationship status, a common aim for the work is required.

To begin, stand or sit facing your partner. If you are standing, you should be close enough to touch your hands palm to palm easily with the elbows bent, but far enough away from each other that, with hands at one's sides, about six inches of space is between any part of your bodies. (If you are sitting, however, you may need to have your knees touching in order to have your hands close enough.)

Now, go over the above exercises again, drawing down energy from above, circulating it through your arms, then up and down through your body. Take a few breaths, then put your hands out and touch the other person. There are at least two ways to do this. You can put both hands up in front of you, facing outward, and touch palms and fingers. Another contact method is to hold your hands out flat, one hand palm up and one palm down. My observation is that the second option seems to work best: to have one person's right hand facing up, slightly cupped, and other's left hand facing down, so that one is moving the energy from right to left, moving deosil, clockwise. Experiment with different ways to transmit the energy through your hands to find what works best for the two of you.

Practice sending the energy around in a circle for a while, or better yet, have a few sessions, perhaps every few days or once a week, until you are both completely comfortable pushing the energy around to each other.

When you feel comfortable circulating energy, stand facing each other and begin to circulate energy around your arms in the most effective way you have found. Then drop your hands to your sides, and take a few deep breaths. Take a step forward, still facing your partner, so that your toes touch. Lean forward and let your foreheads gently touch, then touch hands. Send energy around in your hands for a little while, then let the energy settle in the area of your heart.

Next, one person can let the energy rise up from their heart to the top of their head and out the top of their head, over to the other person's head. (You will need to decide before you start who is going to go first for sending the energy out.) The second person feels the energy come from the first person's head into their body. The energy sinks through the body, all the way to the feet, then out the feet, to the first person's feet. The energy then rises up from the feet to the head, and out again, circulating from person to person several times. After several cycles, allow the energy to rest in the heart.

Next, have the second person start the circle, sending energy out the top of their head and over to the first person.

The ultimate stage in this process is to circulate the energy through the body involving energy centers at the genitals. As previously described, allow the energy to go from the heart to the top of the head, then over to the other person. Instead of allowing the energy to move all the way to the feet, have it move down through the throat, heart, and belly to the genital area. Move the energy out

at that point, toward the genital area of the other person. The second person receives the energy and moves it up through their body to the top of the head, then sends it to the top of the head of the first person. Traditionally, the male sends energy out of the genital area and the female receives it, but there are many variations. Same-gender couples can do this working as well; part of the discussion before this type of exercise is to decide who is going to move the energy out. As with previous exercises, experiment to find which technique works best for you and your energy partner. As before, exhale when you are sending the energy outward.

Two people can do this kind of energy work while engaged in physical sex, if they choose. As indicated, the energy is raised with or without intimate touch. Whether or not you include physical contact, with practice, two people can raise plenty of sexually fueled energy without touching, and with their clothes on.

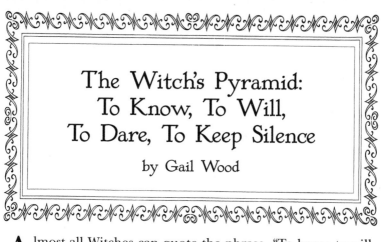

The Witch's Pyramid: To Know, To Will, To Dare, To Keep Silence

by Gail Wood

Almost all Witches can quote the phrase, "To know, to will, to dare, to keep silence" as the Witch's Pyramid and can talk of the links to the four elements of air, fire, water, and earth. Through study, we find a lot of information on this as an important part of the Witch's knowledge of the magical world. However, there is little information on using these oft-quoted phrases in practical applications of magic or spiritual practice. With a beginner's mind, we return again to the primary information of our craft and wonder anew, "What does it all mean?" We discover in the process that there are ways to translate this knowledge into understanding, and with that understanding, to use the Pyramid as part of a dynamic magical life, connected to the elemental realms in deep, mystical union.

The core of our beliefs is that we are embodied sacred beings and that the Divine is housed within our bodies. Our body is our temple in all its physicality, mental acuity, and emotional energy. We combine and recombine the threads of our energies in continuous ebbs and flows that mirror the energies of the universe as a whole. As we learn about ourselves, we learn about the divine transcendent energies of ourselves.

The elements of air, fire, water, and earth are key elements in all nature, present in every being. We humans are no different; we are made up of the four elements, both singly and in combination. The elements combine with our spirit in our bodies to become each one of us in delightful and unique individuality. In our essence we are magical, sacred beings of power and ability.

The Witch's Pyramid is a conceptualization of how those energies operate in our lives. In two-dimensional representations, the pyramid is a triangle, three angles culminating in an upright point. The triangle has multiple meanings in many different symbolic systems, from mathematics to alchemy. In three dimensions, the pyramid is a structure with four cornerstones and four strong pillars to hold the structure strong and solid. The symbol of the pyramid is one of enduring power and deep mystery to ceremonial magicians, the Western occult traditions, and all of us who learned of pyramids in school.

The four sayings associated with the Witch's Pyramid, "To know, to will, to dare, and to keep silence," are the four cornerstones and pillars of our personal temple (our body) and of the temple we create in the astral realms. That saying is the foundation from which we create our magic and move it into the world of manifestation by our will and in accordance with professed ethics. These four sayings correspond with the elements and the integration of elemental magic into our beings, allowing us to connect with the elemental realms of power, mystery, and magic. The individual elements are referred to in a number of ways: the pillars, the cornerstones, the walls of the Witch's temple. Understanding and living this phrase is considered the foundation of all magic and what must be developed in order to gain proficiency in magic. The number four, the number of manifestation, further emphasizes the aspect of stability and foundational knowledge.

The four pillars are written in the infinitive tense, the base form of the verb, the basis on which the word creates its action. Likewise, the Witch uses these four pillars as the seed or creation point to move into understanding or to make magic. Though we usually talk about the Witch's Pyramid in the context of magical and spiritual practice, these qualities apply to all aspects of our lives.

To Know corresponds to the element of air and all the qualities air carries with it. It is about knowledge, studying, researching, and gaining information and using that information to create new understanding and proficiencies. I think this corresponds to the idea of force as applied to universal life energy in the active, invigorating, giving part of energetic flow. In addition to the accumulation of wisdom and knowledge, the Witch is expected to have an inner knowing and to follow the command of the Oracle at Delphi to "Know Thyself." Learning, understanding, inspiration, intuition, imagination, and study are all part of "To Know."

To Will corresponds to the element of fire and all the qualities fire carries with it. It is about discipline and skill, both in life and in magic. Will gives us the energy to get things done and the discipline for continuing focus. I think will corresponds to the form of force as it applies to the universal life energy in the flow that keeps things moving. Concentration, discernment, choosing, focusing, drive, ambition, discipline, and enthusiasm are all part of "To Will."

To Dare corresponds with water and all the qualities water carries with it. Daring allows us to face our fears, to experiment, to risk, to be bold, and to embrace the experiences of life. Daring is integrated with the heart and soul and involves confrontation, the provinces of water. I think daring corresponds with the form of universal life energy in that part that gives the energy of the Universe substance, realness, and manifestation. Boldness, risk, confrontation, embracing, love, spirituality, life, death, and soul are all part of "To Dare."

To Keep Silence is referred to in various ways as "to keep silent," or "to keep silence." I think there is a big difference between keeping silent and keeping silence. Holding the energy of silence is an act of guardianship, an act of power and strength, one that needs stillness, solidity, foundation and stability—all qualities associated with earth. I think this corresponds to the form of the universal life energy in that part that gives the energy a foundation. To Keep Silence means we not only hold the power of not speaking too much or at all but that we also see the magic in the silences between the sounds. Magic comes with the interplay of silence and sound. As we hold the energy of silence, we flow into the rhythms of the unity of force and form. Knowing our stillpoint and inhabiting it is "To Keep Silence."

In some ways, the Witch's Pyramid is not a tool for the Witch's kit, but rather a set of principles to put into place for magical and spiritual practice. When we create magical change, we create change in our lives—both in this world of physical manifestation and in the magical realms of unmanifest energies, often referred to as the astral realms. Consciously or unconsciously, the Witch creates magic in both realms. When the creation is done with conscious intention in both realms, it is woven into the rhythms of the universe. One way to do that is to create your own astral temple, using the Witch's Pyramid as the cornerstones.

Creating and using an astral temple is an ongoing, multipart process and is part of a practice, something that is used and maintained over time, even over a lifetime. On this plane of existence, people have houses of worship, places to go that are consciously made sacred. We also hold events where, in accordance with our beliefs, we create sacred space and commune with what we hold dear and sacred. Temples, churches, groves, and more are all places where we worship, pray, and create change in our lives. Most religions, including Pagan ones, desire individual communion with the sacred. Prayer, meditation, and contemplation are all ways to connect with the sacred. Most people who practice forms of meditation find that some places present themselves over and over again until they start to think of those spiritual places as "theirs." They have created their own sacred space on the astral plane.

People have wondered if the astral temple is an internal temple or an external temple. The answer to that question is that it is both. As within, so without. You carry the experiences of the astral temple in your soul, which is a very intense inner place. By the same token, you travel or journey to your astral temple with your soul. Your astral temple can be a place of solace and comfort, a place of power and strength, a place of memory, a place of meeting, and a place of worship. It is up to you. Whatever it is and will become is up to your own divine being and work. It is magical and beautiful, a reflection of who you are as the Divine.

The temple created on the astral plane can be a place to meet your spiritual teachers and animal allies, keep record of spiritual progress, keep an altar, do devotions, and commune and worship the gods. "Astral temple" is the term; however, your sacred space may well manifest as something different from a temple with columns and a hard floor. It could be a wild place, it could look like a place you know in this world, or it could be something completely alien. An astral temple will remain strong and present in these realms during the times you visit them and afterward. Your astral temple can also get dusty and decline with disuse, so it needs upkeep and use just like a temple on the physical plane.

I find a guided meditation a useful way to build an astral temple.

Take a long deep breath, hold it, and then let it out with a sigh. Take another long deep breath, hold it, and let it out with a noise, releas-

ing all that holds you back. Take another deep breath and release it with a tone. Ommmmm. As the last vibration of that tone reverberates in your body, find yourself in your favorite outdoor spot. Breathe deeply and take in the peace, wonder, and love you have for this space. When you feel centered and ready, look around and find a pathway out of this place.

As you follow the pathway, you realize you are walking into the realms of magic and sacred wonder. You feel the magic surround you and become a part of you as you walk farther along. Many wonders catch your eye and you look intently as you keep moving. At some point, a special place catches your attention and the pathway moves in that direction. As you walk toward it, you realize this place is your astral temple, your place of worship and magic. You walk slowly to it, taking in your experience of this place.

As you walk around and into your temple, you find yourself in the center of the space. You take a moment to find your center and your still point. Then you send your energy out to connect with this space and make it yours.

You turn to the east, the place of new beginnings, inspiration, and ideas. The magic of the east enters your sacred astral space. With long, deep breaths, you feel the breezes of inspiration fill you. The element of air makes its home in your sacred astral space.

You turn to the south, the place of courage, will, and passion. The magic of the south enters your sacred astral space. With long deep breaths, you feel the fires of creation fill you. The element of fire makes its home in your sacred astral space.

You turn to the west, the place of soul, heart, and compassion. The magic of the west enters your sacred astral space. With long deep breaths, you feel the waters of the Universal soul fill you. The element of water makes its home in your sacred astral space.

You turn to the north, the place of stability, rest, and foundation. The magic of the north enters your sacred astral space. With long deep breaths, you feel the stability of earth fill you. The element of earth makes its home in your sacred astral space.

You return to Center, the place of Spirit. You open the gates to the upper realms and feel the celestial wisdom of the Universe fill your space and make its home there. You open the gates of the underworld realms and feel the wisdom of life and death fill your space and make its home there. Standing in the center, you take a long deep breath and draw to you the energies of east, south, west, north, above, and below. With another deep breath, you draw to you the energies of air, fire, water, earth, and spirit. You become the focal point, the crossroads of the energies as you draw deep breaths.

With another deep breath, you pool these gathered energies into your hands. You kneel in the center of the temple and place your hands solidly on the surface and move the pooled energy into your sacred temple. With this energy, you create this astral space as yours.

You lie face down on the surface of your astral temple, with arms outstretched. You feel the melding of the energies as you put your energies into this sacred space. As you breathe deeply, you see the first foundations of your sacred space appear. Now rest there and breathe deeply. You have built enough today. Sit up in your temple and breathe in your sacred space. Imprint its location in your psychic memory. Promise honestly to return to build your temple and what your purposes will be.

When it is time, take a long deep breath. Bid all the spirits in this space goodbye for now with a sincere promise to return. Now turn around and move back the way you came. You move along the pathways and back to your favorite place. Take a long, deep breath and return to this space. Take another deep breath and return to the here and now. Take a third deep breath and open your eyes.

Once you have created your special place in the realms of unmanifest energy and visited it several times, you are now ready to consciously add the cornerstones, the energies of the Witch's Pyramid. I used the Egyptian goddess Seshat, someone sacred to me and my practice. Please substitute the gods and guides of your choice.

Take a long, clearing breath and let it out with a sigh. Take another long breath and let it out with a noise. Take another long breath and let it out with a tone. Ommmmm. Take a long breath that fills you from the top of your head to the tips of your fingers and the tips of your toes. Continue long, deep breaths.

You find yourself in your astral temple. You look around and do some housekeeping and tending to this sacred space. When you are finished, you look around and see the goddess Seshat before you. She looks at you and smiles. She reminds you that part of her work is to lay out the measurements for your pyramid, the foundation of your magic. She

takes out her measuring line and settles down to work. You follow her directions as she tells you what to do in the creation of this pyramid. When she is done, she has you look at it. It is made of a material that has significance for you. Remember.

She then shows you your cornerstone, "To Know." You look at it and examine it carefully. As you are examining it, she pulls from it an object or other thing that has the significance of "To Know" for you. She places this item in your body where it is needed. You breathe in "To Know."

She then shows you your cornerstone, "To Will." You look at it and examine it carefully. As you are examining it, she pulls from it an object or other thing that has the significance of "To Will" for you. She places it in your body where it is needed. You breathe in "To Will."

She then shows you your cornerstone, "To Dare." You examine it carefully. As you are examining it, she pulls from it an object or other thing that has the significance of "To Dare" for you. She places it in your body where it is needed. You breathe in "To Dare."

She then shows you your cornerstone, "To Keep Silence." You examine it carefully. As you are examining it, she pulls from it an object or other thing that has the significance of "To Keep Silence" for you.

She places it in your body where it is needed. You breathe in "To Keep Silence."

The goddess places each object or thing in each corner of your temple and asks you to stand in the center of the temple. As you stand, she instructs you to ground and center and send your energy outward in tendrils to each one: air to fire to water to earth, air-fire-water-earth, air-fire-water-earth, air-fire-water-earth. Around and around until they are in the corners of your temple and you have merged with that energy in the foundation of the temple and in yourself. When you are finished, she instructs you to pull the energies back into yourself.

The goddess then smoothes out your aura with a feather and you feel centered and relaxed, ready to start on a new phase in your path. You breathe deeply as she smiles at you. She turns and writes about this in a book of lore. She tells you she will be leaving this in your astral temple for you to keep as one of your books of magic. "Take good care and add to it," she tells you. Then she is gone.

You look around at your temple and find what you need there. With a long, deep breath, you come back to the here and now. With another deep breath, you open your eyes, grounded in Mother Earth and connected to the Universe.

Once you build your astral temple and work with the cornerstones of your pyramid, you can consciously bring that energy into your spellwork and spiritual practice.

Keeping the Fires Burning: Fire Rituals

by Harmony Usher

Fire is one of the most awe-inspiring forces in nature. Long revered as one of the most powerful elements, fire ignites wonder, excitement, and even fear. Since prehistoric times, fire has been instrumental in the development of the human race. Fire is special to us humans, as we alone use it for survival, cooking, alchemy, light, protection, and ritual. Not surprisingly, fire worship is found in almost every culture in recorded history.

Although fire demands our attention in nature (think of lightning, volcanic activity, and forest fires), we have a fading relationship with this element in our increasingly urban lives. Aside from an occasional barbecue, little of our food is ever touched by flames. Few of us have wood-burning fires in our homes, relying instead on electric or oil heat. In times of high insurance costs and low tolerance for risk, many people have even turned away from wax-burning candles, opting instead for battery-operated or solar-lit imitations. It's no surprise we sometimes forget to honor this powerful force when we are creating ritual and magic in our lives, and when faced with it, we sometimes feel more anxiety than awe.

The Fire of Rebirth

Although there are ample reasons to respect the power of fire, it is important to remember that it is primarily a regenerative force, not a force of destruction. A forest fire, for instance, reduces the buildup of leaves and logs on the forest floor, allowing new plants and trees to flourish. Fire opens up the forest canopy so light can reach the lower levels of trees, stimulating new growth and a greater variety of species. Some trees, such as jack pines, even have strategies to deal with the "threat" of fire. This comes in the form of resin-sealed cones that pop open only when the heat of a fire melts the resin, at which time thousands of seeds scatter to the ground and grow into new stands of pine trees. Imagine that, a species of tree with a

built-in fire survival system! Although birds and small animals may not "prepare" for fire, they often benefit when hordes of insects colonize burned-out logs and trees, creating expansive new feeding grounds.

Humans turn to fire for the purpose of regeneration as well, albeit in a more spiritual than physical fashion. As a result, there are many ways we can harness fire energy to enrich our lives. Most people find that staring into a flame or being in the vicinity of a flickering flame nurtures a spirit of reflection. We light candles in places of worship to honor those who have passed, fostering an atmosphere of respect and remembrance. We can also use flame during meditation or prayer to invite a spirit of calm, create an atmosphere of contemplation, or focus spiritual energies toward change.

Safe Flames

No discussion of fire rituals can begin before considering safety. Never underestimate the power of fire. It is a force that can quickly grow from flickering flame to a force capable of devouring acres of brush. Before any fire ritual, prepare the area with safety for yourself and guests in mind.

If you are using candles indoors, ensure they are placed on sturdy tables, in proper candleholders that catch all dripping wax and do not allow heat to pass through. For rituals involving groups or purposeful movement anywhere near the flame, sturdy holders with sides are preferable to tall candlesticks, which are easily tipped. Do not put other objects close to the flame—I know it is tempting to tuck beautiful fall leaves around festive candles for your Samhain celebration, but don't do it! Remember, a very calm flame can be fed by breezes caused by opening and closing doors, or by whirling dervishes. Also consider your clothing when planning fire rituals, especially if you are the one responsible for lighting or putting out the flame. Fire rituals are not the occasion to be wearing your most flowing clothing—save those for your wind rituals. (I think it goes without saying, but I would humbly suggest you do not combine wind and fire rituals!) A final note about preparation: it's good practice to have a household fire extinguisher close by, and to know how to use it. If you don't have a fire extinguisher, a pail of water under the table or tucked discreetly in a corner is a smart and practical precaution.

If you are doing fire rituals outdoors, choose a still night. Wind and fire are good friends, and when they meet, the party they create can quickly get out of control. Light bonfires or burn offerings in established fire pits that have been used in the past and have shown to be effective at containing a fire. A good area for such a fire pit will be a generous distance from bushes or trees and have no overhanging branches. The ground around the fire area will be dirt or stone, so that embers or sparks cannot set grass on fire. If you are able to run water to the area, do so with a garden hose. If not, bring a couple buckets of water and use these to ensure the fire is completely out before leaving the area.

Begin every fire ritual with a prayer for safety. Honor the flame; humble yourself as you contemplate its capacity to grow, consume, and regenerate. As you light a candle or fire, ask for fire's blessing and benevolence. If you are outdoors, take a moment to ask the wind to remain calm while your ritual is underway. After invocation, use your good sense!

Around the Wheel of the Year

Fire rituals can be created or adapted for any of the sabbat or esbet celebrations throughout the year; it's just a matter of personal preference and meaningfulness. In my circle, Imbolc (also referred to as St. Brigit's Feast) is a favorite celebration for fire ritual. This esbat, which falls between the Winter Solstice and the Spring Equinox, celebrates the Sun's triumph over darkness, and we are always excited to honor the strength of the growing Sun.

The word *Imbolc* refers to the lactation of the ewes, a sign of rebirth and the heralding of the spring lambing season. The lighting of ceremonial fires has long been a part of this celebration, and has certainly become a wonderful time of both celebration and reflection in my circle of friends. Beginning at the Winter Solstice, we begin to cull our lives of those things we no longer want, welcome, or need. We each collect items we wish to burn in a ceremonial fashion at Imbolc, and then meet at a friend's home to light a bonfire, drink hot chocolate and apple cider, and ritualistically offer various personal items to the fire. Items have included paperwork for a business whose time had come to an end (nothing that's needed for tax purposes, of course!), journals full of resentments we were ready to release, and greenery that was a part of deep winter festivities. The use and meaning of the fire is not destruction but transformation, and our wish to change situations that have grown stagnant, disruptive, or harmful to us.

Winter Solstice, Yule, is also a wonderful occasion to use fire ritual. By the middle of December, my children begin reminding me to pick up the white tea lights that will fill our home (we often light upward of fifty candles) on the deepest, darkest, longest night of the year. We lay the candles out during the day and prepare finger foods to enjoy in the evening. The candles are lit at dusk to welcome guests who have come to celebrate the coming return of the Sun with us. No electricity will be used for light during the evening; instead we reflect on the many flickering flames we have come to think of as "little suns" that turn our hearts and minds to the turning of the Earth and the coming lengthening of the days. Safety is paramount when enjoying candlelight to this degree, and safe, well-placed candleholders are essential!

Fire rituals can be adapted for any of the celebrations around the wheel of the year. Feel free to use your creative energy to create rituals that are meaningful to you.

Prayer Fires

One of the simplest uses of fire in ritual is to use this element to carry your prayers, invocations, or wishes to the heavens. To do so, create a small bonfire (with attention to safety) or use a small "burn bowl" or candle, set outside in a safe place away from troublesome breezes or flammables. (For those unfamiliar, a burn bowl is a small bowl, usually made out of brass

or some other metal, with small legs that raise it above the table. In the bowl you place small twigs, dried herbs, paper, or other safe flammables.) When the flame is lit, the smoke rises into the heavens, carrying our wishes and desires with it. Simply stare into the flame and speak your wishes as the smoke rises. Watch the smoke wisp and curl into the night air and allow your spirit to contemplate the vastness of the universe and your place in it. Imagine your desires rising into the darkness to become a part of everything. Visualize the outcome you desire in your mind's eye as you stare into the night sky. You can also write your prayers on a small piece of paper and burn it, again following the smoke's journey into the heavens. Any ash from the burning can be saved for a later wind ritual to be tossed into a breeze, further strengthening your intention and the ritual.

Creative Fire

Fire is said to be at the heart of our human life force and the "creative spark" behind musical, poetic, and artistic expression. Musicians are sometimes described as being "on fire" and artists may be perceived as "smoldering" before a creative urge takes hold and leads to a flurry of activity. Many a blocked artist has described their creative fire as being "put out," or their flame being extinguished. Given the natural connection between fire and creativity, fire ritual is a natural choice for enhancing your own creative energies.

Scrying is the practice of seeking out and seeing things in a particular medium (such as a crystal, water, tea leaves, or flames) and can be a particularly useful kind of fire ritual for tapping into one's creative energy. This can be done with the aid of a bonfire, fireplace, or a simple candle. Sit in a relaxed posture and stare into the flame, allowing your vision to relax and soften. Take deep breaths and enter a peaceful state of mind, taking note of any images that rise in the flame or embers. Consider the meaning of such images, and spend a few moments in silent contemplation, imagining these images coming to pass. Speak words such as "Fire, fire, burning bright, ignite the flame within tonight." After the ritual, return to your creative pursuit with renewed energy and passion.

Fire Signs and the Stars

In astrology, we find three fire signs: Leo, Aries, and Sagittarius. Individuals born under these signs are often powerful, confident people who move quickly and, at times, fiercely through their lives. They tend to be action oriented, and may tire easily of lengthy intellectual discussions. They are often very creative and interested in change. If you practice with people born under these signs, you may notice they have a strong desire to engage in fire rituals, and there is some benefit to allowing them to lead such rituals for a group.

~

Regardless of your need, the time of year, or your astrological sign, fire rituals bring energy and power to a circle and can be instrumental in inviting creativity, change, and power into our lives. As you journey through your year, keep the fires burning and respect the power of the flame.

Powerful Effigy Magick

by Melanie Marquis

Rioters burn them in the streets. Mourners find comfort in their likeness to the dead. They lie in tombs and stand in shrines, covered in offerings, paying tribute to fallen kings and calling out to ancient gods. From the English custom of setting fire to effigies of public enemies past and present on Guy Fawkes Night, to the Sri Lankan tradition of burning an effigy of the demon king Ravana in symbolism of evil's defeat, effigies are used in cultures around the world for purposes ranging from the political to the deeply spiritual.

An effigy is simply a three-dimensional representation of a person or a personified entity. This can be anything from a tiny cloth voodoo doll to a giant clay funeral sculpture. As humans, our psyches respond strongly to depictions of the human form, and using effigies magickally offers a deeply personal and direct channel through which to access powerful energies within us. Effigies can be used to transform the self or to banish the bad. They can be big or small, detailed or crude. Effigy magick has no set rules or limits. Although often set on fire, effigies can be destroyed or manipulated in other ways, as well. Regardless of the method used, effigy magick is fire magick. These human likenesses fan the flames of magickal power, acting to transform, to illuminate, and to transform the stagnant and dead into the fluid and living. Try these rituals to get your imagination going, and then create your own ways to harness the ancient power of effigies.

Out with the Old

Are you at a crossroads in life, about to make a major shift into a new and better phase of development? Acknowledging such occasions with a ceremony helps manifest a smooth and positive transition. Whether you're dedicating yourself to a new spiritual path or reinventing yourself to begin a more satisfying career, an effigy can make a striking addition to any initiation rite. Putting fire in the mix raises the magickal mercury even higher, and

burning an effigy of your old self is a memorable and effective way to shift gears into a brand-new you.

Since burning a life-size effigy made of synthetic materials would release a lot of polluting fumes, make a miniature effigy out of natural materials instead. Create your form with cornhusks, twigs, and leaves. A twig with a forked end makes an instant torso and legs. Tie a second twig crosswise onto the middle of the first twig and you've got the arms. A leaf with a face drawn on it makes the head. Cornhusks and additional leaves can be attached to make hair, clothing, hands, and feet. You can add a bit of your real hair to make the effigy magically effective. Draw symbols or write words on the leaves and husks to represent the old you that you're leaving behind. If you're not sure what to write, go with a simple "the old me." The effigy can be used alongside other elements of an initiation ceremony, or it can serve as a complete rite on its own. Either way, when you're ready to destroy the effigy, make a small, contained, approved outdoor fire and toss the figure into the flames. Watch your old self turn to ash, then envision the new you rising up from the flames.

Releasing Emotions

Effigies can also be used to let go of past pain, guilt, sorrow, or anger that no longer serves you. Detaching ourselves from hatred or hurts long carried is an intense process. It can happen in an instant, but it can also be beneficial to shed those scarred emotional layers more slowly, in a way that lets you explore your memories and gather further knowledge and insight.

A biodegradable effigy made of fruits and vegetables banishes the energies encased therein over time, as nature slowly consumes the produce. You can use a single fruit or vegetable to make the effigy, or you can combine several items, piecing them together with thin twigs. Carve your name or initials into the figure to magically mark it as yours. As you handle the effigy, think of the past pain, sorrow, anger, or guilt that you want to destroy. When the figure is complete, place it outdoors. Have one close friend stand to the side and watch as you face the effigy and speak aloud to it. If you're alone, call on the birds and squirrels and wildlife to be your witnesses. Explain why you want to be rid of the negative emotions attached to that particular part of your past. Say goodbye to the effigy and leave it outside where it will be munched on by the animals and broken down by the elements. Over the next several weeks, take some time every few days to write a sentence or two describing your current feelings about the past emotions you are working through. As the effigy returns to nature, your spirit will release its burden.

Worry Not

Using a communal effigy to banish excessive worry makes for a fun group experience. Get a few friends together and have everyone bring a piece or two of old clothing. Use the clothes to create a scarecrow-style effigy, pinning together pants and a shirt and stuffing it with rags or newspaper. You can make the head with a shirt sleeve or with the toe end of a pair of pantyhose. Just cut off about twelve inches, tie off the end, and stuff it. Give the dummy a generic face with plain features so that it can act as an effigy for everyone in the group—just paint a simple face with a worried and anxious expression. On the body of the effigy, have each person write something that causes them excessive worry. Words like *money, sickness,* or *emergencies* might be appropriate. Next, stand hand in hand, forming a circle around the effigy. Say in unison, "Be gone, worry!" Put on some upbeat music that everyone enjoys. Dance carefree around the effigy, taking turns walking, dancing, and stomping on it, shouting out curses against potential troubles and the anxieties such troubles cause. After everyone has danced a good jig, take the effigy apart and recycle or donate the clothes.

World Issues

Effigies can also be used to magically combat global problems. Ills that plague humanity such as hunger, war, or human rights abuses can be embodied into an effigy and symbolically destroyed, sympathetically effecting change on a worldwide scale.

Make the effigy out of dough, as large as you can. Five or six batches of dough, each made with 1 cup flour, ½ cup salt, ¼ cup of water, and 1 tablespoon of vegetable oil will make a decent-sized effigy. Put the dough all together on a large floured surface such as the dining room table or kitchen floor. Mash down the dough and roll it out fairly flat, to about 1-inch thickness. Cut around the edges to make a gingerbread man figure. Carefully slide thin cardboard or poster board under the effigy and carry it outside. Place the figure on the ground and pat it out more so that it's even larger. Push stones or other objects into the dough to create a mean face. Use the end of a stick to scratch the name of the ill you wish to banish onto the effigy. Leave it outside for several days until it hardens completely. Then call up some like-minded friends and give everyone a hammer. Smash the effigy and envision the demise of humanity's bane.

Effigies for the Living

Effigies are often made to honor the dead, but why not make one to honor the living? Find a cloth or plastic doll that somewhat resembles you, and decorate it so that it shares some of your more unique characteristics. Draw on any tattoos or moles, stick earrings in the doll where you have piercings, and cut and style the doll's hair to resemble your own. Then do something to the doll to make it symbolize an even better you, adding a token that represents your ideal self. You could add a crown, give it a superhero cape, wrap it in jewels, cover it in magical symbols, dress it in clothing associated with your desired profession, or whatever else might appeal to you. Stand the doll

upright in a safe place. Visit this shrine to yourself as a monthly ritual. Gaze at the doll and take a moment to forgive yourself for any shortcomings. Then take a moment to celebrate your true self, thinking of at least one recent accomplishment or positive development in your life, feeling pride in at least one of your personal traits. Challenge yourself to imagine greater success and fulfillment. Place offerings around the effigy, surrounding the little you with flowers, coins, stones, shells, or other appealing objects. Treat the effigy with love and respect, an outward symbol of your sacred inner spirit. Your confidence will get a boost and your soul will gain nourishment, opening the way for magically enhanced good fortunes to befall you.

~

As varied as the cultures that create them, effigies are versatile and serve many functions. Now that you know some of the ways effigies can be used magickally, try developing your own techniques. You will awaken a power deep within your spirit, a power that connects the modern day individual to the ancient wellspring of human potential.

Mars and Anger

by Gail Wood

*Anyone can become angry – that is easy. But to be angry
with the right person, to the right degree, at the right time,
for the right purpose, and in the right way; this is not easy.*

—Aristotle

The way of anger is not an easy path. All of us feel anger
at times, from the mildest irritation and resentment to
all-consuming rage and fury. Most people would advise us to
leave our anger behind, to forgive, to forget, and to move on;
this is very worthy, healthy advice. Still others will tell us that
well-placed anger is justified and can motivate us to create
change in ourselves and in our society; again, this is very true.
Each day we choose how we relate to our anger and how we
manifest it in the world. Anger burns with a bright fire that
can warm us or destroy us, and it's up to each one of us to
choose how we handle anger. By approaching our anger magically and with the help of the gods, we can manifest a life in
which anger is a healthy part of our being.

A few years ago, one of my students, an incarcerated
Pagan, wrote to me and said that he was dealing with his
anger by working with the Roman god Mars. He didn't give
much detail other than it was an important and active part
of his spiritual life. Prison is probably one of the most fertile
places for the destructive power of anger to breed, grow, and
destroy. It takes a powerful god such as Mars to assist us with
this potent emotion so that we are able to use anger for our
growth and not for harm.

As most of us have learned, the Roman god Mars is a
warrior god and the lover of Venus, the goddess of love. His
associations with battle and war led astronomers to name the
blood-red planet in his honor, echoing the honor and reverence he received in the glory days of Rome. Mars was revered
in the Roman Empire, second only to his father, Jupiter, in
prominence. He was the patron of the city of Rome and the

father of its founder, Romulus. As the god of war, he was accompanied by Fugar and Timor, the personifications of fear and flight. Where the Greek god of war, Ares, was cruel and brutal, Mars was much beloved and widely worshipped even as a warrior.

Perhaps this reverence and affection was present because, before he became a warrior, Mars was an early chthonic god, a deity of the fertile Earth, vegetation, and springtime. He was a protector of the boundaries in agricultural life, the fields, the farmers, and the cattle. As the Roman Empire grew, Mars' role expanded as he became a god of death and finally of war. His early history is rooted deeply in the everyday life of fertility and death, and then as protector and warrior. As a springtime god, his festivals were always in the spring, a time when battle campaigns began. The first spring month of March is named for him.

An evolved picture of Mars includes a strong, competent man attending to the important parts of growing life, which includes protecting the boundaries of our individual lives. His connection to fertility and death brings to mind the ancient mysteries of the universe, where life and death meld together. His chthonic power comes from fertility and growth, and his warrior energy is that of raw power and strength. His warrior self teaches us to protect what is ours and to resist the aggression of others. Modern-day warriors do not need to be aggressive or conquer the realms of others. Just as an evolved Mars combines the chthonic energy of the Earth with the raw power of strength and protection, so in our lives we combine our understanding of the sacred worlds with contemporary "street smarts." Our life conquest is to break down the barriers between our true Self and our conscious Self—to seek true understanding of our deepest soul and our place in the universe as divine and sacred beings. In that quest, we need to know ourselves and how we work with harsh and tough emotions, particularly anger.

Anger is a potent and powerful emotion, one that can be understood, managed, and harnessed for our own development and survival. The accompanying emotions of fear and flight are ancient qualities essential for our survival. Fear reminds us to be alert to threatening situations, and flight gives us one strategy for survival. Anger allows us another strategy: to fight for our own survival. Physically, our heart beats faster and adrenalin floods our system when we are angry or afraid, allowing us to act quickly without elaborate thought.

Anger is raw energy, and to live in the presence of so much untamed power can be physically, emotionally, and socially destructive. So this wild energy must be tempered by the more civilizing qualities of discernment and judgment. Without the veneer of discernment, anger can become uncontrolled, uncontrollable, and destructive. Unfortunately, in most cases, what we destroy is our own precious self or something dear to us.

Over the years, I've learned that working and dealing with my anger requires a myriad of responses and techniques. Being a Pagan, I seek ways to integrate my responses with my deities and my worldview as well as the practical concerns of living in modern society. Anger, I've learned, never really goes away because we do need it. It's like peeling an onion—there are layers of what anger is and a multitude of responses. There are three main ways of dealing with anger and we do this through both unconscious and conscious means. The more conscious understanding we bring to the situation, the better equipped we are to handle these instinctive, emotional responses.

Express Your Anger

We can express our anger, and we choose whether that expression is healthy or unhealthy. Ideally, expression can take the form of a strong, positive statement of your needs that does not hurt others. That kind of expression requires some control over your emotional response and depends on your ability to be articulate about the situation. When I can't think constructively or when the situation doesn't allow that kind of response, I must admit that sometimes I just go into the kitchen, choose a coffee cup I don't like, and then go outside and smash it to bits. My anger is then well expressed, with

harm to none. I thank Mars for his attention and ask him to transform that anger into constructive thought. It doesn't usually solve the problem, but the emotional and angry response is now under better control. Finding good, safe ways such as this to express your anger will be much more helpful than reacting with name calling, rash actions, or harsh words.

Because anger has a strong physical response, many times our expression needs to be a physical one. Our primitive, atavistic instincts are for flight or fight. Instead, dance. I usually set up an altar to Mars with lots of red, his color, and representations of his totems, the wolf and the woodpecker. I have wine and bread and make a libation bowl. I play music with a strong drumbeat, and I begin by standing still and breathing deeply. I call Mars to come to me in the form of a woodpecker and to peck through the layers of my being and reveal the sources of my anger. As that happens and the music intensifies, I dance. Sometimes it's jumping up and down and visualizing the emotions falling off me like so many pieces of pecked wood. Sometimes it's howling and growling as I give voice to my emotion while I move. I dance until I know it is done. I thank Mars for his presence and his assistance. In honor of him, I put the libation bowl outside for the creatures that honor him still.

Suppress Your Anger

The second means of dealing with anger is suppression, which is a two-step process: to hold in the anger, and then refocus and direct it to more positive behavior. The danger here is that suppression often turns anger inward toward yourself, which can harm your physical health, your worldview, and your relationship with yourself and others. Our society supports suppressing many of our strong emotions without providing good tools for converting them into something more positive. Pagans have the good fortune to have many techniques in their spiritual toolkit, as well as deities and spirit guides to assist them.

Visualization is a great technique for this strategy of dealing with your anger. You can visualize the anger as red energy in your body, then pull it off with your hands and place the energy in a fire or bowl of water. Then visualize the anger being converted to a more soothing color, such as blue. Repeat this as often as necessary. Sometimes the situation is complex or your emotional response is very intricate, with layers of concern. Here is a small ritual and meditation for those times. Please adapt the meditation to your own preferences and needs.

Anger Visualization

Create an altar with libations and offerings to Mars, using a red candle to represent his power and strength. I often wear red when I do this. Cast the circle and call in the spirits according to your tradition. Call in Mars as warrior and protector. Take some time to write out or draw your emotions on a sheet of paper, which you will leave on the altar. Make yourself comfortable for meditation.

Take a long cleansing breath, hold it for a second and let it out. Take a second long, deep breath and let it out with some noise. Take a third long breath and let it out with a tone. As the vibrations from the tone vibrate in your body, find yourself in a clearing surrounded by trees in the twilight of the evening. There's a fire burning in a cauldron in the center of the clearing and a circle of benches around the fire. A wolf is howling in the background.

On one of the benches, you see a powerful man wearing the garb of springtime. You know this is the god Mars and you notice he is reading the sheet of paper from your altar. He sees you and stands, beckoning you to come to him. As you go, you notice that he has a woodpecker on his shoulder and two wolves, a male and a female, by his side. He takes your hand and leads you closer to the fire.

He has you lie down there on the ground beside the fire, placing the paper from your altar beside you. As the warrior god, he talks to you of the situations in your life and the anger there. As he speaks, the woodpecker begins to peck away at these layers of anger. Situations, failures, and poorly expressed emotions fall onto the paper beside him. The anger you feel in all its permutations—resentment, annoyance, fury, and more—fall in little bits as the woodpecker peck-peck-pecks away at you. "Breathe deeply," he says, "as you experience this." When it is done, the woodpecker flies back to his shoulder.

Mars then talks to you of boundaries, the ones that are already in place, both useful and useless. He then talks to you of the boundaries you must set, and the boundaries you must tear down. As he talks, the two wolves circle you, the male moving sunwise around you and the female moving moonwise. Moonwise, your territory is being unraveled as needed, and sunwise, your territory is being established. Around and around they go, until Mars has finished speaking. They stop and nuzzle you gently as pack, as family, and then move back to the edges of the circle.

Mars stands you up and sweeps the last bits of anger from your being, moving them onto the paper. He folds the paper and hands it back to you. He then places a medallion of black onyx around your neck, saying you can use that to absorb anger as you deal with your current situation and beyond. You thank him and bow in deep reverence. When you stand upright, they are all gone, and you are beneath the starry night, the red planet prominent in the sky.

Take a deep breath and come back to the here and now. Take another deep breath and open your eyes. Take a third breath and reconnect to the stability of the Earth and your own center.

Go to the altar and safely burn the paper with the candle flame. Raise a cone of power while the paper burns, sending the energy out into the universe for your own protection and healing from anger. Say a farewell to Mars, thanking him for his assistance. Dismiss the directions and take up the circle according to your tradition. Take the libation bowl and the ashes outdoors. Leave the libation for the creatures of nature and bury the ashes in Mother Earth to be purified.

The processes of the ritual will help you create a new situation for your anger as you redirect it from harming you and into a more fulfilling form. In this way, *suppression* ceases to be a bad word but merely another strategy for dealing with your own potent power.

Calm Your Anger

The third technique for dealing with anger is to create a calm inner life. When your inner life and your inner response is one of peace, your outward response can also be more calm and constructive. As a warrior god of an extraordinarily successful empire, Mars was, by necessity, a great strategist. By creating a calm inner life, you can develop long-term strategies to deal with whatever life brings to you. Sometimes anger is not situational but rather a conditioned response to outside stimuli. If you work to recondition yourself, you will change your response to fearful or bad situations.

There are a number of techniques for creating a calm inner self, many of which are already part of the modern Pagan's knowledge. Reframing, a common psychological and communication technique, allows us to reposition our understanding. When my student first told me that he channeled his anger through Mars, my initial reaction was not positive. My knowledge of Mars was my narrow view of his history and some assumptions I made based on the cruelty of other warrior gods. I just assumed Mars was like those other gods. However, as I researched Mars and began to work with him, I discovered a more expansive view of Mars, one based on his chthonic persona and the reverence given to him by farmers, country folk, and ordinary citizens, instead of the media-influenced view of an armor-clad warrior who wields the sword and spares no one. As I worked with him, my frame of reference expanded to see a god who is strongly connected to the sacred world and the universal rhythms of birth, death, and rebirth. He isn't an easy god by any means, but he is a strong, powerful, and clear-eyed strategist who is forthright and honest about the forces around and in us. By doing some research, I was able to reframe my negative associations and mitigate my angry response to my student's study of Mars.

Humor is another strategy for creating a calm inner life. When confronted with a difficult situation, it's always good to figure out a way to laugh about it; if there is nothing humorous about it, find something else to laugh about. The physical action of laughter alleviates the tension brought on by the stress of anger. The wolf totem of Mars is especially useful in changing your physical responses. Simply howling like a wolf moves the stress out of your body and creates a completely new vibration. Of course you need to pick a prudent time and place for howling. Your emotional state might well be tense and angry at the beginning, but as your body begins the howling or laughing, you find that it feels good, so much better than the tense, angry state your body was in before, and you can move your emotions and your body out of stressed mode and into a calmer place.

Relaxation techniques, grounding and centering, and connecting to the calm center of ourselves and then moving into the flow of the universal energy are also good techniques for creating inner calm. It is the chthonic persona of Mars, the man of power who is lover of Venus, goddess of love and beauty, who has helped me re-envision my inner self. With him as earth god, the red color that is associated with Mars softens and becomes infused with lighter white, pink, and purple. Visualize Mars as a vegetation god, surrounded by plants, totems, and all sorts of growth. Speak to him of your anger and the problems surrounding your reactions, and he will respond. Don't expect him, even in this persona, to give you easy ways out of your dilemmas; however, he will help you to become strong and powerful in your own right. Seeking peace as an alternative to anger is an act of incredible power. By seeking inner calm and peace, your inner world begins to work in harmony with your outer life after time and practice.

~

As you work with your anger and incorporate the wisdom you gain from Mars, you will find that there are many imaginative ways to express and redirect your anger. The American journalist Dorothy Thompson once wrote, "Peace is not the absence of conflict but the presence of creative alternatives for responding to conflict." With the help of deity in the form of Mars and his totems, there are many creative and magical ways to re-create our lives as we become strong and powerful as divine, physical beings.

Healing with Fire

by Paniteowl

Working with the elementals can be a daunting task when people choose to walk the Pagan pathways. Earth, air, fire, and water each have their own complexities, and each can be used in a variety of ways to enrich our lives. Fire, to me, is the most underrated element when it comes to understanding its power and effect. Before working with this fantastic element, we must first overcome the warnings and fears instilled in us by well-meaning people who teach us that fire can hurt us. Well, yes, it can! But it can also help us in many more ways than we credit it with.

Fire is the planet's "birthing" element. When volcanoes spew their molten lava, they are creating new land and giving structure to the Earth. Perhaps the most striking examples can be found on the islands of Hawaii, where one can walk atop the crust and get up close and personal to an active volcano. Although I found it interesting, I will admit that I was quite uncomfortable while exploring a volcano some years ago. I'd really rather watch a video of crust creation from the comfort of my recliner!

Walking across the cooled lava flows may give you the feeling of walking on the Moon. The stark, gray/black swirl of melted rocks and the enormity of the field is spiritually awe-inspiring. This is the visual reality of the Earth giving birth to new land. Is it scary? Of course it is. Yet it is beautiful as you see the patterns of the birth waters that create the land. The lush vegetation of the islands shows us what to expect in the future for the lava fields. Fire creates, and the Earth is enriched with the help of air and water. The elements work together to bring beauty and balance.

Each year we follow the news reports of wildfires in many areas of the United States. Homes are threatened or

lost, and the financial losses are enormous. Yet within a few years, the land recovers and plants thrive in the ashes of what was there before. There are some seeds that require the intensity of a forest fire in order to sprout and reestablish their species in the now fertile soil. Knowing this, one wonders why people build expensive homes in the areas that naturally need to burn off. For centuries, farmers have used fire to "burn off" fields in order to replenish the soil and restore the balance so that crops will flourish. I'm sure they adopted the helpful practice after seeing how fertile an ash-enriched field can become.

We can take the information shown to us by the natural forces to better understand how fire can help our human bodies to replenish and heal within. We too are "of the Earth," and the examples we see in nature give us clues as to the powerful healing aspect residing in the element of fire.

Fire can heal! I know that's a simple statement, but let's look at some experiences most of us have had when we've been ill. We get a fever, and we know to drink lots of fluids to keep ourselves from getting dehydrated. You'd think this was more about the element of water than fire, but the fever is our body's way of telling us something is wrong. The heat generated by our white blood cells fighting an infection is the natural way fire acts in the body to keep us in balance. A fever is a healthy sign, one to which we must pay attention. A fever forces the water out of our system through sweating, and in order to help the fever fight infection, we flush our body with liquids to encourage the discharge of those nasty germs that are making us feel so crummy. The sign that we're on the road to recovery is when the fever "breaks," and the fire that has rushed to our defense dies down and eventually flares out. Knowing how fire works within our bodies can enhance our own healing energies. The more we know, the better we can direct our own energy.

When we have a sore muscle, there is heat in the area that is affected. Again, the fire of our nature is telling us there is a problem. We apply cold packs and rub liniment into the area, but it's really healed when the heat has left the muscle. Fire has again done its job to encourage healing. Knowing what to look for, and on what to focus, helps the healer work more efficiently.

Although our "fur-kids" can't tell us when they are hurting, we know by feeling their noses. (Okay, this may not always be the case, but frequently, it is a simple, non-invasive diagnostic tool.) Cool means fine, hot means our animal needs help. When an animal is injured, the first sign is often a limp, or a twitch when touched in a certain spot. This area often feels hot to the touch. Again, the fire within is giving us a warning and has already begun its healing work. At times like this, it is entirely appropriate to light our candles to encourage the healing power of fire. By lighting candles and acknowledging fire as being part of the healing process, we are practicing sympathetic magic on an elemental level. Does it work? Yes, most emphatically, it does! However, we are modern Pagans, and a visit to the vet is also very much in order. As the ancient Pagans used whatever they could to effect a healing, we are fortunate in having many more devices and medications available to us today that we can and should use. Ignoring the tools available to us today is, in my estimation, cruelty to our animals.

There are many disciplines of energy work, and perhaps one of the best known is the Reiki tradition. It's a fact that both practitioners and clients consistently talk about the "heat" felt from the hands of the Reiki Master when he or she is working on a client. The Master feels it, and the client feels it. The Master is focusing energy in a specific manner, and healing is recognized by the heat that is transferred. The tool of fire can be used very specifically and is easily recognized by the participants in this method of healing. There are other disciplines, but at the heart of each is the trained practitioner learning to manipulate and move energy. The "heat" expressed in a treatment is a sure-fire sign (pardon the pun) that our efforts are indeed working.

Traditional medicine uses fire to cauterize wounded flesh. The searing or sealing of torn vessels has saved lives for hundreds of years. We may not have to bite on a bullet and suffer a hot branding iron nowadays, but with the help of modern medicines, we can use fire more effectively than in ancient times. Thank the gods for modern painkillers! Hot pads and hot poultices are used to bring focus to an infected area. Maybe some of you remember the old mus-

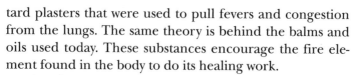

tard plasters that were used to pull fevers and congestion from the lungs. The same theory is behind the balms and oils used today. These substances encourage the fire element found in the body to do its healing work.

Another way to recognize the healing aspects of fire is to look at how we go about our daily lives. Whether we cook over an open fire or a gas range or even an electric stove, we are purifying our foods through the act of heating. In other words, we are transforming meats and vegetables into a safer state of being. The trick, of course, is to find the balance of enhancing the food without overcooking. Remember, fire can burn! Finding that balance is the talent of the kitchen Witch. A few years ago, I got a new stove, just before an annual gathering. The stove is unique in that the top burners are gas, while the double ovens are electric. It's referred to as a dual fuel unit, kind of like a hybrid vehicle. I love this stove! Yes, to me it is magickal, and I have done more cooking from scratch with it than I did for many years before. Since it was a novelty, many of those who gathered with us were finding opportunities to use my new toy. One woman who was baking monkey bread got a small burn on her wrist as she was taking the baked bread from the oven. She looked at me with chagrin and apologized for leaving her DNA on my stove! It made me laugh that she would worry about "imprinting" or "contaminating" my stove by being burned. (However, it did start a long discussion about using other people's tools, whether magickal or mundane.) Invariably, the discussion evolved to grounding ourselves, and being respectful while working with fire.

Finally, I'd like to talk about what may happen when you are working with the element of fire on a regular basis and truly understanding its capabilities. The help you get from this element can manifest in many ways. The best way to explain it is to tell you a true story that really highlighted our connection with this element.

Recently we had the honor of welcoming a number of new practitioners into our Trad. We had invoked the elements and it seemed that fire was more attentive than the others. We took this as a sign to focus on this element this year as part of our training. During the ritual, I had encouraged each of the members to reintroduce themselves to fire, and we played with the flames in the fire pit. A month later, the three-year-old daughter of one of our members became ill. Yes, there was fever, but also red eyes, red palms, and redness on the soles of her feet. Her mother took her to the emergency room but was not comfortable with the level of expertise shown by the ER doctor. She was sent home with a prescription for antibiotics and told to wait a few days before bringing her in again if there was no improvement. That night, the mother could not sleep, so she began to search the Internet for clues using her daughter's obvious fiery symptoms. She's not very Web savvy but found her way to the Mayo Clinic site, and there was an article on Kawasaki disease that seemed to fit all her daughter's symptoms. The following day, she brought her to a renowned children's hospital. She was fortunate that a specialist in children's infectious diseases happened to be on the unit that day. He took one look and pronounced "Kawasaki," then had her admitted immediately. She was started on an IV therapy program and spent the next four days in the hospital.

Although the little girl is still recuperating, she's well on her way to a successful recovery. In researching this disease, we've found that there is a ten-day window of opportunity to avoid the long-term effects of permanent heart damage. This little girl will have to be monitored often this year, and if there are no problems showing on her EKG, she will still need an annual EKG to ensure that there will be no residual effects. Knowing this, there is a worry, of course, but the knowledge gives her parents access to tools to monitor her well-being.

After reviewing the events and talking with the girl's mom, we can see where the element of fire directed the mother to keep looking for answers and not settle for the opinion of the first doctor she saw. In the mother's own words, she felt "driven" to do her own research, and she admits she has no idea how she found herself on the Web site for the Mayo Clinic. Although she felt that Kawasaki was indeed the culprit, she read through many, many articles before going back and studying the disease more thoroughly. The validation by the doctor at the children's hospital, and the subsequent treatment, was, to her, a validation of the element of fire directing her to find out what was wrong with her child. It was very much an example of using sympathetic magick to help heal. But the sympathy was coming from the fire elemental, rather than from the

mother. It helped her doubt what she had been told. Her daughter's continued severe fever and redness encouraged her to find some alternatives. It drove her to take her child to the right place, at the right time. As she sat by the bedside of her child, she recognized that her fire elemental was right there with her and aiding in the healing.

∼

As you work with the elements, please don't limit their ability to aid you in your magickal and mundane practices. Connecting on a personal level will help you understand not only the elemental, but also its interaction with your mundane life. Make it your friend, your partner, your familiar—whatever term is comfortable for you—but by all means recognize that when it comes to healing, the fire elemental can be one of your most important support systems.

Water Magic

Waterguard: Spells for Purification and Protection

by Elizabeth Barrette

Water is life. It forms the basis for all living creatures on Earth and makes up a large portion of our bodies. Both freshwater and saltwater provide habitat for fish, birds, plants, and many others. Water is also one of the four magical elements whose energies help define and empower our craft.

Sadly, many threats—from pollution runoff to global warming—compromise the integrity of water as a source of life and power. Water can only sustain us if we take good care of it. The responsible practice of magic involves understanding the forces that fuel our work, communicating with the spirits that oversee them, and acting to defend the Earth as well as making appropriate use of its bounty.

The Element of Water

On the physical plane, water is H_2O: two atoms of hydrogen bound to one atom of oxygen. Water exists in all three states—solid, liquid, and gas—at various places on Earth. On the human plane, water corresponds to intuition and the emotional self. Spellcraft employs water energy to purify or change things. Water can also take and hold energy imprints, as in homeopathy. Spirits and deities associated with water may be generous and life-giving, but they tend to have a stormy temper if offended.

Water is also unique in that it transforms itself through the other elements. Air of water manifests as fog, mist, and clouds—forms that conceal and enchant. Fire of water manifests as steam and hot springs—forms that simmer and boil, activating the passionate range of emotions, hence the term "torrid affair." Water of water manifests as rain and streams—forms that run clear and wash away impurities. Earth of water manifests as mud and ice—forms that can either bind fast or lubricate dangerously. Using these elemental aspects in spellcraft allows you to fine-tune the energies for a more precise effect.

Spells for Purification

Water energy purifies because physical water cleans things—it's a metaphysical extension of a physical property. Therefore, many water spells involve purification of energy, people, or objects. You can also work magic to purify water itself.

Clean Water Spell

Obtain a worry stone of clear quartz or glass. Charge it by visualizing clean, clear water. When you do activist projects relating to water, or when you visit any body of water, rub the stone and refresh your visualization. Chant:

> *May this water be clean and pure. May it support life.*
> *May its energy grow fresh and strong. So mote it be!*

If you wish, you may also invoke a deity associated with the relevant type of water, such as Chac for stopping acid rain or Yemaya when visiting the ocean (see "Working with Water Spirits" on page 312 for more deities). Because this spell is so discreet, you can even do it in public with nobody noticing.

Refreshing Rain Spell

When you feel tired and grungy after a hard day, use water to refresh yourself. For this spell, you need a blue glass bowl, your wand, and some rainwater. (You may put the bowl outside during a storm to catch rain fresh for the spell, or you may catch a large amount of rainwater in a plain jar and save it for later use.) Pour the rainwater into the blue bowl. Gently tap the side of the bowl with your wand, then put the tip of the wand into the water and stir. Chant:

> *Water clean and water bright,*
> *Make my spirit feel all right.*

Set down the wand. Rinse your hands in the water, lifting it and letting it trickle back into the bowl; pat your face with your wet hands. As you listen to the trickling water and feel it on your skin, concentrate on washing away the negative energy and drawing fresh power from the element of water. Finish by pouring any leftover water outside onto the ground.

Ocean Tide Spell

This spell addresses more serious levels of negativity, such as residues left by malicious entities or hostile magic. It employs the power of the ocean and the outgoing tide, so if possible, cast the spell when the nearest salt water tide is going out. For this magical bath, you will need ½ cup sea salt and several drops of essential oil, plus a recording of ocean waves. Choose a purifying oil such as eucalyptus, lavender, lemon, rosemary, or witch hazel.

Fill your bathtub with hot water. Add the sea salt and a few drops of essential oil (just enough for a subtle fragrance). Turn on the ocean recording, then get into the bath. Lie back and relax. Invite the oceanids—who can manifest in any salt water—to join you. Soak for a while. Listen to the sound of the surf. Imagine playing in the waves with frisky nymphs, and let the salt water wash away all the negativity.

When the water cools, stand up and pull the plug. As the water drains away, visualize the tide going out and focus on sending all the negative energy with it. Thank the oceanids as they leave. Finish with a quick rinse in fresh water to wash the salt off your skin.

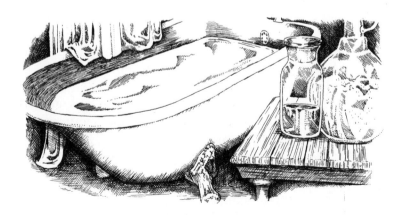

Spells for Protection

Although protection does not top the list of associations when people think of water, some aspects of this element lend themselves very well to this purpose. In environmental and political geography alike, rivers, lakes, and other bodies of water form natural boundaries. This makes water energy very good at keeping out unwanted influences.

Watershed Preservation Spell

A watershed spans the area that drains into a particular body of water, such as a lake, wetland, or ocean. By taking good care of the watershed on which you live, you can protect your water supply and befriend the local water spirits. Depending on where you live, you may work with limniads (mountain lakes or springs), undines (streams, rivers, or lakes), or oceanids (oceans).

Begin by visiting the nearest body of water. Introduce yourself to the spirits there and invite them to follow you. Borrow a bottle of water from the lake, river, or ocean. Set up your altar with aquatic symbols (blue cloth, river stones, seashells, mermaid pictures, and so on) and a clear glass vase. Pour a little of the borrowed water into the vase, about one-seventh full. Encourage the water spirits to watch what you do. Then do one practical thing to protect your local watershed, such as donating money to a wetland park or volunteering for river or beach cleanup.

Continue this process for the next six days. Pour a little more water into the vase and do one practical thing. At the end of the week, your vase should be full. Return the borrowed water to its source. Thank the water spirits for their attention and remind them that you are their ally. Ask them to lend their power when you work water magic and to be nice to the humans who are taking care of the waterways.

You can cast this spell more than once, such as on a quarterly or annual cycle. Over time, you will form a close connection to the local watershed and its spirits. If anything threatens it, they will help call your attention to the threat and boost your efforts to deal with it.

White Water Warding Spell

To protect your home, you will need to gather a bottle of water from a fast-running creek or river in your area. Put the water in a white vase or bowl. If you live in a house, you'll be walking around the outside of your yard or house; if you live in an apartment or other small space, you'll be walking around the inside of your room(s). As you walk, sprinkle the water and chant:

Swift, white water running free,
Keep all harm away from me.
If harm tries to pass by thee,
Wash it down into the sea.

Visualize a river rushing and roaring around the boundary of your home. Imagine that any negative energy or unwelcome entities get swept away from you.

Chill Out Spell

Use this spell when matters have boiled over, and you want some person(s) to calm down and think before saying or doing anything more. (You can cast this spell for yourself and/or for other people, depending on your tradition's rules for magic.) For this spell, you will need a picture or other symbol of the overwrought person(s), a symbol for the contentious matter, blue thread, a plastic freezer carton, and some water.

First, hold the symbols of the person and the issue together and tie them with blue thread. Then say:

Mind over matter,
Cool down the chatter.

Put the symbols inside the freezer carton and fill the carton with water. Then say:

Power of water, fresh and cold,
Put words and deeds safely on hold.

Place the carton of water in the freezer. Visualize ice forming to inhibit hasty, hot-headed words or actions that might be regretted later.

Leave the carton in the freezer for one to three days, enough time for the matter to settle down. Then take it out and let it thaw. Dump out the water into your yard or a body of water, allowing communication to flow.

∽

Water magic relies on the emotional self and the soul, along with natural bodies of water, for its power. You can use water energy to cleanse and protect yourself, your home and things, and the waters of the Earth. The healthier our wild waters, the more power they can share with us and the healthier we will be as well. The closer your relationship to the water spirits, the more likely it is that they will manifest when you need them and lend their energy to your magical workings. Therefore, a successful water Witch regularly sets aside time to work for the protection of water bodies and to commune with the spirits of water.

For Further Study

Asiya. "Water Correspondences." Asiya's Shadows. http://www.asiya.org/article.php/WaterCorrespondences (accessed June 23, 2009).

Black, Enodia. "Ice Magick." Llewellyn Journal. http://www.llewellynjournal.com/article/1330 (accessed June 23, 2009).

Cunningham, Scott. *Earth, Air, Fire & Water*. Woodbury, MN: Llewellyn Publications, 1991.

———. *Earth Power*. Woodbury, MN: Llewellyn Publications, 1983.

CyberAngler. "Tide Predictions." http://www.cyberangler.com/weather/tides/ (accessed June 23, 2009).

de Villiers, Marq. *Water: The Fate of Our Most Precious Resource*. Boston: Mariner Books, 2001.

Emoto, Masaru. David A. Thayne, tr. *The Hidden Messages in Water*. New York: Atria Books, 2005.

iSerenity. "iSerenity Environments" (specifically, environmental sounds "Waterfall Whisper," "Roaring Ocean," "Wailing Whales," "Thunder and Lightning," "A Warm Relaxing Shower," "Rain," and "Bubbling Brook"). http://www.iserenity.com/environments.htm (accessed June 23, 2009).

Twig Boat Magick

by Melanie Marquis

It seldom rained where I grew up in southern Arizona, but when it did, I would race outside after the storm to play a special secret game. Kneeling on the wet sidewalk, a pile of sticks at my side, I'd sit with my back to the house and watch the rain stream along the gutter, carrying away my little twig "boats" as I tossed them into the stream, each imparted with its own significance. Whether you call it Pooh sticks (from *The House at Pooh Corner*) or a simple childhood pastime, there is something truly magickal about twig boats. From cauldron stirring to wandwork to scratching mystical symbols on the dusty ground, twigs are essential tools in magick. Gifts from the sacred trees that shed them, twigs are full of magickal power, and twig boat magick unleashes this force. Combining the energy of twigs with the energies of that most creative element, water, produces real results. Twig boat magick is easy magick that really works, providing a versatile medium through which to magickally better your life.

Pick Up Sticks

The first thing to do is select your twig. You can let your intuition choose—walk outside and pick up the stick you find most appealing—or you can take a more methodical approach, choosing twigs based on thickness, age, length, flexibility, color, texture, shape, or type of wood. A heavier, thick twig is good for magick intended to slow or to bring strength. A thin twig is preferable for magic to bring swiftness or to lighten burdens. A straight twig will keep matters on a forward course, while a bent or curved twig can cause a U-turn in circumstances. A twig with a forked end is useful in magick meant to bring clarity to a decision between two options. Forked twigs are also good in spells with two targets, for instance, a spell to improve both work relationships and family relationships. A flexible twig eases transitions and encourages transformation, change, and adaptability. A sturdy twig that can't be bent is good for magic to guard, to bring determination, or to preserve the status quo. Light-colored twigs can be used for "positive" magick such as attracting and healing, while dark-colored twigs can be used for banishing or defensive spells. Older twigs are used to shed the old or to bring the end of a cycle, while young twigs bring fresh ideas and new developments. Twig texture can also be considered: smooth twigs are good in spells to make things run smoothly, while rough or thorny twigs are useful for disrupting negative patterns. In magick to reveal hidden truths or to increase spirituality, a twig with its bark peeled off provides effective symbolism. For long-term spells, choose long twigs, while short twigs are best for fast-acting magick.

You can even choose twigs based on wood type and tree lore. Pine is good for purification and prosperity, while holly is useful in magick dealing with underlying energies, spirituality, and psychic power. Oak brings action, energy, and courage. For love magick, mimosa, willow, or magnolia are preferred. You can take into consideration as many or as few attributes as you like when selecting your twigs, but your emotional response should be your ultimate guideline. If it feels like a good twig to use, it is.

Once you've chosen your twigs, it's time to let your magickal imagination set sail. Explore some of the basic ways to use twig boats in magick, and you'll soon be able to adapt and apply these methods to help achieve any goal.

To Attract

Twig boat magick can bring you your heart's desire. Infused with your wish and enchanted to attract it, an inconspicuous little twig boat will send out a powerful call to the life force on which it sails. Decide what you want to attract, then make a list of symbols you associate with this goal. Your list might include glyphs, colors, plants, names, numbers, keywords, or any other correspondences. Select the symbols you want to incorporate into the spell, and choose a twig to act as the vehicle. Enchant the twig by imparting to it the energies of those chosen symbols, sprinkling it with herbs, painting it with natural dyes, covering it with glyphs and words of power, or scratching certain numbers or patterns of notches into its bark. Thus charmed, the twig is now open to the guidance of your will. Hold the twig in your hand and fill it with intent. Envision the granting of your wish, and imagine the powers of nature coming into perfect alignment to bring you what you want. Say aloud, "Bring me this!" Toss the twig into a river or stream, and watch the magick glide merrily on its way.

To Banish

Flowing water cleanses as it carves through the landscape, and twig boat magick offers a powerful way to banish negativity. Whether you're feeling a little glum or you have a major crisis on your hands, troubles are banished more quickly and more completely when twig boat magick is employed. Covered in a magick coat, a twig boat sent downstream will carry off your burdens as the water washes it clean.

Create a mixture of mud and herbs chosen to symbolize the trouble you wish to banish. Select the herbs based on the plant's astrological associations, or keep it simple and use pepper or a similar spice as a representative of general negativity. Put some dirt in a large bowl or pot and add enough water to make a mud with the consistency of thick pancake batter. Cast in the herbs, thinking of your desire to banish your troubles. Stir counterclockwise, imagining harmful patterns reversing, baneful powers waning to nil. Carefully finger paint the muddy mix on an especially thorny or sharp-ended twig. Envision the "dirt" in your life being carried away by the cleansing river. Throw the twig into swift moving water as you say, "Wash away, mud!" and envision positive change.

Fast and Slow

Twig boat magick can be used to slow things down or to speed things up. A stick in mud slows progress and causes detours, and a twig boat sunk in shallow waters will help impede actions or occurrences you wish to halt. Sum up as completely and concisely as possible what you are hoping to hinder, and write this on a thick, heavy twig, followed by the word "stop." Bury the twig boat vertically like a sunken ship in the bed of a slow-moving river or stream, asserting aloud that the situation is stuck in the mud and cannot progress.

For swiftness in achieving your goals, choose a slender, springy twig and empower it with your wish, thinking of what you want coming to you quickly. Write the words "soon it will be!" down the length of the twig. Choose some herbs to represent resources you need to achieve your goal. Need more money, or more energy? Try cinnamon. Need cooperation, trust, or good health? Choose rosemary. Rub the herbs on the twig, thinking of how the river will carry off these particles to seek out and gather those elements you need for success. Toss the twig into fast-moving water and watch it speed away.

Stick Together

Looking for a magical way to attract love, or to bring two people closer together? Choose two twigs, one to repre-

sent each person or theoretical person the spell hopes to influence. You might have a specific person you want to be closer to, or you might have a desire to get closer with a lover as of yet unknown. How you prepare the twigs depends on your magickal goal. If you are looking for romance, use one twig to symbolize the type of partner you're looking for, and one twig to symbolize you. Write your full name on the twig that signifies you, and write the characteristics you look for in a love match on the other twig. If you are hoping to mend a broken friendship or encourage a faraway friend to move to a nearby town, write your full name on one of the twigs and your friend's full name on the other twig. Tie the twigs together, bundling them side by side. See yourself closer to your magickal goal; imagine standing next to the person or sort of person you seek. Toss the bundle into a lake or pond and say, "From now on, together!"

Branching Out

Twig boat magick offers endless variety and unlimited opportunities for personalization. Think up your own ways to magickally manipulate twigs. Decide for yourself what it would symbolize to snap a twig in two, what it would manifest to spear a leaf on the end of a twig. Would certain types of twig boat magick be best performed in an ocean or in a pond, in your bathtub, or perhaps in a mud puddle? Powerful hunches are the stuff new magick is made of, and whatever works for you personally will work in your magick. Although the great tree of magick is indeed universal, each part of the tree we inhabit is also individual, this branch angled toward the Sun, that branch bursting with new leaves. Each twig, and each magician, has unique powers and potential.

Polarity and Magic

by Deborah Lipp

Humans love to divide, define, and sort. From something as simple as yet another iteration of "there are two kinds of people in the world" (those who split the world into two kinds of people, and those who don't), to something as complex and intricate as the Kabbalah, we are constantly sorting, assigning, categorizing, and cataloging. Furthermore, this is a cross-cultural phenomenon; *everyone* does it.

Why? Because reality itself is a series of categories, beginning with the very simplest one: Is/Is Not. How do I know I'm typing on a computer? Because my computer is surrounded by Not Computer, my keyboard is sitting on Not Keyboard, and my fingers wiggle in an atmosphere of Not Fingers. Without Is/Is Not, there is no reality, there is simply an undifferentiated Oneness. And that Oneness may well be Nirvana, but sure it's hard to get anything done when you don't know where anything begins or ends, including your car keys. In order to wrap our human brains around the vast universe, we must separate things into categories, and Is/Is Not is the most basic of all.

That undifferentiated Oneness is, in more concrete terms, the universe as it existed before the Big Bang of creation. From that point on, we get *things*, we get a universe of this/that, either/or, and Goddess/God.

What is Polarity, Exactly?

Although we can begin by dividing the universe into Is/Is Not, polarity is more specific than that. My keyboard is not really *opposite* to my fingers, despite being Not Fingers. Polarity, specifically, is an energy and a way of describing the universe that depends on opposites in a state of balance and tension.

You can get all scientific about it (and Pagans who are focused on hard science certainly do), talking about positive and negative charges, attraction and repulsion, getting down to the atomic level. Historically, occultists have tended to describe polarity in terms of magnetism. Everything has a positive or negative charge, and the interaction between opposite charges creates power. In

magnetism, opposites attract with a power that can be irresistible. Take polar opposites—negative and positive—and place them on terminals with a wire between and you have a battery, an energy source.

There are many examples of polarity that don't require you to have paid attention in your high school science classes. There is polarity between day and night, between cold and heat, and, quite obviously, between male and female.

From a magical point of view, the basic principle is this: energy flows whenever polar opposites interact.

Opposite forces bind together, creating an energy source. Finding ways to connect opposites is a source of power. This basic truth is intensely useful in magic and ritual.

East Meets West

Many occult concepts of the Far East diverge widely from Western concepts. Western astrology is entirely unlike Chinese astrology, and the Western four (or five) elements do not correspond to the five Chinese elements.

But the Western magical concept of polarity is strikingly similar to the Eastern concept of Yin and Yang.

The familiar symbol for Yin and Yang is a circle divided into dark and light sections that fit together. In the dark section is a spot of light, and vice versa. Here we see two comments on polarity: first, that the dark and light sides are parts of a greater whole—the circle that surrounds them; second, that each contains its opposite—Yang (light, male, day, extroversion, hot) contains a spot of Yin (dark, female, night, introversion, cold), and vice versa. Nothing, then, is purely one or the other.

In Eastern philosophy, the "yinness" or "yangness" of a person or thing changes based upon its current relationship. Gray is Yang (light) in relation to black, but Yin (dark) in relation to white.

Polarity and Gender

Gender is normally the first perception of polarity that we all share. When a baby is born, we may ask, "Boy or girl?" even before we remember that the more important questions are "Healthy baby?" and "Healthy mom?" Social perception divides everything in the world according to gender.

In Yin/Yang philosophy, Yin is female and Yang is male, but of course Yin contains Yang, as Yang contains Yin. Similarly, in Western Occultism, the polar energies of gender are thought to reverse as we traverse the planes of existence: female energy has a negative charge on the physical plane, positive on the lower astral, negative again on the upper astral, and so on.[1]

Polarity, Love, Sex

We started out talking about the Oneness of the universe, and now we're talking about sex. They're not that far apart. The universe divides into Is/Is Not, and one way we understand that is through gender; female is Not Male; male is Not Female, and society gets very stressed out about anything that complicates that formula. Two people coming together in ecstatic sexual union seems, momentarily, to erase the divided nature of reality and make us one again. This sexual/polar tension is described by Aleister Crowley in the *Book of the Law*[2] like this:

1. Janet Farrar and Stewart Farrar. *The Witches' Way: Principles, Rituals and Beliefs of Modern Witchcraft.* London: Robert Hale, 1984.

2. Aleister Crowley. *The Book of the Law, Liber al vel legis.* York Beach, ME: Weiser Books, 1987.

For I am divided for love's sake, for the chance of union.
This is the creation of the world, that the pain of division is as
nothing, and the joy of dissolution all.

Crowley is definitely going straight for the sex here, and the love as well, but he also alludes to something a little less obvious: the push/pull of polar tension, the desire to be both this and that.

This *and* that. Because if we are not divided, we cannot play with the division, we cannot gaze with love and mystery at someone who is ultimately Other. Without division, we cannot create; we can only be.

Of course, the joy of dissolution doesn't exist only with heterosexual union. We can find polar energies in any relationship that breaks apart (we are two individuals) and comes together (we are ecstatically One). Love and sexual ecstasy are experiences that transcend the binary nature of gender, and teach us something of polarity: division and dissolution is love's true nature, not the labels we put on the divided parts.

The Space Between

One concept that is incredibly important in working with polarity is that of liminal space—the space between two states. Thus, twilight and dawn are times of immense power, because they stand between night and day. People who transcend typical perceptions of gender and gender roles, GLBT people (gay-lesbian-bisexual-transgendered), are often considered to have liminal power as well. Shamans were historically known as powerful individuals who could navigate the space between the human realm and other realms.

Using Polar Power

Looking at a twenty-four-hour day helps delineate ways of working with polarity. The times of greatest occult power are noon and midnight, when each pole is at its peak, and dawn and dusk, when the undefined space between poles holds sway. The same is true of the year: equinoxes and solstices mark between-space, dividing seasons and astrological signs, while the four holidays known to Wiccans as the Greater Sabbats are centers of their seasonal moments—Beltane is the height of spring, Lammas the peak of summer, Samhain the center of autumn, and Imbolc the dead of winter.

In other words, polar power happens when a polar energy is fully itself, and it happens in the balanced liminal state between poles.

Crowley's quote gives us another clue as to accessing polar power: the pain of division and the joy of dissolution, or, the pain of division *followed by* the joy of dissolution. What does this mean?

Polar objects, energies, and people can be divided in ritual and magic, and then brought together. They can be balanced, or they can be forced out of balance. They can be separated, and then reunited.

Balance

In general, if you're working with polarity, you should start with as much balance as possible, so that a shift in that balance will make ripples in the energy. For example, make sure everything on your altar is in perfect balance. A cup is female/Yin, an athame is male/Yang. If you add another male tool, what female tool will you add?

You can balance people, of course, by physical gender or by the roles they play in ritual. You can balance colors ("hot" with

"cool"), and you can even balance your incenses (any reference book on herbs and magic can give you the gender of your incense ingredients).

Wicca generally balances tools, people, and behaviors. For example, in some rituals, men and women do not hand things to each other; touching is always passed through the polar filter, so if there are three women and one man in a rite, that man is kept busy—visualize passing a cup around the circle, where the man has to tuck himself between every pair of women, or walk the cup around so only polar opposites touch.

Another way you can engineer this is for men, and only men, to handle all female tools, and vice versa.

In a women-only or men-only ritual, you could experiment with removing all the opposite-gender tools from the altar, so as to work only with the single pole represented by one gender. Or, you could choose to remove all the *same*-gender tools and have the people themselves represent that pole; a women's circle could have only male tools in use, allowing the women to form specific polar relationships with each tool.

More common, though, is for the altar to remain balanced and the ritualists to find a polar balance within themselves; women finding, perhaps, a better connection to their own Yang.

Balance is powerful in and of itself, even without a shift in energies. It creates a sense of wholeness and power, and the closed circuit of Yin-to-Yang can crackle with electricity.

Separating and Coming Together

Oh, the pain of division, followed by the joy of dissolution. It's kind of like a pressure cooker—without a lid, it's just heat. Heat is powerful, but *with* a lid, it's an explosion waiting to happen. And that's *powerful.* The lid, in this case, is the separation; the artificial pulling apart of two opposites that attract, so that when they at last come together, wham! Water never tastes so good, sleep so luxurious, or conversation so lively as when you've been without it for a long time.

When I perform a handfasting for a man and a woman, I encourage the bride and groom to be apart for at least three days prior to the ceremony; no sex, no sleeping together. Absence truly makes the heart grow fonder. During the ceremony, all instructions to the bride are given by the Priestess, and all instructions to the groom are given by the Priest. Everything for the bride is female, everything for the groom is male, and at last, during the ceremonial blessing of cakes and wine, the bride holds a female tool (the cup) and the groom holds a male tool (the athame), and, having had every physical and symbolic aspect of their polarity separated for as long as possible, the athame is plunged into the cup, while the loving couple gazes into each other's eyes. Wham!

Liminal Space

When using liminal space, you are using the absence of normal notions of polar power to find a new source of power. It is the space of mystery. Dawn, which is neither day nor night; New Year's Eve, which is neither this year nor next year; and androgyny, neither male nor female, are all examples of the anti-polarity that can be used in magic and ritual.

Because liminality is ambiguous, it is thought to contain the capacity for freedom and change. You are not stuck in your proscribed role during liminal time, and so it can be a time of transformation. Rites of passage are specifically liminal rites; during the rite, you are neither child nor adult, single nor married, initate nor non-initiate, or whatever passage is being marked. Thus you are in a highly receptive state in which you can be changed utterly. When Wiccans cast a circle that is "between the worlds," they are consciously creating liminal space so that power can be raised and transformation can occur within.

Perhaps the most powerful liminal states are pregnancy and childbirth: In pregnancy, you are not quite yet a parent, and yet not *not* a parent. In labor, you are still not quite yet a parent, and yet not quite just pregnant either. Every mother can recall the power of this magical, stressful, exhausting, and powerful "third being" she has been.

Liminal space is also blended space, where poles combine in ways that may be counterintuitive, baffling, or unexpected. A rarely discussed example of this is in the celebration of the Pagan holiday Imbolc (February 1 or 2). In many Pagan celebrations, and even in the mundane Groundhog's Day that occurs at the same time, springtime and warm weather are the focus. Yet it is often the darkest and coldest part of winter (in the Northern Hemisphere, in temperate regions). In direct opposition to Imbolc on the wheel of the year is Lammas, or Lughnasadh, on August 1 or 2. Here, at the peak of summer's heat (again, in the Northern Hemisphere), death and darkness are often the focus. These two holidays use liminality by introducing the opposite of the obvious as the core of the rite; the darkness during light, and

the light during darkness. Yule is a festival of lights despite occurring on the longest night of the year.

Another example is that of ritual cross-dressing. This is found in numerous British Pagan festival traditions,[3] and functions to bring a transitional (as well as a transgressive) blending of polarities to Pagan celebrations.

Sex and Sexuality

When people talk about polarity, they mostly head straight for the sex. By now we've seen that polarity is more than that; it's an energy, experienced in days and nights, in seasons, and in transitions. It's an energy symbolized in magical tools and magical behaviors.

Nothing, *nothing* so powerfully channels the energies of polarity as do the things that happen with gendered bodies. Polar energy is a part of physical gender, it is a part of sexual arousal and sexual fulfillment, and it is a part of love. People sometimes mistakenly assume that all three of these things (gender, arousal, and love) always align the same way, or should do so, or that polarity-based systems *think* they should.

Let's start by talking about the physical body. Our bodies generate magical energies, just as they generate pheromones and other secretions. Polar energy is generated from the physical

---

3. Ronald Hutton. *Stations of the Sun: A History of the Ritual Year in Britain.* New York and Oxford: Oxford University Press, 1996.

body: female/Yin energy from women's bodies, and male/Yang energy from male bodies.

In Wicca and other occult paths, this energy is used by having people work in partnerships of a man and a woman. Many people consider a romantic couple the ideal partnership; others prefer their magical partner and life partner to be two different people.

My magical partner is a heterosexual man who is married (and quite monogamous!) to one of my best friends. She, in turn, works magically with a gay man. Obviously, neither of these working partnerships is romantic or sexual, but they generate a great deal of gender polarity, and that polarity is not dependent on sexual orientation any more than it is dependent on romance.

What do working partners do? Basically, any magic and ritual at all, if performed by such a pair, accesses the magical power of polarity to heighten the event.

In any relationship between friends, there is a complementary quality. My partner has, in personality, many Yin traits—he is gentle, compassionate, and soft-spoken. He is also optimistic and musical. I, on the other hand, have many Yang traits—I am forceful, extroverted, and comfortable making and enforcing rules. I am also a little cynical and highly verbal. His male Yang and personal Yin complement my female Yin and personal Yang. The polarity that we share is individual to our relationship, and it works for us.

It's important to recognize that the energy of polarity is arousing; indeed, *any* energy is arousing. It's not at all unusual to become aroused at a drum circle, or at a concert, or even when working on a particularly fascinating project—the movement of energy and the awakened life force touch us sexually just as they touch us everywhere else. Polarity is an extra "oomph" of arousal on top of that. We need to be conscious of this if we're working with a partner with whom it is inappropriate to fool around, so that we can process the feeling without acting on it or being overwhelmed by it.

Where do transgendered people fit into a gender polarity system? I have not found any hard and fast rules. Some transgendered people will choose to eschew polarity work entirely. Most seem to find that their bodies resonate energetically to their inner gender, even if their physical genitalia don't match. The truth is, we know little about *how* gender energy is generated or about its relationship to the physical; we also know little about why a person is transgendered and how *that* might relate to biochemical energy. I think it's a situation in which unigendered people (people born in a body that matches their gender experience) need to listen to and respect the experience of transgendered people, and not try to come up with Two Sizes Fit All rules.

Because there is such a thing as gender polarity, a lot of people assume that sexual polarity is, by definition, heterosexual. Not so! Sexual polarity is the ebb and flow, the I and Thou of pleasurable interaction culminating (sometimes, anyway) in union and dissolution. Penetration, for just one obvious example, is inherently polar, no matter how it occurs, regardless of whatever body parts happen to be employed. Even in sex within a heterosexual couple, polarity can be played with and exchanged; if you think of Yin as "receptive" and Yang as "active," you can see that there are moments during most sexual experiences where poles are traded between partners.

Sex magic is not necessarily polar, but polarity energy can be added to the power by consciously choosing balance, separation, and merging. Likewise, sex is not necessarily a part of a polar working, but it can be added when both partners are willing.

Finally, let's talk about love. Referring again and again, as I do, to my favorite Crowley quote, I know that the pain of division is *all about* love. Love, ultimately, is our living, mortal experience of transcendent Oneness. We live our lives separate and apart, except for those moments when we touch the infinite by truly merging with another human being. In the act of making love with a beloved, we feel our souls and bodies are one within ourselves and with each other. This goes beyond polarity, back to the basic notion of division: Is/Is Not. We both are and are not our beloved.

Love, again, is not confined to gender, nor to romance. When I look within myself, I know I have experienced transcendent love in the arms of a partner, but I have also experienced it as the mother of a child, and most profoundly, I have felt it in my love of the gods. In Wicca, love of human for human is used as a means to access the transcendent love that brings us closer to the Divine.

The Healing Magic
of the Dinnshenchas

by Michelle Skye

It is not easy to find information on the Dinnshenchas[1] (pronounced Din-sheen-k'has), Irish faeries in service to the goddess Aine. When searching through the traditional old faery standards—Kathryn Briggs, Lady Gregory, W. B. Yeats, Robert Kirk, Thomas Keightley, and W. Y. Evans-Wentz—they are curiously absent. In fact, it is not until more modern times that you see the dinnshenchas briefly mentioned in dictionaries and encyclopedias on the citizens of the faery realm.[2] They abound across the Internet as well, always elusive, always on the very edge of the information, as if they were an afterthought—"Oh, and by the way, there are these faeries in Ireland known as the dinnshenchas."

Some scholars in the metaphysical community, upon finding information notably scarce, would scoff at the existence of the dinnshenchas, preferring to rely upon the information in moldy leather books with dusty pages. And while I am a lover of leather books (although not of mold), I prefer to think of the dinnshenchas as unrealized, untapped energy that has yet to be fully understood here in the mortal realm. Think about it. Scientists discover new plants and plant species all the time. In India alone, from 1954 to 2008, 850 new plants have been discovered![3] And that's right here on planet Earth, where we can see and touch and

---

1. Not to be confused with the Irish place name stories of the same name.

2. See Edain McCoy's *A Witch's Guide to Faery Folk* (St. Paul, MN: Llewellyn, 1996), p. 206 and Ann Franklin's *The Illustrated Encyclopedia of Faeries* (London: Vega Publishers, 2002), p. 66.

3. Web Newswire, "Richness of Biodiversity ~ Plant Discoveries – 2008," Business desk, May 28, 2009, http://www.webnewswire.com/node/455765 (accessed September 2009).

smell everything! The possibilities in the infinite, in the Otherworld, are staggering.

Yet, even as I drag the dinnshenchas out of secrecy kicking and screaming, part of me wonders if they don't prefer anonymity. They are shape-shifters, after all, comfortable in many guises. Some sources claim they are small, ugly men, others call them dwarves, and still others claim no known physical form. In my work, they have taken the form of women clothed in streams of light. They are small or big, as the situation suits them, and they always seem to be moving quickly. Due to their speed, it is hard to get a good look at them. The long hair and light dresses that my human eyes see may actually be the trailing form of their essences, spread out behind them like a long comet's tail as they burst from one place to the next. In my work, they almost always appear to be yellow or flamelike in color, with tinges of peach or sherbert orange.

The dinnshenchas' main mission is protection. They protect cattle, animals sacred to the goddess Aine, and women, especially women who are in precarious situations. In the eighth-century text "The Battle of Mag Mucrama," Aine was forced to lie with the warrior King Ailill.[4] Her rape connects Aine, and the faeries serving under her, to all women undergoing violence and devastation at the hands of men. For this reason, the dinnshenchas not only protect women, but they also avenge them when they have been wronged. Just as Aine fought against Ailill by biting and mutilating his ear, the dinnshenchas punish those who have hurt and wronged women. At the same time, they serve to bolster the strength and resolve of the women who have been abused, helping them to heal from the experience.

If you, or someone you know, have been through a violating experience, the dinnshenchas can offer a measure of peace and calm. They will not be a substitute for professional therapy but can, instead, be a supplement to more traditional ways of healing. After all, you're only going to go to the therapist a few times or maybe just once a week, so that leaves plenty of hours empty.

Being fire faeries and light faeries, serving a goddess who is associated with the Sun, the dinnshenchas are most attracted to

---

4. Michelle Skye, *Goddess Alive*, Woodbury, MN: Llewellyn, 2007, p. 96–97.

candle magic or any activity utilizing bright and shiny items—quartz crystals, mirrors, reflecting bowls, brass chimes, and so on. I also believe they have a connection to the broom tree. Broom is powerful healing tree that is mentioned in many ancient Celtic poems and books. It blooms in summer with a profusion of small yellow flowers, linking it to the Sun and the light aspect of healing. At the same time, broom is mentioned in the Welsh poem "The Cad Goddeu" or "The Battle of the Trees." In the poem, broom is seen to fight and become hurt in the ensuing battle. Yet broom lives on, just as all who have been wounded—emotionally, physically, and mentally—live on, nursing their wounds until they can become whole again. To me, broom is the perfect companion for a healing journey through the labyrinthine passageways of abuse. It is a tree of hope as well as a tree of strength.

Candle Healing

Candle healing magic works to connect the wounded person to the energy of fire. Fire is lively and energizing and exciting. Fire is life, in one of its most elemental forms. It can be scary to allow fire into your life after an abusive experience. After all, our initial response is to close down, close up, and shelter our fragile psyches. We want to protect ourselves, emotionally and physically, from ever encountering a similar experience. And, while this is a normal reaction, eventually it is necessary to begin to open up again. We, as human beings, cannot stay closed off forever, otherwise we suffer from depression and loneliness. Humans are social animals; we need to interact with each other in heartfelt, meaningful ways.

You can begin with any color candle you wish. Perhaps you choose pink for divine love or green for healing or red for stability and security. It doesn't matter, as long as you feel comfortable with your choice. Since I work a lot with the chakras (energy centers in the body), I would probably begin with a red candle, as red is the color for the first chakra. As my healing progressed, I would open up the chakras in order, infusing each with fire energy through the appropriately colored candle.

Whatever color you choose, take some time when you are alone to prepare your candle. Hold your candle and state aloud your intention of healing and welcoming the energy of fire. Take

some time to really feel connected to this intention. When you feel ready, rub your candle with oil and light it. Watch the flame dance and sway. Feel the flame's heat. Hear the gentle pop or fizzle as the candle wax melts. Imagine that any resistance to healing melts away from you just as the wax melts away from the flame. The first time, try to stay connected for at least five minutes, building up time incrementally as you continue the candle exercise throughout the upcoming days or weeks.

Before you snuff out the flame, cup your hands around the base of the candle. Slowly pull your hands upward, following the length of the candle. When you get above the flame, hold your hands there, gathering the fire energy. You may feel the warmth of the flame or you may see an actual ball of energy pulsing between your hands. Take that energy, that warmth, and place it inside your body by laying your hands on yourself. You can place them on your heart, your stomach, on a corresponding chakra, or on any place that feels like it needs the warmth of fire. Allow the energy to seep into your body, awaking and enlivening you. When you are done, snuff out the candle and save it for another time when you'd like to welcome the healing energy of fire.

Reflective Healing

There are so many ways to perform healings using reflective surfaces, but one of my favorites is deceptively simple and profound. First, find yourself a small, hand-held mirror. It should be small enough to easily fit in your purse, in the back pocket of your jeans, or the glove compartment of your car. Try to find a mirror that you find visually appealing, whether in color, design, or decoration.

Anoint the reflective surface of your mirror with oil. It can be any scent that calls to you personally, but I recommend cinnamon oil. Cinnamon is a spice associated with fire and the Sun. It harmonizes nicely with the energy of the dinnshenchas, working with their goals of protection and healing, while adding an element of success. It also has a lovely, strong smell that will remind you of these goals throughout the day.

After you have anointed your mirror and allowed the oil to dry, gaze into the reflective surface. You may only be able to see a small portion of your face due to the size of the mirror, so be sure to focus on your eyes. When you are gazing into your own eyes, say "I love you," three times. You can do this aloud or inside your head, but it is important to actually formulate the words. Take your time with the speaking or thinking of the "I love you" phrase, as you are reminding yourself that you are worth loving. You are letting yourself feel love in safe surroundings. You are telling yourself that you deserve love, for you are a child of the Divine.

You can choose to get out your mirror and say "I love you" as many times as you feel are necessary. Don't force yourself but also don't limit yourself. This is a powerful affirmation that should be done only when you feel ready. Once you do it, you will be amazed by the positive changes that take place in your psyche and in your life.

Tree Healing: Scotch Broom (*Cytisus scoparius*)

(Do not confuse Scotch broom with Spanish broom or butcher's broom, as they are all different plants. All brooms can be toxic if ingested in large doses and should be avoided by anyone who is pregnant or has hypertension.)

Scotch broom is not any easy herb to find dried and packaged.[5] Your best bet may be to consult your local herb shop. Note that Scotch broom is native to Europe and considered an invasive species in the United States, as it will crowd out native plants and destroy habitats. Scotch broom is fairly common on the East and West Coasts of the United States—where you may be able to harvest it wild—but hasn't yet spread very far into the interior of the country. It is not recommended that you plant Scotch broom in the Americas. An herbal shop may have it on the shelves and, if not, they may be able to special order it for you.

Once you've found your dried Scotch broom, use it as an incense. You can burn it by itself or in conjunction with other herbs (perhaps lavender for relaxation or chamomile for peace and calm). Whenever you begin to feel stressed and anxious, unable to cope with the many emotions whirling inside you, take five minutes out of your day for a "Broom Incense Break." Fill a bowl with some sand (or use an incense charcoal holder), and place your charcoal disc on the sand or incense holder. Light the charcoal disc and, once it is glowing, sprinkle on some broom. Breathe in the scent and breathe out your anxiety. Continue adding the dried herb onto the charcoal disk. Continue to breathe. Continue to release. Once you are feeling more centered and relaxed, dispose of the disk and store your herbs in a cool, dark place.

For each of these healing techniques, feel free to call on and ask for the aid of the dinnshenchas and the goddess Aine. They are here for you and are willing to help. Here is a small invocation for you to do by itself or along with the healing techniques described above.

I call on the magic of the dinnshenchas—
Protecting, healing, and supporting.
I honor you, as I honor your goddess, Aine,
And as I honor myself.
May your strength be with me now
And in all my times of trial.
Blessed Be.

---

5. I did, however, find some online at: http://www.capricornslair.com/broomtopcut1.html

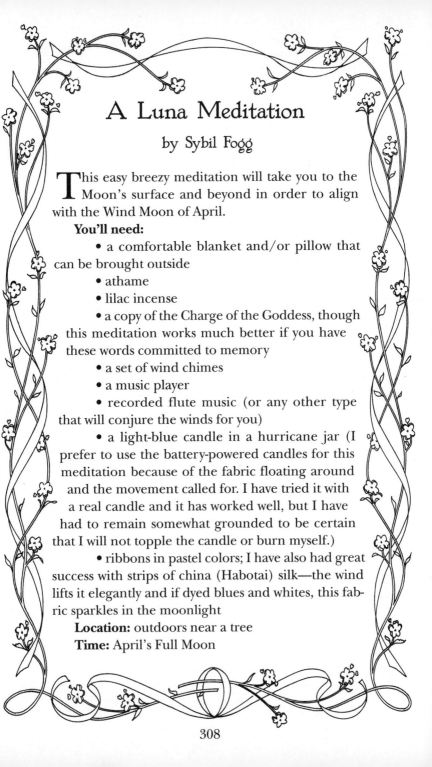

A Luna Meditation

by Sybil Fogg

This easy breezy meditation will take you to the Moon's surface and beyond in order to align with the Wind Moon of April.

You'll need:

• a comfortable blanket and/or pillow that can be brought outside

• athame

• lilac incense

• a copy of the Charge of the Goddess, though this meditation works much better if you have these words committed to memory

• a set of wind chimes

• a music player

• recorded flute music (or any other type that will conjure the winds for you)

• a light-blue candle in a hurricane jar (I prefer to use the battery-powered candles for this meditation because of the fabric floating around and the movement called for. I have tried it with a real candle and it has worked well, but I have had to remain somewhat grounded to be certain that I will not topple the candle or burn myself.)

• ribbons in pastel colors; I have also had great success with strips of china (Habotai) silk—the wind lifts it elegantly and if dyed blues and whites, this fabric sparkles in the moonlight

Location: outdoors near a tree

Time: April's Full Moon

To prepare: Lay out the blanket and pillow in an area that is illuminated by moonlight and hang the ribbons by tying them around a tree branch. Hang the wind chimes as well. Burn the incense and prepare your chosen music.

Ritual

Cast the circle in the way you normally do. Then sit on the blankets with the candle in front of you, and light it. Gaze into the candle's flame and clear your mind.

Listen for the wind chimes over the music. Really work to hear them clearly until all other sounds are drowned out. Use this concentration to move into yourself. Feel darkness surround you so that all that is visible is the flicker of the candle. Follow the twinkling of the wind chimes. Go deep with the sound.

Embrace your inner self and feel light fill you. Grow with light and sound. Your arms are stretching, your muscles strong, your feet powerful. You could leap to the Moon if you wanted. Now, it's time to follow your instinct.

Spend some time traveling to the Moon in your imagination. Whether you need to go there via a spacecraft or by flying, go with the flow. Sometimes I have let my mind take me deep into this journey, and travel through space has been akin to swimming. The darkness and thickness of the air reminds one of the womb and I have felt great support by accepting the Great Mother's embrace and letting go.

Once you have arrived at the Moon, walk around. Explore. Make mental notes of all that is around you. What does the air smell like? What does the ground feel like? Is there water visible? Is it hot or cold? Are you warm enough?

Raise your arms in front of you and feel the air around you shift as your hands move above you. There is a breeze starting at your feet and working its way around your ankles, knees, hips, thighs, waist, chest, shoulders, neck, chin, and ears to the top of your head.

On the physical plane, allow your body to rock with the air pushing it. Sway back and forth. Roll your head around your neck. Lift one shoulder up toward your ear and then push it back, down, and around forward. Do the same with the other shoulder. Repeat as many times as you feel necessary. Push your chest from side to side. Push a little farther so that you feel your spine working. Let every movement continue together.

On the spiritual plane, guide the winds with your hands. Catch it between your palms. Bring it to your chest and heart and disperse it by laying your palms against your body. Repeat as many times as it takes to fill your soul with the Moon's winds. Feel yourself filling with the Goddess. Imagine you are covering your being with a silver and blue shimmer. Feel this glitter work its way into your skin.

Make sure your body in the shared existence is still alive. Move onto your knees and continue swaying back and forth. Make a wide circle with your torso. Push yourself from side to front to side to back and

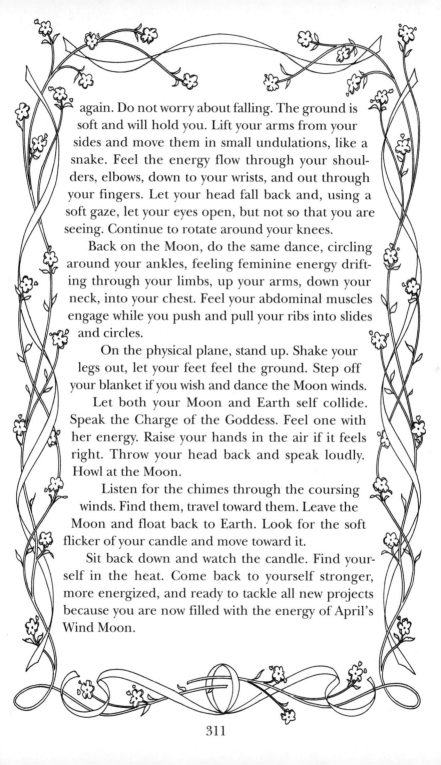

again. Do not worry about falling. The ground is soft and will hold you. Lift your arms from your sides and move them in small undulations, like a snake. Feel the energy flow through your shoulders, elbows, down to your wrists, and out through your fingers. Let your head fall back and, using a soft gaze, let your eyes open, but not so that you are seeing. Continue to rotate around your knees.

Back on the Moon, do the same dance, circling around your ankles, feeling feminine energy drifting through your limbs, up your arms, down your neck, into your chest. Feel your abdominal muscles engage while you push and pull your ribs into slides and circles.

On the physical plane, stand up. Shake your legs out, let your feet feel the ground. Step off your blanket if you wish and dance the Moon winds.

Let both your Moon and Earth self collide. Speak the Charge of the Goddess. Feel one with her energy. Raise your hands in the air if it feels right. Throw your head back and speak loudly. Howl at the Moon.

Listen for the chimes through the coursing winds. Find them, travel toward them. Leave the Moon and float back to Earth. Look for the soft flicker of your candle and move toward it.

Sit back down and watch the candle. Find yourself in the heat. Come back to yourself stronger, more energized, and ready to tackle all new projects because you are now filled with the energy of April's Wind Moon.

Working with Water Spirits

by Elizabeth Barrette

Numerous spirits and deities are connected with water. Elemental spirits are typically sorted by the type of water they inhabit. Lesser elementals are bound to a particular pool, stream, or other specific body of water. Greater elementals may manifest more freely, either within any type of water body or wherever water is available. Deities typically relate to their home culture and region, but some range more widely. They may oversee water in general, types of water bodies, or specific water features.

Chac: The Mayan god of rain, thunder, and lightning is also called "He Who Gives Food to Others." He gave maize, or corn, to the Mesoamerican cultures. Today, some Christian Maya farmers still pray to Chac for rain in times of drought.

Gwragedd Annwn: Unlike many water spirits, these Welsh faeries are benevolent. They love children and like human women, so they are very helpful to mothers. They keep magical gardens and villages beneath lakes. They are very beautiful. It is said they sometimes take human husbands, but will flee if mistreated. Their faery nature shows in odd behavior (laughing at funerals is a famous example) and according to legend, they can bear children, so these traits may appear in humans with fey ancestry.

Hapy: The Egyptian god of inundation oversaw the Nile River and its annual flood cycle. The floods fertilized and irrigated Egyptian fields, making it possible for people to grow more food there. Honor Hapy if you live near a big river whose changes dominate local life.

Latis: This English lake goddess later gained associations with mead and other intoxicating beverages. She represents knowledge and the responsible use of water for human needs. Brewers pray to her for a lively brew.

Limniads: These water nymphs live in mountain lakes and springs. Their name comes from the Greek *limh,* meaning "pool." Limniads of cold lakes and springs tend to be aloof and indifferent to human needs. Limniads of hot springs can be exuberant and passionate but careless of human fragility.

Merfolk: These water spirits take a half-human, half-fish form. The females are called "mermaids" while the males are called "mermen" or "tritons." They usually live in salt water, although some mermaids have been reported in rivers or lakes. Mermaids can sing to enchant human men, often to their deaths; they may be indifferent to or jealous of human women. Mermen can blow conch shells to control sea animals and the weather. Although some merfolk are friendly, they often come

into conflict with humans, so associating with them poses some risks. Related subtypes, such as the lorelei, can be wholly dangerous.

Naiads: Greek water nymphs who live in lakes and ponds. Among the most common water spirits, naiads can work well with people if treated respectfully. They stick to natural bodies of water.

Nereids: The fifty daughters of Nereus are water nymphs associated with the seas. Traditionally, propitiatory rites would encourage them to bring fair currents and abundant fish, and to withhold harm from ships and sailors.

Nixies: Also called nix, these freshwater spirits inhabit rivers and lakes. They cause mischief, such as untying or tipping small boats, scaring away fish, or splashing people with cold water. They cannot control the weather, as can some greater elementals, and they are rarely as dangerous as the aquatic huntresses.

Oceanids: The many daughters of Oceanus and Tethys are water nymphs connected with the oceans. More than three thousand of them maintain the oceans and also supervise lesser bodies of salt water. They have the ability to manifest in any salt water, including a bowl during a ritual (a good reason to use real sea salt). They can influence the currents, fish and ocean mammals, and sometimes even the weather. They may appear shy or passionate, as changeable as the tides. Although usually kind to mortals, they can unleash devastating anger on those who offend or abuse them.

Poseidon: The Greek god of the ocean often appears as a merman riding a chariot drawn by dolphins or fish. He commands all marine life and the weather over the oceans. He fancies beautiful women.

Undines: These water spirits take charge of all fresh waters such as streams, rivers, and lakes. However, they can manifest in any freshwater, including man-made bodies, such as wells, garden pools, or even a chalice of water during a ritual. Undines tend to be playful and carefree. The more powerful ones are more serious.

Water faeries: These spirits can pose great danger, especially to children. They come in many forms, but typically inhabit deep, still water or rushing rivers. The kelpie, for instance, resembles a horse or pony and carries its unsuspecting riders to their doom in its lake. Peg Powler is a green water hag who lives in the River Tees and drags people in to drown them.

Yemaya: In Yoruban and Afro-Caribbean traditions, she is the *loa* or ancestral goddess of the ocean, the fish, and the ties of family and community. Fishermen pray and make offerings to Yemaya in hopes of receiving fair weather and abundant fish.

For Further Study

Conway, D. J. *Magickal Mermaids and Water Creatures: Invoke the Magick of the Waters.* Franklin Lakes, NJ: Career Press, 2008.

Fairies World. "Spirits and Elements, Goblins Elfs and Gnomes." http://www.fairiesworld.com/spirits.shtml (accessed June 23, 2009).

Hawkins, Jaq D. *Spirits of the Water.* Sequim, WA: Holmes Publishing Group, 2001.

Divining Bowls

by Elizabeth Hazel

D ivining bowls can be made and used in many different ways, and are a terrific coven craft and kid craft project. This article offers a starting point for constructing divining and oracle bowls; you can explore and experiment with these and apply your personal taste, abilities, and creativity to this project. I've made several divining bowls over the years using a variety of techniques, craft materials, and surface designs, and have found them to be surprisingly effective devices.

Divining bowls are used in a random way to predict the future, and are unabashedly predictive tools. Unlike tarot cards or astrology, the past and present aren't considered: it's all about the future. Although there are many different possible methods, stones are usually thrown into the bowl. The future is determined by examining the position of the markers. Water, wax, ashes, or other elemental methods are further options.

Before designing a divining bowl, reflect on the elemental technique that suits you. If you're an earthy type or want to construct a traditional divining bowl, plan to toss stones or markers into the bowl. If you're a watery type of person, consider different methods for using water in or on a divining bowl. A fiery person can try incense or ashes, and an airy person may toss feathers or paper markers that dance on the surface of the bowl.

The surface of a divining bowl is covered with symbols or images. You can customize it for ritual uses, spiritual preferences, or just for fun. A traditional Witch may choose to decorate a bowl's surface with Witch runes or witchy symbols, whereas a heathen may use other runes. If you're using the bowl for a fun party game, words or familiar images offer quick and easy interpretations. Tailor the design to the purpose of the bowl, and adapt the design to the type of marker that will be used for divination.

Before starting this project, do some sketching and hone in on your personal preferences and objectives, as this will affect the materials you use and the divining techniques you select.

The Bowl

Start by making or buying a bowl. Platters with flat surfaces work very well if you're going to throw stones, as a large part of the surface can be decorated with images and the stones won't automatically slide toward the center. Find a ceramic, glass, wood, or plastic platter, plate, charger, tray, or a low-lipped bowl with a good-sized, flat center. The "bowl" doesn't have to be round; squares, ovals, and rectangles work, too. Crafters with access to a kiln can craft a bowl and markers out of clay. A divining bowl can even be constructed from a cardboard lid with low edges. Ceramic planter bottoms work very well, and are inexpensive and easy to decorate. If this is a kid's project, try using paper plates and three pennies. Make a creative choice that fits your style and intention, as well as your budget.

Design Elements

As options are unlimited, sketch a design for your divining bowl. Decide on the symbol set, and on how you want to divide the space on the surface of the bowl. One way to orient your bowl is to indicate the cardinal directions at the edges. The surface can be divided into sectors by quartering the space, with a pentagram, or with convex curves that bulge out from the edges. Specific meanings can be attributed to different spaces; for instance, zones could be labeled yes, no, soon, distant, void/nothing, and so on. Sectors can be filled with distinctive colors, and this can be an additional source of meaning.

The next step is to place symbols across the surface using paint, permanent markers, fabric, felt, or paper. If you prefer not to draw or paint, cut out pictures from magazines, or from computer-generated images or clip art. Exceptionally crafty Witches may choose to embroider a design on fabric. A fabric surface can be laid over the surface of a platter. If using fabric on its own, construct a flat "pillow" lined with quilt batting so markers will land on a lightly padded surface. (Although this is a slightly different project, I've embroidered lovely rune pads with design elements that add meaning to a rune cast.)

Symbols or images should be jumbled and scattered across the surface of the bowl. Symbol sets include runes (ogham, Witches' runes, and other alphabets), alchemical or astrological glyphs,

or numbers. You can also decorate the surface with meaningful shapes: star (hope), Moon (dreams), triangle (ideas), ray (inspiration), flame (swift results), square (stability), lightning bolt (unexpected events). These symbols work well if you're cutting and pasting shapes. You can also paint (or cut and glue) more specific images—four-leaf clover, heart, hands, rainbow, butterfly, spider and web, cat, dog, tree and leaf, rose or flower, dark clouds, rain, coins, snake, dove and crow, sword, mailbox, phone, or faces with clear expressions. Words are another option: yes, no, wish, trouble, happy, tears, money, debts, go, friends, stop, magic, or protection. A Celtic Pagan may scatter symbolic tree leaves across the surface. If you're into Victorian lore, cover the surface with different flowers and use a "language of the flowers" guide for interpretations.

For those who prefer a more integrated bowl surface, design a Tree of Life with various symbols scattered around it, or put different words or symbols on the leaves. Tarot readers can put the four suit symbols into quadrants, and scatter numbers around them. This is an amusing variation on tarot reading, as the markers will indicate cards to pull for a reading.

Symbols should be distributed evenly across the bowl's surface. With time and use, you'll become more adept at interpreting the meaning of the images in your divining bowl and can change and expand your original symbols' definitions.

Finishing the bowl will depend on the materials being used. If the surface has been painted, spray a finishing coat of clear polyurethane to protect it. Permanent pens on a planter bottom or cardboard don't need any further steps. If paper cutouts have been used, coat the images with a layer of decoupage or a light coat of clear polyurethane. (Experiment with a sample first; some spray paints may cause printed inks to run.)

Markers

Markers, or game pieces, offer endless choices. In the earth realm, quarter-sized flat stones work well, as do the flat glass beads used in flower vases. Or find three equal-sized flat tumbled stones. You can make all of the pieces identical, or make them distinctive. Symbols can be painted on the stones, for example, an *X* for yes, an *O* for no. (Red nail polish is good for this, and sticks well to stones and glass.) A third stone can be left blank to indicate a matter that isn't yet decided or subject to chance. Coins have heads or tails that can be read as yes/no. Regular dice, astro-dice, or markers with runes are also alternatives.

If you decide to use fire with your divining bowl, write a question on a small piece of paper, pierce it with an athame, light it on fire, and allow the ashes to float down to the surface of the bowl. Ashes falling from a sage smudge can be used in the same way. You can also use joss sticks, as the ashes fall in clumps rather than into piles of powder. Find an incense holder that will hold the incense stick straight so the ashes can fall in any direction.

There are different methods for using water with your bowl, too. Water can be sprinkled across the surface using an aspergillum (a bundle of fresh herbs, generally rue). Or fill the bowl with water and cast stones into it. If you want to combine fire and water, burn a candle and allow wax to dribble onto the surface of the water. Analyze the shapes and position of the wax drips.

Feathers, helicopter maple seeds, or flower petals can be used as markers in air divination. Similarly, quarter-sized cardboard disks can be made for casting and will float a bit before landing.

It's best to use three or five markers; too many markers will overcomplicate the divination process. Divining bowls are most effective when the markers highlight just a few symbols or zones on the bowl's surface. If divining bowls are new to you, start with a simple bowl concept. After you get the hang of using divining bowls, you can create more complex or intricate oracle bowls.

Casting Fortunes

Once a divining bowl is ready to use and you've decided on the markers you're going to use for divination, cleanse and consecrate the bowl. If your bowl is waterproof, wash it in cleansing salts. If not, smudge it with sage.

The easiest way to use a divining bowl is in a fun, uncomplicated way. Simply shake the markers in your hand or in a dice cup, toss them onto the surface of the bowl, and read the outcome. You may find that standing and dropping the markers from directly above works better than a seated throw. Examine the symbols highlighted by the cast, and think about what those symbols might predict about the future.

If you prefer a more involved practice, you can design a divining ritual. This might start with casting a protective circle around the divining bowl and evoking a particular totem or spirit to help answer a question. If you have a specific question, write it on a piece of paper and place it beneath the bowl before casting.

Get a small notebook to write down the date and results from your casts. Over time, this record will help you learn more about what your bowl's symbols mean.

$\sim$

Since divining bowls are easy to use, consider passing around a divining bowl at a sabbat ritual. These bowls are wonderful Yule gifts, and can be customized for your friends. You can make a Muggle-friendly divining bowl to take to psychic fairs, parties, and baby/bridal showers. Kinky Witches can create a divining bowl with options for erotic fun. A divining bowl can be beautiful or primitive, simple or elaborate, highly esoteric or mundane. The only limits are your creativity, the materials you select, and the rules you create for using it. Cast away and be blessed!

Owning the Fullness of Your Magical Power

by Tess Whitehurst

Sometimes we can get carried away with the obviously "fun" aspects of magic: the glittery light of a crystal, the shrouded mysteries of former lives, or the hypnotic beat of a ritual drum. And these are of course important things! But when we ignore or overlook the pain that we're still carrying around from our childhood, or the anger from an old romantic relationship, or feelings of fear or victimhood from any sort of violence that we've experienced, we're not fully in possession of our power. We're literally giving our power away to these old experiences and wounds.

I'm not for a moment suggesting that you should tell yourself or anyone else that it's "okay" that you were mistreated' in any way. What I *am* suggesting is that you should forgive, because in essence, when we don't forgive, we're saying that someone or something else has power over us. Not only that they have power over us, but also that they have the power to diminish *our* power: "You did this to me, and *because of you*, I am forever damaged and weakened."

When we forgive, on the other hand, we're reclaiming this power. We're saying, "It's not okay that you did this, but my power is not diminished because of it. In fact, I'm even more powerful that I otherwise would have been, because I've found it in my heart to forgive you and to release myself from the power you seemed to have over me."

For many years now, I've made a point of forgiving to the very best of my ability every old hurt that presents itself. And I, like almost everyone, have had a lot to forgive! I'm a child of divorce; was often attended by seemingly uncaring babysitters and step-parents; was sexually molested; was held at gunpoint during an attempted kidnapping; and experienced a physically abusive relationship.

Despite all that I've already forgiven, it seems to be a lifelong practice—but one that gets easier over the years, and one that is well worth the time and effort. Every time I let go of an old hurt, I'm flooded with feelings of happiness and joy as I feel my natural power come rushing back to me. I've also found that consciously releasing old patterns and wounds has allowed me to actually have a harmonious long-term romantic relationship, to walk city streets with confidence, and to have mutually respectful and loving family relationships. Below are some of the techniques I've used to support the process of healing old wounds and forgiving old grievances.

Old Grievance Inventory

The Old Grievance Inventory is basically a roadmap to your power. To create it, get out your journal or notebook and write three headings: "Other People," "Self," and "The Universe" (or whatever name you use for the Divine).

Under the heading "Other People," take your time and think of the people who still make you feel angry, hurt, sad, frightened,

or disempowered in any way. Write the person's name and then write what you feel they did or did not do. Most people have a lot of parental issues, especially at first, so don't be afraid to honestly record your hurt feelings about your primary caregivers.

Many people are also angry with "God," "the Goddess," or "the Universe" for the death of a loved one, a traumatic event, or just "the way things are." If this is the case with you, be honest with yourself about it, withhold self-judgment, and write it down under the appropriate heading.

You might also be angry with or disappointed in yourself for something you think you did or did not do. If so, under the heading "Self," write the issue or issues you have with yourself. This isn't the time to analyze; just write it down.

With all of these, don't overlook something just because it might seem strange. These "strange" grievances can often be the most powerful things to forgive. For example, I once realized that for many years I had been angry with myself for "not saving the world." Talk about weight on my shoulders! Another time, I realized that I was angry with my mom for deciding to have me. You can see the profound healing potential in forgiving that one, right?

You might be angry with a parent for putting a pet to sleep twenty years ago, an old flame for breaking up with you, the universe for being so unfair, or yourself for not spending more time with a loved one before he or she passed on.

Creating this list might take awhile, so be patient with it. And don't feel stressed out about remembering every tiny little thing: just write down all the stuff that comes to mind right now. After all, you can (and should) return to this process again and again throughout your lifetime.

Now that you know where your power is wrapped up in these old hurts, you can perform the following ritual and begin to reclaim it.

Banishing Ritual for Forgiveness and Healing

This ritual is intense and can be time-consuming, so I suggest setting aside an entire evening for it. You might even have to do it in several parts, which is fine.

This should be performed during the waning Moon. Through-out the ritual, drink plenty of water. This will assist you in clearing negativity from your body and energy field.

Using your Old Grievance Inventory, create a story, poem, or piece of visual art for each item you listed. Each written piece can be a few lines, a page, or several pages. For the visual art, you can paint, sketch, or create a collage. Just get something on paper that feels powerful to you and holds the energy of the grievance. And whatever you do, don't worry about whether or not it's "good" art. That's not the point!

Once you've finished, place your artwork in a stack. Pick up one piece and take some time with it. If it's visual artwork, look at it and really go into the imagery. If it's writing, read it out loud, putting feeling into it, even crying if necessary. Then, say:

*I am willing to release my attachment to this grievance and
to reclaim the power that it holds.*

Now, safely burn the grievance in a fireplace, fire pit, or cauldron. Notice how the flames purify the grievance of its negativity, transforming it into the positive energy of heat and light. As this happens, feel your power come rushing back to you. Repeat with each item.

When you're finished, wash your hands, guzzle at least two large glasses of water, clean up any mess you might have made, and then take a shower or bath.

Now you've released yourself from the grip of these old situations! Some of them will clear out of your consciousness fairly quickly, while others might seem to hang on a bit longer. But be assured that you've made serious headway in letting go of each issue and reclaiming the power that's rightfully yours. It's now just a matter of time.

Forgiveness Visualization

This exercise can be done alone or at least one Full Moon cycle after performing the above banishing ritual.

Light a green candle and some frankincense incense. You might also want to play soft, ambient music. With your Old Grievance Inventory nearby (or just keeping the items in mind if you haven't made a list), sit or recline comfortably. Close your eyes, take some deep breaths, and consciously relax your entire body, paying special attention to your heart, stomach, shoulders, and throat.

Imagine you are walking on a mountain path on a beautiful day. Notice the leaves moving in the gentle breeze, see and feel the ground beneath your feet, and inhale the fresh mountain air. Though you're walking uphill, you don't feel tired or winded at all, just more and more invigorated. Continue to walk upward, and as you do, notice the meadows and forests in the valley below you as they get smaller and smaller. Look up at the sky and notice how clear and blue it is. Eventually, you reach a beautiful, ancient-looking, intricately carved gate. You gently push it and it swings open to a bright, grassy plateau at the very top of the mountain. You notice a large fountain, brightly colored flowers, and birds singing sweetly in the trees. You walk past the fountain to look over the edge, and when you get there, you're amazed by how high you've climbed. It's almost as if you're looking down from the highest point on Earth. You sit down and make yourself comfortable so that you can gaze out at the sky above and ground below.

Very slowly, a giant movie screen comes into focus and seems to hover in the sky at eye level. Now, the first person under the "Other People" heading on your list appears on the screen. In this movie, they're doing the thing that hurt you so badly. Inwardly, you ask yourself, "How could s/he have done such a thing?" As if the movie screen heard your thought, it now rewinds to a time in this person's past during which s/he was hurt or disappointed, a time that formed his/her future actions toward you. It rewinds again and shows another episode in this person's life that created pain and discouragement. You might begin to feel compassion and understanding at this time. Then the movie moves forward again to the starting point and beyond. Now you see the person in his or her most beautiful and ideal future, healed and whole. An angel appears and begins showering gifts upon this person, everything they most deeply desire in the world. See the person laugh and cry with joy. If you can, feel happy for them. When this feels complete, move to the next person on your list and perform the same visualization with each.

Now, you appear on the screen. You're doing the first thing you wrote on your list under the heading "Self." From your current top-of-the-world perspective, you quickly realize that even though the movie is showing you, it isn't really you. In other words, you see that you're something eternal

and infinite, not this tiny little projected picture that seems to be carried away with some drama from the past. This realization allows you to watch the movie of yourself with compassion, almost as if it's someone else. Now go through the same visualization with yourself that you did for the other people on your list.

As the "movie" ends, relax and reflect on what you've seen. As you gaze down at the Earth far below, you suddenly realize that the drama of life has a purpose: it allows us to unravel old hurts and grow stronger. Even when things seem to make no sense or to be totally wrong, they have a positive potential for healing and growth. As you're thinking this, you look back to the screen and notice that the only name on the credits is the name you use for the Divine Presence. You perceive that not only this movie, but also your entire life experience has been orchestrated by this Presence. Then you understand that in truth, you are one with this Presence and that you have (on some level) known this all along. This causes you to laugh with joy. Suddenly, nothing seems as serious or as horrible as it once did. You feel free.

Take a few minutes to bask in this feeling. Then imagine that you stand up, walk to the gate, and slowly meander back down the path. When you arrive at the bottom of the mountain, conclude the visualization and open your eyes.

Clearing Clutter

I believe that clearing clutter is the single most important magical act that we can possibly perform. Why? Because magic is about sensing and working with the connections between everything:

external and internal, physical and emotional, sacred and mundane. And clutter in your home represents clutter in your life: stagnant places in your mind, body, emotions, and energy field.

And so, when it comes to forgiveness, clutter clearing is essential. Releasing what you *don't* want (from both your home and your life) creates the space for what you *do* want. In this case, you *don't* want grudges, grievances, negativity, and general disempowerment. You *do* want clarity, joy, and the full scope of your magical power.

I suggest that you supplement your other forgiveness work with a thorough clutter clearing of your home. You can take your time with this, but it's important to begin so you can get your energy moving in the right direction. If you feel overwhelmed, start small: commit to clearing out one room, one closet, or even one drawer. Something is always better than nothing, and you'll be surprised how much energy you can generate by clearing out a single drawer. It often inspires you to keep going until you've cleared an entire room.

Make sure to get rid of gifts you've never liked, clothes that don't make you feel wonderful, old papers you don't need anymore, broken things that you aren't willing to fix, unfinished projects that you aren't willing to complete, home decorations or furniture that you don't like or that have negative associations for you, books you'll never open again, anything else that you don't love, need, or use, and—perhaps most important—pictures or gifts that remind you of old, unpleasant times or relationships.

You'll be surprised how much clearer, lighter, and more positive you feel after you let go of the extras. Make sure to drink lots of water as you clear, as you'll be simultaneously releasing toxins from your body. (Because, remember, *everything* is connected.)

The "Start Your Engines" Clutter-Clearing Ritual

Use the following ritual if you need a little extra support with emotional clutter clearing. Take a brisk walk outdoors for at least twenty minutes. Then put two drops of hornbeam flower essence (available online and at most health food stores) into a glass of water. Hold the glass in both hands and imagine very bright white light coming down from above, entering the crown of your head, going down to your heart and out through your hands into the glass. Think the words *clarity*, *energy*, and *release*. Then guzzle the whole glass. Finally, light a white candle and start clearing.

Healing and Self-Love Ritual

As you move through these stages of release and forgiveness, you'll likely go through waves of emotions, sometimes negative ones. This is because you're bringing old emotional toxins to the surface so that you can release them and heal from them (the same concept as a hangover).

During this process, it's important not only to release the old hurtful and negative feelings that you've been carrying around, but also to replace them with positive and empowering ones. This is a ritual to help you do both.

You'll need:
- ½ gallon aloe juice
- 1 cup mint tea or fresh mint leaves
- a large bottle of drinking water
- a green candle
- frankincense and myrrh incense

On the day of the New Moon, draw a bath. Add the aloe juice and mint to the bathwater. Light the candle and incense and place them near the tub. Hold your hands over the tub, close your eyes, and say:

Archangel Raphael, please infuse this bath with vibrations of healing and love.

Soak in the tub for at least forty minutes. As you soak, think positive and loving thoughts about yourself while drinking the bottle of water. If you notice your mind wandering, gently bring it back by mentally stating the following affirmation:

I love myself deeply and allow myself to heal.

Personal Empowerment Ritual

At any stage of your forgiveness process, the following ritual can support your efforts to retrieve and increase your personal power. It's most effective when done on a regular basis.

Every morning during the waxing Moon, light a red candle as you say:

As I light this flame, I summon the source of my power.

Sit comfortably and hold up your open palms so that the flame warms them. Imagine that the flame is your infinite power source. Envision and feel your power entering through your palms and filling your entire body and energy field. When this visualization feels complete (it should only take a few moments), open your eyes and extinguish the candle.

The Beauty of the Blessing Bowl

by Janina Renée

Whether simple or ornate, used as a decoration or a utilitarian object, a bowl is a vessel that you can fill with good things—including your imagination! It is no wonder that delightfully crafted bowls are popular home decorations, and are regularly featured in catalogs and gift shops and at art shows. In addition to many different types of pottery and glass vessels, there are bowls fashioned from wood, hammered pewter, and natural rock (such as rose quartz or lapis lazuli). Many of these are described as "blessing bowls," revealing a trend in the creation of public and private rituals.

One of the most common practices is to fill a bowl with cards or slips of paper with written wishes and blessings. Some individuals and families do this to count their blessings (often as a daily ritual), by jotting down things they are thankful for. Watching the bowl fill up is a visual affirmation of how genuinely fortunate a person can be. For celebrations, such as baby and bridal showers or at birthday parties, individuals might write out a bunch of blessing wishes, inspirational messages, good thoughts, and even warm memories of the recipients, and then present them in a nice bowl as a gift. Alternatively, a bowl with colorful cards and slips of paper may be set out at the event, with all of the guests invited to put in their own good wishes. Later, the lucky recipients might add a few of their own wishes and affirmations for themselves.

Hand in hand with putting the written blessings in the bowl is drawing them out. Thus, on special occasions or at times when some cheering up is needed, the recipient of such a gift can read some of the blessing notes to be reminded that he or she is loved and blessed. Bowls with preprinted blessing cards are also available commercially, so that anyone can draw them as a daily practice, or pass them on to others. This practice of exchanging blessings is also becoming popular with certain groups, such as religious communities, where a large blessing bowl may

be kept in a lobby or fellowship room so that members can contribute positive messages and draw them out at any time they wish.

Instead of or in addition to putting slips of paper into blessing bowls, many people like to add crystals; other natural objects such as collected rocks, seashells, and seedpods; and various small objects with symbolic meanings. (Some will first fill the bowl with sand, to make it easier to position certain objects, as well as to bring in the connecting element of earth.) This is especially popular with persons who maintain home altars, and may be done in combination with other practices—such as prayer, candle-lighting, or placing the bowl before a religious image as a way of turning one's wishes over to the Sacred. Blessing bowls can also be arranged to benefit other people. For example, to send healing wishes to a friend, you could put their picture in a bowl along with other objects that have some connection to them and then add crystals, healing herbs appropriate to their condition, and so on. You might place candles in the center and arrange the other objects around them.

As bowls are able to contain water and other fluids, blessing bowl rituals can involve dipping and anointing, pouring actions, and libations.

A traditional example of a water-pouring ceremony is the Thai wedding custom of binding a bridal couple's hands over a large vessel; the other celebrants bless the couple by pouring water (often from a conch shell) over the couple's hands. As all of the water runs together harmoniously, the couple is symbolically united. (This also makes an interesting statement about how our friends contribute to our sense of self, both as individuals and as married pairs.) For luck, the guests may put other items in the blessing bowl, such as fruit, rice, and eggs.

Sometimes a blessing bowl is passed around as part of a commemoration or a religious ceremony. For example, celebrants may take turns holding the bowl while their neighbors dip their fingers in to anoint themselves or others, or wash their hands as part of a ritual cleansing. Bowls of water or oil may also be set out so people can perform these acts individually, whenever they desire.

For some Neopagan groups, a bowl is a necessary ritual implement, both for blessing ceremonial participants and making common offerings. In the first case, liquid such as water or mead is poured into the bowl and blessed with words and/or gestures, and a little is then sprinkled over each of the celebrants; a leafy twig or a sprig of herbs may be dipped into the bowl for the purpose of sprinkling. For offerings, the blessing bowl may be passed around during toasts, and each person pours a little of his or her own drink into it. The bowl is afterward poured out onto the ground, perhaps at the root of a tree, as an offering to the spirits of Mother Earth and Nature.

While these celebration practices inspire group harmony, blessing bowls also serve as tools for solitary contemplation. The ritual act of adding symbolic objects to one's blessing bowl, as mentioned earlier, promotes individual insights. Other meditative actions include pouring water into a bowl to release stress, gazing at floating candles in a water-filled bowl, and slowly emptying a bowl as symbolic of emptying the mind. If you take certain foods or dietary supplements for health and healing, you might want to put them into a blessing bowl as a way of signal-

ing your subconscious mind that this is something special; likewise when you are serving healing foods to loved ones.

Even an empty bowl, just sitting on a shelf, is more than a mere decoration. It is an inspirational object because it is simple, humble, and ready to serve. It is receptive and feminine. It can even be a cosmic symbol—consider how the dome of the sky resembles an overturned bowl! Feng shui practitioners set out empty bowls to receive positive energy, which is why exquisite bowls are popular Chinese home decorations.

An empty bowl can also inspire ritual gestures. For example, tomorrow morning you could step out your front door, hold out an empty bowl, and praying to your own deity or the Power of the Universe, make the statement, "I am ready to receive whatever this day may bring—let my bowl be filled with whatever I need to meet the challenges of this day!"

The Shadow as a Spiritual Force

by Raven Digitalis

This article and meditation focuses on an aspect of spirituality that spans numerous traditions across cultures, is viewed in a myriad of forms, and is applicable to Neopagan practice and philosophy. That element can be called "Shadow."

Shadow, as a spiritual force, manifests in many forms—just as does as its equal-opposite counterpart, Light. At the same time, is there really any division between darkness and light, black and white, good and evil? Or does reality operate and fluctuate in varying shades of gray? Why do we have distinctions such as these in our reality? I've come to believe that easy-reference labels can be beneficial for purposes of identification and discernment. On the other hand, it's all too easy to latch onto labels of any sort and become dependant on them—which changes *discernment* into *judgment.*

Some spiritual systems teach that identifying something under *any* of these extremes (dark/light, black/white, good/ evil, and so on) is spiritually counterproductive, and inaccurate, and limits thinking. In this view, looking at reality with an eye of categorization only leads to hierarchical thinking, distorted views, and divisive mental cataloging. Many spiritualists tend to perceive reality and all its facets as a massive grayscale. All is One. While monotheistic religions tend to draw strict lines of division between "this" and "that" (generally the sacred versus the profane), polytheistic religions tend to recognize the duality in all things but still see both sides of the spectrum as sacred and holy in their own right.

In terms of the force we label "Shadow," its existence is highly interpretive. What can be termed Shadow for one person may or may not be termed the same by another. Going back again to monotheistic viewpoints, Light is often aligned with the sacred, while Shadow is aligned with the profane. As Neopagans, we realize the folly in this type of extreme dualistic thinking: reality makes no distinction between extremes, and is indeed constantly fluctuating between them. There would be no day

without night, no life without death, no joy without sorrow . . . both are equally sacred, and both must be examined to cultivate spiritual wholeness. Neither Shadow nor Light can be neglected if one is wishing to make one's life a truly holistic spiritual experience. Witches, magicians, and spiritual seekers of all varieties must examine *all* sides of reality's divine spectrum.

The word *shaman* originates from the Tungus people of Siberia (Russia) but is now frequently used to refer to particular practices of indigenous people across the globe, often Native American shamanism, Amazonian shamanism, Aboriginal shamanism, and so on. Part of the shaman's role—which can be seen in a variety of forms across the globe, yet all with similar characteristics—is to voyage the depths of darkness to uncover the light of awareness, revelation, and insight. Shamans are initiated through pain and trauma or have inherent abilities borne from living on the edge of a society (by some necessity, such as having a disability). Shamans were and are venerated for their abilities, and are often simultaneously feared for their power. When shamans and shamanistic practitioners help clients, they often work to heal them from a platform of interpersonal darkness. Parallels can be drawn between this idea and

Jungian psychology: it's from the repressed, deeper portions of the Self that Shadow accumulates (to degrees either healthy or unrestrained), and it's from this deeper Self that the Light of Awareness is born.

Contrary to popular misinterpretation (even within some Neopagan circles, sadly), the force of Shadow is not purely destructive, evil, or manipulative. At the same time, "black magic," predatory sorcery, and manipulation *can* be aligned to the Shadow side . . . but there's more to it than that. Much, much more. Can dreaming or astral projection be classified as positive aspects of "Shadow"? Yes, certainly! Can illusions of perception, such as a false mask of compassion, be classified as negative aspects of "Light"? Absolutely.

I have personally come to see the Shadow under a number of forms and tend to catalog them in a certain spectrum. Below is a review of my own perceptive divisions of Shadow and what can be included in each. I examine a number of these points in my book *Shadow Magick Compendium*, but not all of them. These lists can easily be expanded and even rearranged and altered to some extent by any reader who has their own personal interpretations of Shadow and Light.

Internal Shadow: The Internal Shadow is the darker side of human nature and is psycho-spiritual. Herein exists portions of the emotional body that have been repressed by the mind. When denial occurs, thoughts are pushed to the back of the mind and into the unrecognized Internal Shadow. When darker emotions palpably arise, such as sadness, anger, and apathy, it may be considered a conscious surfacing of the Internal Shadow. Just the same, a person may be objectively aware (or at least somewhat aware) of their darker characteristics, which is the first step in magickally and spiritually working with one's Inner Shadow.

External Shadow: One's External Shadow can be seen as a projection of the Internal Shadow. Gone unrecognized, the External Shadow can manifest through projection. For example, a person may believe that no one thinks they are smart, when the truth of the matter is that they do not accept their own intelligence. External projection can arise in limitless ways, from many repressed beliefs. Also included in this definition of the External Shadow are the shadows of others. In other words, any aspect of "Shadow" that is not your own can be considered external. External Shadow work relies on external forces, yet connects with and affects one's internal reality, such as with fasting or godform assumption (invocation). Demonic evocation, Qlippothic pathworking, binding, and cursing magick can also be categorized here.

Astral Shadow: The astral plane is an etheric reflection of the physical world, and it carries energies that are generally invisible to the untrained eye. The astral is also a realm of guides, guardians, and ancestors. Thoughtforms, deities, dreams, and etheric beings exist on the astral plane, and magickal workings concerned with these forces can be considered operations of the Astral Shadow. Naturally, the astral plane carries currents of darkness that are directly linked to the shadow of the human psyche and the natural world. The astral plane and physical plane are intricately connected by the Web of Life—the threads of Wyrd—which connects all portions of reality (both seen and unseen) to each other. Many of the deeper mysteries of the Witch are indeed greatly astral, etheric, or energy-based.

Shadow of Nature: The food chain may be considered part of Nature's Shadow, as one life form must feed on (destroy) another to survive. The "death" side of "life and death" can be viewed as a Shadow of Nature. The destructive aspect of Nature may be included here, such as natural disasters and poisonous plants. Additionally, shadowed aspects of Nature— eclipses, the infinite night sky, the dying season, and the dark Moon—may be considered the Shadow of Nature.

Social Shadow: The unseen, hidden, suppressed, or overlooked aspects of our culture and society fall under this category. In my own definition, the Shadow of Society is predominantly *not* positive. Skewed cultural worldviews, underhanded corporate crime, religious fanaticism, and self-serving politics can be considered a part of the Social Shadow. The Social Shadow is greatly shaped by the Internal Shadow, which is to say that devastating sociopolitical crime is often no more than horrid projections of peoples' inner fears and psychoses. Personally, I feel that the most devastating aspects of the Social Shadow are the two extremes of fanaticism and apathy.

A Meditation on the Shadow Self

The following is a meditation designed to access fears associated with darkness. This is not in reference to physical darkness, but to darkness as a vibration. The vibration of darkness contains repressed fears, forgotten memories, and subconscious habits, many of which influence our everyday lives. Of course, this does not make internal darkness inherently bad or malicious, but something essential to navigate for personal development.

Swiss psychiatrist Carl Jung termed this aspect of the psyche the "Shadow Self." In reality, it can take years, if not a lifetime, to accurately study and come to terms with our internal shadows. Mysticism and magic are ways to better *Know Thyself*, and the meditation that follows is a suggestion as one step in the process. Please read through the meditation a number of times so you are able to perform it by memory.

Procedure

Situate yourself in sacred space, and have some comfy pillows to lie on. Be sure to perform this meditation in darkness; the witching hour (midnight) is preferable. If you can perform this on a New Moon, all the better. Light a single black candle to partially illuminate the space, and cast the circle in your usual way. Summon the elements and dedicate the circle to your patron and matron gods (if you have any) and the spirits of the nighttime.

When you feel connected, lie on the pillows and declare your intent. Say something like:

Behold! Great spirits of obscurity and darkness, I now wish to enter the Shadow of my mind. I do not fear the darkness, but rather embrace it as a force of creation and mystery. Sacred spirits of the inner planes, I humbly ask that you guard me and guide me into myself, that I may grow and learn with patience and accuracy.
So mote it be.

With your eyes closed and your body comfortable, visualize the room around you. Allow your mind's eye to focus on the room from your perspective and feel the placement of your body in the room. Become aware of your environment and visualize your body for what it is: a temporary vessel for your spirit.

While performing visualization, practice deep breathing. Take deep breaths in through your nose and out through your mouth. Continue to alter your consciousness and become psychically aware of your body and the environment. Take a decent amount of time to expand your perception.

Now sufficiently aware, envision your astral body descending through the floor and into the ground. Descend only a few feet beneath the soil. You are comforted by the sensations of

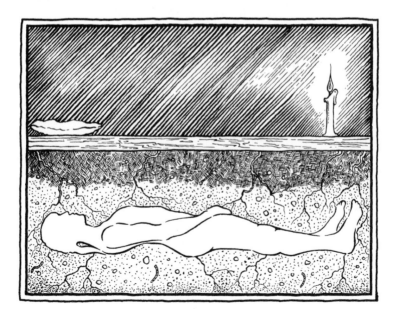

peace and stillness in this place. Open your psychic senses and feel the burrowing creatures and worms. Feel the roots of trees and plants brushing your body. Feel the damp soil, recognizing it as a center of nourishment and (re)birth.

At this point, knowing that you are safe and protected by the bounty of the living Earth, bring to mind two or three occurrences in your life that caused you great amounts of pain and emotional suffering. Take some time to remember these; some things may pop into your mind immediately, while others may be shrouded and even willingly repressed. If you happen to remember a large number of painful experiences, you may wish to write these down after the meditation so that you can perform the meditation again with different focuses in mind. Focus on the most traumatic, painful, and emotional experiences you have endured in your life. If tears surface during the meditation, allow yourself to cry. Process each experience individually, remembering them even if you have already worked through them in the past. Claim your power.

Sort through each issue individually. For each one, take plenty of time to recall the specifics of each situation: How exactly did you feel at the time? What was your role in the situation? Were you a victim? How has the situation affected your personal development? How has it influenced your life, both positively and negatively? Are any of your current patterns of behavior or modes of reaction connected to the event? Spiritually, what could be possible reasons for having to endure the experience? What can you do to resolve your pain attached to these occurrences?

When you run through the event in your mind, you should feel a return of emotional weight. Now, envision your astral body—still submerged in the ground—covered with a dense, black tarlike substance. This represents the extent to which your mind still holds onto the event, the extent to which it plagues you now. When ready, visualize a soft, healing blue light emerging from your heart chakra, radiating through your body and eventually to the dense astral matter surrounding your body. Envision this light conquering the astral junk, permeating through it. With a strong exhalation, envision the black substance breaking away from your aura, plummeting down into the soil. Envision the healing light surrounding your astral body, guarding against the tar's return.

Once you have performed this with each painful occurrence, visualize your astral body rising up from the ground, through the floor, and back into your physical body. Wiggle your fingers and toes, breathe deeply, and come to center.

To close, state your intention, saying something like:

Sacred spirits here this night, I thank you for protecting and comforting me as I journeyed layers of my mind. I ask that I be able to understand and release these issues by continuing to face them bravely and accurately. Thank you for attending this rite. Blessed be.

Take some time to come back to your body, and close the circle as you normally would. It's a good idea to write about your experiences afterward and spend additional time meditating on the intricacies of each experience of the past. Do whatever it takes to peacefully come to terms with the experiences of your past—each and every one of us has endured trauma to one degree or another, and every one of us deserves to heal and claim our power. Nothing is ever fully released; our experiences are simply come to terms with and accepted. Everything in life, no matter how dark and painful, can hold profound lessons beneath the surface.

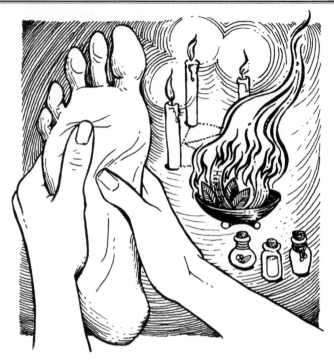

Foot Massage Magic

by Suzanne Ress

Have you ever put a penny in your shoe for good luck, or had a special pair of shoes or socks you considered lucky? During the Yuletide season, children all over the world leave a pair of shoes or a sock out to be filled with gifts and sweets by Saint Nick, Santa Claus, the baby Jesus, Befana, and other mysterious entities.

To empathize with someone else, we say one needs to walk in her shoes, and the twelve-inch standard measurement generally used in the United States called a foot was originally determined by the length of an average man's shoe.

Shoes, and socks, are powerful magical symbols because they contain our feet, which are what connect us to the Earth, where all magic originates.

In the days when people wore only sandals and their feet were their principle mode of transport, Jesus Christ insisted on washing his disciples' feet, saying that, "One who has bathed does not need to wash, except for the feet, and is entirely clean" (John 13). The Chinese healing system of reflexology uses pressure points on the soles of the feet to stimulate energy flow within various specific body parts. Dreaming of yourself or someone else walking barefoot in places where shoes are normally worn symbolizes a free spirit, humility, and honesty. Have you ever heard the saying, "shoes make the man (or woman)"? Evidently, our feet, and footwear, can symbolically sum up the whole person they carry around!

All too often, in Western culture, we tend to ignore our feet (unless they hurt), unaware that by giving them some attention in the form of a massage spell it is possible to unlock pleasant new doors to self-fulfillment.

Before explaining the basic massage technique and some specific massage spells, I would like to make sure readers understand that when giving a foot massage to oneself or to a partner, it is very important that the entire experience be relaxing and pleasant. Therefore, if the foot or ankle to be massaged is in pain due to accident or injury, or is in a chronically painful state such as arthritis, do not attempt to perform massage spells on it, as this could do more harm than good. Also remember that not everyone has the same level of sensitivity to touch, and what feels good to one person might be painful to another. No massage spell should ever be the slightest bit uncomfortable, so make sure the communication channels with your partner(s) are wide open.

The power of foot massage spells lies in their ability to bring someone to a very relaxed, almost trancelike state, where the magic can take effect.

In addition to using massage spells to obtain what you need, it is essential that active, conscientious efforts in the direction of the desired result are made.

For most of these massage spells you will need some or all of the following:

- candles (of the appropriate color)
- essential oils and a carrier oil, such as almond, olive, or jojoba
  - paper, and appropriately colored, or invisible, ink
  - dried or fresh herbs (of appropriate type)
  - a firebrick or charcoal brick
  - drums
  - a basin in which to wash the feet prior to massage. This basin must be made of stone, wood, ceramic, or glass. Avoid plastics, but, if inevitable, line the plastic basin with burlap, linen, or cotton cloth before putting in water and other ingredients. Also, a natural or manmade fountain can be used. If at all possible, wash them in the same place as the massage. If feet are to be washed in a different area than where the massage/magic will take place, swaddle the feet during transport in linen, cotton, silk, wool, or burlap.

The Magic Rituals

All the massage spells follow the same pattern using different scents, colors, and words.

For Success in Obtaining Work

This should be performed on the night of the New Moon. Make a massage oil of 1 drop frankincense essential oil, 1 drop sandalwood essential oil, and 1 drop veviter essential oil in 1 tablespoon jojoba oil.

You will also need 3 dried bay leaves; 3 green candles; a small strip of paper torn from a desirable section of the help-wanted ads of a newspaper, or a handwritten (by the job seeker) description of the sort of employment desired. This should be in black ink on a small strip of white paper.

First, wash the feet in a basin of warm salt water with unscented neutral or balanced-pH soap (neither acidic or basic—these are sometimes classified as "mild" soaps). Dry the feet carefully with a white cotton or linen towel.

Anoint the three candles with a little of the massage oil, and place them in a triangular formation close to, but a safe enough distance from, the massage area. The person receiving the massage should be lying down comfortably on his or her back. If this is not possible, or if this is a self-massage, sit in a relaxed and comfortable position.

Crumble the dried bay leaves and burn them in a small crucible or on a firebrick or charcoal block with the strip of newspaper or handwritten paper. Make sure both items burn down completely to ashes.

Put a few drops of the massage oil on the palms of your hands and begin by gently stroking each foot from ankle to toe, slowly, ten or fifteen times. Stroke also the heels and soles of the feet.

Your hands and fingers should have enough massage oil on them at all times to enable them to slide smoothly over the feet, so add more as necessary.

Next, make large circles, always moving from ankle to toe, all over the feet. Gradually make the circles become smaller, so you are finally using only your index and middle fingers to make them as large as a quarter. Circle clockwise on the right foot, and counterclockwise on the left. Gently rotate each toe using your thumb and index finger. End with more ankle-to-toe stroking.

The massage should take twenty to thirty minutes. Your massagee may have fallen asleep, or should at least be in a very relaxed state by this time. Without disturbing the person if they have drifted off, rub most of the cooled ashes over the soles of the feet, visualizing him or her happily occupied doing the desired job. Reserve a small amount of ashes to sprinkle inside the shoes to be worn while job searching. Take a few minutes to relax and meditate on your friend in a new job. Then blow out the candles, and, if you have performed this spell inside a magic circle, open the circle.

For Improved Athletic Performance

This massage is best done on a sunny day outdoors at midday.

Make a massage oil using 2 drops essential oil of neroli, 2 drops essential oil of frankincense, and 2 drops bergamot essential oil in 1 tablespoon of olive oil.

Obtain 4 red candles and 4 orange candles. On one of the orange candles, carve the initials of the name of the person desiring improved sport performance.

Prior to the massage, the feet should be washed in warm salt water with 4 tablespoons orange flower water and a sprig of woodruff.

On a small strip of yellow paper, have the massagee write *Fortis Corporis, Potenta Venit* in black ink ("Strong Body, Potency Come"). The strip of paper should then be rolled up tightly and anointed with four drops of the massage oil.

Place the 8 candles in a straight line from east to west, alternating colors, a safe distance away but in full view of both massager and massagee.

Using the fire from the flame of one of the orange candles, burn the rolled and anointed strip of paper to ashes along with 2 dried and crumbled bergamot leaves and 2 dried and crumbled lemon verbena leaves (lacking these, use finely chopped dried orange peel).

Visualize the person performing the sport very competitively. The movements of this massage are the same as the previous one, but at the end, you should gently pinch the soles of both feet all over. Rub some of the cooled ashes over the soles using small circular motions. Reserve some of the ashes to be sprinkled under the insoles of the shoes to be worn during sport practice or training. If the sport is done in bare feet, save some of the ashes to rub on the soles of the feet just before a big performance or competition.

For Winning the Heart of a Desired One

This massage should be done on a Friday evening, by the light of many ivory or white candles.

Wash the feet by candlelight in a warm rose water bath with fresh rose petals. Prepare a massage oil, also by candlelight on the same Friday evening, using 2 tablespoons sweet almond oil as the carrier with 1 drop of jasmine essential oil, 1 drop rose oil, 1 drop neroli oil, and 1 drop gardenia oil.

Have the massagee write the qualities of the desired lover in green ink on a small square of pink paper, and his or her own name in a circle around it. He or she must then pierce the paper in three points with a needle, to form a triangle shape around the words. Sprinkle three drops of the massage oil onto the paper and fold it in half to make a triangle.

Place several dried pink or red rose petals (preferably from a rose cut at dawn on Midsummer's Eve, but any red or pink rose will do) inside the folded paper, and burn it to ashes.

Proceed with the foot massage. If possible, listen to soft, romantic music that both people enjoy. Visualize the desired lover while massaging, but do not speak of him or her or utter any names. After the basic massage is done, spend some time rubbing the feet from toe to ankle, with a heartbeat rhythm. Rub the cooled ashes all over the feet and then kiss both of the big toes three times each. The feet should not be washed for at least twenty-four hours.

For Overcoming Insomnia

This massage must be given in the evening, just before bed time, in total silence, preferably indoors.

Prior to the massage, the insomniac must write out a list, as long as possible, of all his or her worries, fears, problems, and preoccupations. This list should be written on black paper, using black or invisible ink, and then placed outside the bedroom door under a rock.

Prepare a warm infusion foot bath of chamomile, linden, and hops, with 1 cup of warmed milk added. Allow the massagee's feet to soak for five to ten minutes.

Make up a massage oil using warmed almond oil and 3 drops essential oil of lavender. Have the insomniac lie in a very comfortable place (their own bed, if possible), and take your time giving a long, slow, and drawn-out massage.

When the insomniac is peacefully asleep, you should tip-toe outside and take the piece of black paper from under the rock. Crumple it into a tight wad and throw it into a public recycling bin, far from the insomniac's house.

To Find a Lost Object

You will need 4 white stones the size of plums and dried mallow leaves (these can be taken from tea bags).

Before the massage, wash the feet in warm salt water with pH-neutral white soap, then wrap them in white cotton or linen and prepare to begin the massage.

Light 4 white candles, and place them in the cardinal directions to form a circle around the massage area. Place one stone next to each candle.

Use a warm salve made of 1 tablespoon melted pure beeswax emulsified with 1 tablespoon olive oil. For the first five minutes of the massage, sing or chant the following, "What is lost shall soon be found, what was gone shall come back round." If possible, have a third person nearby but outside the circle, softly drumming a little slower than a heartbeat.

Once five minutes have elapsed, there should be total silence, with all persons present visualizing the lost object. After about ten more minutes of silent massage, pick up the stone representing north. Gently and slowly roll the stone with the palm of your hand from the ankle, over the back and bottom of the heel, and along the sole of the left foot. Rub and press the stone all along the bottoms and tops of the toes. Repeat for the other foot. Return the stone to its candle and pick up the west stone, repeating the same procedure, then the south stone, and finally the east stone.

Last, take a small handful of dried mallow and pass your hand over the flame of each candle at a safe distance, starting at the north and moving to west, south, and east. While you are doing this, you should say slowly one more time, "What is lost shall soon be found, what was gone shall come back round."

Sprinkle some of the mallow into the seeker's shoes, which should be worn until the lost object is found.

A Few Additional Massage Ideas

For gaining riches and financial stability: Use basil, mint, sandalwood, and ginger oils and herbs, and the colors green and gold or yellow. Perform the massage on a Sunday, under a bright Sun.

For good luck wherever you go: Use mint, basil, and clover (leaves and essential oils), red candles, and a red ribbon or silk scarf. This massage should be given on a Friday evening, during a waxing or Full Moon.

For healing a sick person: Wash the feet in a rosemary infusion. The massage oil should be made of hyssop leaves soaked in olive oil for twenty-four hours. Use a blue candle and have the sick person write a petition for wellness on a strip of white paper in blue ink. This strip of paper should not be burnt but soaked in the rosemary infusion, then dried and preserved until the sick person heals.

～

These are just a few examples of foot massage spells that can be practiced on a partner, or on oneself. Using this basic structure, you can invent your own magic foot massages for other purposes. Make sure to use the appropriate colors and herbs if you choose to modify these spells for other purposes.

Once you start paying a little more attention to your feet and a partner's feet, not only will you spend some enjoyable and relaxing moments together, you'll also begin to unlock some of the ancient magic we all have within us.

Your Guide for Healthy and Natural Living

Enhance your sex life with natural aphrodisiacs. Spice up meals with herbal butters. There are hundreds of ways to get the most from nature's most versatile plants inside *Llewellyn's 2011 Herbal Almanac*. Featuring over two dozen articles, this treasury of innovative herbal ideas spans five categories: gardening, cooking, crafts, health/beauty, and myth/lore.

In this edition, you'll discover how to creatively cook asparagus, cure headaches, add color and texture to your garden, craft essential oils, gather wild herbs, collect seeds, create homemade gifts, boost the health of your pets, make your own pesticides, treat fibromyalgia, and much more. From crafts to prickly lettuce to the last rose of summer, this practical almanac is your gateway to the herbal kingdom.

LLEWELLYN'S 2011 HERBAL ALMANAC
312 pp. • 5¼ × 8
ISBN 978-0-7387-1131-7 • U.S. $10.99 Can. $12.50
To order call 1-877-NEW-WRLD

Shadowscapes Tarot

Renowned fantasy artist Stephanie Pui-Mun Law has created a hypnotic world of colorful dragons, armored knights, looming castles, and willowy fairies dancing on air—a world of imagination and dreams.

Lovingly crafted over six years, this long-awaited deck will delight all tarot enthusiasts with its wondrous blend of fairy tales, myth, and folklore from diverse cultures around the world. Featuring breathtaking watercolor artwork that fuses Asian, Celtic, and fantasy elements within the Rider-Waite structure, each exquisitely wrought card draws upon universally recognized symbols and imagery. A companion guide also presents evocative stories and insightful interpretations for each card.

Creating a Safe Haven for Home & Family

Everyone wants a home that is safe and protected. With this friendly and accessible guide to psychic protection and defense, you can ensure the safety and well-being of your home and loved ones.

Bestselling author Richard Webster presents this extensive collection of time-tested and practical methods for psychic protection. Learn to activate the shielding properties of gems and crystals, pendulums, candles, amulets and charms, incense and herbs, the body's chakras (energy centers), and more. Webster's simple yet powerful activities and rituals enable you to block psychic attacks, release negativity, strengthen your aura, and engage in prayer and angel communion to create a safe, nurturing, and harmonious home.

Simple Charms & Practical Tips for Creating a Harmonious Home

Every inch and component of your home is filled with an invisible life force and unique magical energy. *Magical Housekeeping* teaches readers how to sense, change, channel, and direct these energies to create harmony in their homes, joy in their hearts, and success in all areas of their lives.

In this engaging guide, energy consultant and teacher Tess Whitehurst shares her secrets for creating an energetically powerful and positive home. Written for those new to metaphysics as well as experienced magical practitioners, *Magical Housekeeping* will teach readers how to summon success, happiness, romance, abundance, and all the desires of the heart. By guiding changes in both the seen and unseen worlds simultaneously, this dynamic and delightful book will help to activate and enhance readers' intuition and innate magical power.

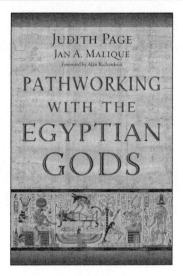

GET MORE AT LLEWELLYN.COM

Visit us online to browse hundreds of our books and decks, plus sign up to receive our e-newsletters and exclusive online offers.

- Free tarot readings • Spell-a-Day • Moon phases
- Recipes, spells, and tips • Blogs • Encyclopedia
- Author interviews, articles, and upcoming events

GET SOCIAL WITH LLEWELLYN

Find us on **f** Find us on Facebook Follow us on **twitter**

www.Facebook.com/LlewellynBooks • www.Twitter.com/Llewellynbooks

TELL US WHAT YOU WANT!

At Llewellyn our aim is to keep pace with your passion for lifelong learning and magical living. Please help us to understand and serve you better by taking our short survey (approx. 5 minutes).

Please go to

http://www.llewellyn.com/surveys.php

to complete the online questionnaire and let your voice be heard.

Thanks in advance for your feedback!